DIARY OF THE SINAI CAMPAIGN

DIARY OF
THE SINAI CAMPAIGN

Major-General Moshe Dayan

SCHOCKEN BOOKS • NEW YORK

CONTENTS

ILLUSTRATIONS

Between pages 184 and 185

The publishers would like to thank Bamahaneh, Tel Aviv, and the Israel Government Press Office for making these photographs available.

MAPS

All the maps were drawn by Eli Shafir, Haifa

FOREWORD

THIS book is based on the diary for the years 1955–7 kept by the office of the Chief of Staff. The entries covered fully not only the military items which reached the Chief of Staff's table each day, but also the political context in which they were set.

This diary is not, of course, presented here in its entirety, nor has the shorthand style of the original text necessarily been followed. Some sections have been eliminated, others shortened, still others expanded. Much additional material has been included from the written reports of the units taking part in the campaign and from the accounts I received in talks with the commanders.

In dealing with the political aspects, I have followed the direction of Mr Ben Gurion, who was Prime Minister and Minister of Defence when the happenings described in this book took place, and who felt that the time had not yet come for publication of the full record of the developments preceding the Sinai Campaign. However, responsibility for everything written here, both the facts and the judgements, is mine alone.

I must emphasize that this book presents the events from my personal perspective, and is not to be regarded as taking the place of an official history of the Sinai Campaign. It does not cover every single deed associated with the campaign performed either on the fighting fronts or in the rear. It gives no expression, for example, to the activities of the Regional and various formation Commands, nor, above all, of the General Staff, either in the planning or the operational phases of the campaign.

If I were to thank by name all who were helpful, directly and indirectly, in the preparation of this book, the list would be long indeed. I wish, however, to place on record my special appreciation to Lieut.-Colonel (now Colonel) M. Bar-on (Morele), who served as head of the Chief of Staff's office in 1956, and to Captain Neorah Matalon (now Mrs Neorah Bar-Noah), who was then secretary to the Chief of Staff. It is thanks to their vigilance and industry in gathering the material at the time that the writing of this book was made possible. Thanks also go to Lieut.-Colonel Avraham Ayalon, head of the Historical Department of the Israel Defence Forces, and Lieut. (Miss) Michal Botrimovitz, who were helpful to me during the period when the book was being written. To the others in the ranks of the Israel Defence Forces to whom I am indebted, I offer my warmest thanks through the present Chief of Staff, Major-General Yitzhak Rabin.

Moshe Dayan
ZAHALA, ISRAEL
SEPTEMBER, 1965

CHAPTER ONE

*

THE BACKGROUND

1

THE Sinai Campaign was the product jointly of a sharpening of the politico-security conflict between Israel and her neighbouring Arab States, and of the Anglo–French decision to establish control of the Suez Canal Zone by force.

If it were not for the Anglo–French operation, it is doubtful whether Israel would have launched her campaign; and if she had, its character, both military and political, would have been different.

Conversely, if the Arab States, led by the ruler of Egypt, had not pursued a policy of increasing enmity towards her, Israel would not have resorted to arms, even when the Suez crisis between Egypt and Britain and France exploded into a military clash.

The connection between the Anglo–French action in Suez (Operation 'Musketeer') and the Israeli campaign in Sinai is dealt with in the diary; but some words need to be said about the developments which led to the decision of the Israel Government to fight.

Declarations by the Arab rulers proclaiming their intention to attack Israel and wipe her off the map were renewed shortly after the signing in 1949 of the Armistice Agreements between Israel and the Arab States at the end of our war of independence. Not only did they refuse to translate these Agreements into a durable arrangement for peace, as they were committed to do, but immediately after the cease-fire, they started border incursions and raids against Israeli civilians.

At first, this was regarded by the Government of Israel as a hangover from the war, and though she demanded of the Arab

States adherence to the terms of the Agreements, she followed a policy of patience and restraint.

In the second half of 1954, however, the anti-Israel terrorism was intensified. In the succeeding months, it became clear to the Israel Government that these were not isolated incidents prompted by individual whim, but an organized operation undertaken with the knowledge of the Arab Governments and at the initiative and on the responsibility of Egypt. Israel's security situation steadily worsened, reaching a point of gravity in 1955-6 unknown since the war days of 1948.

The basic causes of this tension were three-fold: Egyptian preparations for an all-out war against Israel; Arab acts of terror by trained guerrilla bands; and the blockade of Israeli shipping in the Gulf of Akaba.

2

The decisive intimation to Israel of approaching Egyptian attack was the arms deal concluded between Czechoslovakia and Egypt in September 1955. By this transaction, Egypt received a large quantity of modern weapons, and the Israel Government considered this a preparatory step by the Egyptian ruler towards the fulfilment of his ambitions against her. She also judged that the very possession by the Arabs of arms superior in quality and volume to those available to Israel would spur them to exploit this military advantage and hasten their attack.

The Czech arms received by Egypt included 530 armoured vehicles – 230 tanks, 200 armoured troop-carriers and 100 self-propelled guns; some 500 artillery pieces of various types; almost 200 fighter aircraft, bombers and transport planes; and a number of warships – destroyers, motor-torpedo-boats and submarines.

By the standards of arms acquisition in the Middle East at that time, the scale of this deal was very much larger than anything known before. Added to the weapons already in Egypt's possession, it wiped out in a flash the shaky arms balance which existed between the Arab States and Israel. Up to then, Egypt had close to 200 tanks, and so did Israel. Now, Egypt's armoured force alone, apart from the armour in the other Arab States, had an ascendancy over Israel's of nearly four to one. This was true also of the air force. Before, Egypt had eighty jet warplanes as against Israel's fifty. Now, the number of Egyptian jet fighters and bombers shot up to 200 – four to one. In artillery, naval vessels and infantry weapons, the Israel picture was no better. It was not only the disparity in quantity but also the superiority in quality which decisively upset the arms scales. The Migs and Ilyushins which the Egyptians received were at least two stages ahead of the Meteors and Ouragans then in our possession; and their modern T-34 Soviet tanks were infinitely better than our old Sherman Mark 3s.

With the strengthening of his military power, Colonel Gamal Abdul Nasser's prestige rose among the Arab peoples, and he became the recognized and outstanding leader of the Arab League States. On 19 October 1955, the Joint Egypt–Syria Military Command was established, and in October 1956, Jordan, as expected, became its third partner. The State of Israel thus found herself hemmed in on three sides, south, east and north, by Arab armies subordinate to a single Command, and her Government could be under no illusion as to the aggressive purpose of this united military organization – nor against whom it was directed.

3

The penetration of Israel's borders by infiltrators bent on theft, sabotage and murder had been heartily approved by the neighbouring Arab Governments ever since the establishment of the State of Israel in 1948. But in April 1955 came the decision by the Egyptian General Staff to use acts of terror and sabotage as a means of warfare, and to this end it set up a special formation called 'fedayun'. [The literal translation of this Arabic term is 'self-sacrificers'.] The fedayun were under the command of the Intelligence Branch of the Egyptian Army in the Gaza Strip, and were organized in three camps (Camps 9, 10 and 16) near the seashore, west of the city of Gaza. At the time of its establishment, this unit numbered some 700, and the intention was to enlarge it and operate fedayun branches in the other Arab States – Jordan, Syria and Lebanon.

In addition to their regular monthly wage of nine Egyptian pounds, fedayun troops received a cash bonus for every crossing into Israel and a further special payment for every 'successful' action – murder or sabotage. Fedayun service also carried with it other perquisites, as is indicated in the following letter sent by the Chief of Egyptian Army Intelligence in the Gaza Strip, Colonel Mustafa Hafez, to the Governor of the Strip, interceding on behalf of a certain Yunes Mabrak who was up before the local courts charged with murder:

To the Administrative Governor-General:

1 The above-mentioned [Yunes Mabrak] is a representative of our office and one of the most faithful; he is a man who can be entrusted with important and dangerous missions. He was an example of heroism and supreme courage in his dedication and readiness for self-sacrifice on behalf of Egypt and the Egyptian armed forces.

2 The above-mentioned volunteered for the Palestinian fedayun forces and, infiltrating into Israel, carried out with his comrades acts of sabotage, dynamiting and killing. The following are some of his actions which are worthy of praise:

A On 29 August 1955 he carried out the following deeds:
    i Killed three workers in an orange-grove at Bet Hanun.
    ii Murdered a mechanic in the electric power station near Al Kabeiba.
    iii Blew up the main pylon of the 'Voice of Israel Overseas' radio station. (Map Reference 12721448.)
    iv Attacked the farm settlement of Juala (M.R. 12781438) near Zarnoga in the vicinity of Al Kabeiba, in which one man was killed, four were wounded, one building was destroyed and damage inflicted on the village co-operative store.
    v Ambushed a convoy of vehicles at M.R. 12951486.

B On 30 August 1955 he carried out the following deeds:
    i Ambushed a vehicle near the village of Ajur and killed three people. The vehicle was destroyed.
    ii Attacked the village of Tzumeil (M.R. 13001190) and blew up one of the buildings.
    iii Ambushed a vehicle on the Plugot–Bet Govrin road.
    iv At the same site, he ambushed three army vehicles.

3 Since the above-mentioned is one of the accused in the murder trial No. 26/55, and taking into account his wonderful deeds, we request that merciful consideration and appreciation be given to his past record of sacrificial actions so that a way may be found to help him as far as possible. It will also be

possible to use him in the future if he sees that the authorities appreciate the results of his courageous deeds.

We therefore request that you deal compassionately with our representative and that you close the file against him.

Mustafa Hafez,
COMMANDER, PALESTINE INTELLIGENCE

Towards the end of 1955 and during 1956, the acts of terror and sabotage by fedayun units increased, disturbing the ordered pattern of life in Israel, particularly among the new immigrant villages in the border regions.

An idea of what was happening may be gained from this list of fedayun incidents which occurred in the southern part of the country on five days in April 1956:

7 April 1956
Water pipeline blown up between Ashkelon and Yad Mordechai.
Civilian jeep fired on at Ahuzam; one Israeli civilian killed, one wounded.
Civilian truck fired on at Shuval; one killed, one wounded.
Army truck fired on at Tel Kuneitra; two wounded.
Army truck fired on and set ablaze near Ahuzam; three wounded.
Another army truck fired on near Ahuzam; two wounded.

8 April 1956
Hand-grenades thrown into a house and a vehicle in Ashkelon; one killed, three wounded.
Two civilian vehicles fired on at Ahuzam; one killed, two wounded.
Hand-grenades thrown into house at Shafir and another house blown up; one wounded.
Hand-grenades thrown and automatic fire opened up at house in Kibbutz Gal-on; one wounded.

9 April 1956
Army command car struck mine at Beerotayim, and two additional mines found near by.
Hand-grenades and automatic weapons attack on work camp of Water Company at Ketziot; two killed, three wounded.
Army command car fired on at Kibbutz Bet Rayim; one killed, one wounded.
[On this day, however, four fedayun bands ran into Israeli

7

ambushes and were engaged. Near Yad Mordechai, two fedayun were killed and one was captured; one Israeli soldier was wounded. Near Bet Govrin, four fedayun were captured, two of them wounded. Another fedayun group was ambushed in the same area that day and two were killed. Near the sand dunes of Nir Galim there was a running skirmish between an Israeli border patrol and a fedayun band of five; all five were killed, as was one Israeli soldier.]

10 April 1956
Army command car struck mine at Magen; three wounded.
Army vehicle struck mine near Kisufim; three wounded.
[On this day, too, other fedayun were foiled: one group ran into an Israeli ambush near Khirbet Likia, losing one killed and two captured; another group was ambushed near Bet Govrin, but managed to escape.]

11 April 1956
Command car struck mine south of Kerem Abu Iraq; one wounded.
Civilian bus and civilian truck shot at on Tel Aviv–Ramla highway; six wounded.
Shots fired into synagogue of agricultural boarding school at Shafir; six pupils killed, two wounded.
Hand-grenades thrown into two houses in village of Ahi'ezer; three wounded.
Border patrol car shot at near international airport of Lod; one wounded.

4

The Israel Government could not, of course, remain indifferent to these actions and accept them with equanimity. It was clear that there would be no end to this terrorism as long as the Arab Governments, particularly the Egyptian, could harm Israel without endangering their countries and their armies.

Israel therefore adopted a policy of reprisal, or, more accurately, of military reaction (for this did not take the same form as the fedayun attacks on civilians). After a wave of fedayun murder, an Israeli army unit would cross the border and strike at a military objective – an Army camp or a police fort – in the Arab territory from which the terrorist detachment had come.

The purpose of this policy was to show the Arabs that while Israel might be unable to protect the life of every tractor-driver ploughing a field close to the border, or prevent the mining of a dirt approach-track to an immigrant village, the country responsible for the saboteurs would not get off scot-free. When an Israeli force operated inside Arab territory without the local army's being able seriously to challenge them, the Arab military failure was openly demonstrated to their own people. Thus, instead of raising the prestige of the Arab régimes, the end result of fedayun actions was to shake popular trust in them and in their armed forces.

This process of action and counter-action brought the Arab Governments face to face with the choice either of strengthening their fedayun attacks in Israel, and so repairing the damage to their prestige in the eyes of their public, or of abandoning this course completely and thereby avoiding the provocation of Israel Army assaults which left in their wake blown-up camps and police forts and tens of killed among Arab troops and police.

It is possible that the Arab régimes would eventually have followed the second course and dropped their policy of terrorism, but during 1955–6, events snowballed. Both the fedayun operations and the Israel Army actions they triggered increased in frequency and scale. Moreover, since an Israeli reply could always be expected, the neighbouring state from which the fedayun had crossed into Israel knew what lay in store and could take appropriate steps, concentrating additional forces in army and police bases near the border ready to repel the attacker. This of course turned minor forays into battles whose range went on widening until, in the end, artillery and armour were involved.

Developments reached a pass by the end of the summer of 1955 and there seemed to be no way out. The explosive pattern of Arab terror and Israeli reaction heightened the tension between the two sides and produced an eve-of-war atmosphere. The Egyptian ruler, sensitive of his reputation, was loath to put a stop to the actions of the fedayun whose fame had by now spread among the Arab world as 'avengers of conquered Palestine'; but at the same time, the Israeli military response served as an ultimatum to the Arabs: to preserve the peace or to slide into war. In the month preceding the Sinai Campaign, between 12 September 1956 and 10 October 1956, Israel Army units, reacting to murders by the fedayun, carried out four assaults in which they blew up the police forts of Rahawah, Garandal, Husan and Kalkiliah. Israeli casualties (killed and wounded) in these actions numbered more than 100 and Arab casualties about 200. This was not yet war, but it certainly was not peace.

5

One of the basic issues in the conflict between Israel and Egypt was the freedom of Israeli shipping through the Red Sea. To get to the Red Sea, vessels leaving the port of Haifa on the Mediter- ranean need to pass through the Suez Canal, and ships leaving Eilat, Israel's southernmost port, must cross the Straits of Tiran. It was Egypt's policy to bar these waterways to Israeli shipping and thus deny Israel direct naval communication with East Africa and Asia.

Israel is not rich in natural resources, and among the few minerals she does possess, potash and phosphates take first place, and are exported primarily to the countries of the Far East. Blocking the naval routes to this region was thus not only a front rank political issue for Israel but also a grave blow to her economy and a brake on her development.

Since there was no question that this blockade was illegal, and a violation of the Suez Canal Convention [signed in Constantinople in 1888], of international law, of the Armistice Agreements and of the United Nations Charter, Israel had raised the matter at the UN. And, indeed, on 1 September 1951, the UN Security Council considered the Israel complaint and adopted a resolu- tion calling on Egypt to lift the blockade. Not only did Egypt ignore this decision, but at the end of 1953, she issued additional restrictive regulations banning the passage of *all* goods to and from Israel, even cargo of no specifically military value, such as food, and even if carried in non-Israeli vessels.

With the publication of these new regulations, Israel again brought her complaint to the Security Council. It came up for discussion on 29 March 1954, but the Soviet Union exercised the veto and the subject was dropped from the agenda.

The Israel Government did not give up the struggle and on 28 September 1954, at six in the morning, the Israeli vessel *Bat-Galim* reached the southern approaches to the Suez Canal.

It was thought that if the Egyptian authorities refused her passage, the United Nations would be compelled to consider the case and oblige the Egyptian Government to respect international law and allow freedom of transit to Israeli ships through Suez.

But this assumption was not realized. The Egyptians seized the *Bat-Galim* and incarcerated her crew. Again the problem came before the Security Council, in December 1954 and January 1955, but without effect. The end of this vain attempt to secure Egyptian acceptance of international legal obligations was that Egypt confiscated the *Bat-Galim* but returned its sailors – overland, through the Gaza Strip – on 1 January 1955, after they had spent three months in an Egyptian jail.

Failure to open the Suez Canal to Israeli shipping produced a mood of disappointment and anger in Israel; but no one considered that this matter could be handled in any way other than within the diplomatic framework. This, however, was not how Israel viewed the problem of passage through the Straits of Tiran.

These Straits link the Red Sea with the Gulf of Akaba, a gulf whose shores are divided among four countries – Egypt, Israel, Jordan and Saudi Arabia. Such waterways, which are bounded by coasts of more than one territory, are obliged by international law to be free to the vessels of all nations, and no part of them can be claimed as territorial waters by any of the states sharing their coastline. These states have no right to control shipping passing through.

But Egypt chose to ignore this principle of international law and interfered with vessels seeking to move between the Red Sea and the port of Eilat. In 1953, she introduced blockade regulations against Israeli shipping, and established a coastguard unit at Ras Natsrani. This unit, backed by coastal guns, now stopped all vessels entering the Straits, and subjected them to examination and search to ensure that they were not Israeli ships.

At the beginning of September 1955, Egypt decided to strengthen and broaden the scale of the blockade. She notified all shipping and air companies that passage through the Gulf, whether by sea or air, was passage through Egyptian territory, and that anyone wishing to use this route had to give seventy-two hours' advance notice and receive permission from the

11

Egyptian authorities. As for Israel, her ships and planes would not be allowed at all through or over the Straits of Tiran since, the statement said, Egypt considered herself to be in a state of war with her. Following this announcement came the stoppage, in addition to shipping, of flights by the Israeli airline 'El Al' from Tel Aviv to South Africa, which formerly had flown over the Straits.

Widening the scope of the blockade of Suez and Tiran, and extending it to our air link with Africa, was the last straw.

On 22 October 1955, while I was vacationing in France, I received a cable from the military aide of Ben Gurion instructing me to come home immediately. (Ben Gurion had returned to the Cabinet from his temporary retirement at Sde Boker and was again Minister of Defence, but not yet [again] Prime Minister.) The cable read: 'The "old man" rose from sickbed this morning. (He had been ill for two weeks.) His first request was to see you. He wants you to come immediately. Cable time arrival.' Next day I met Ben Gurion in his room at the President Hotel in Jerusalem. I reviewed the security situation and the current problems we faced. At the end of the talk, he, as Minister of Defence, instructed me, among other things, to be prepared to capture the Straits of Tiran – Sharm e-Sheikh, Ras Natsrani and the islands of Tiran and Sanapir – in order to ensure freedom of shipping through the Gulf of Akaba and the Red Sea.

Ten days later, on 2 November 1955, Ben Gurion returned to office as Prime Minister. In presenting his new Cabinet to the Knesset, he gave a general policy address, and when he came to the section on defence, he said:

The forays from the Gaza Strip alone caused 153 casualties in killed and wounded during the first nine months of 1955. The Egyptian representatives at the UN have openly declared that a state of war continues between Egypt and Israel. The Government of Egypt has violated basic international law governing the freedom of shipping through Suez, on which there was also a specific resolution of the Security Council. *Thus Egypt now seeks to seal the Red Sea route against Israeli vessels, contrary to the international principle of freedom of the seas. This one-sided war will have to stop, for it cannot remain one-sided for ever.*

The Government of Israel is ready faithfully to respect the

12

Armistice Agreements in all their terms and details, preserving them in the letter and the spirit. But this duty is also binding on the other party. An agreement which is violated by the other side will also not be binding on us. If the armistice lines are opened by them to saboteurs and murderers, they will not be found closed to our defenders. If our rights are assailed by acts of violence on land or sea, we shall reserve freedom of action to defend those rights in the most effective manner.

We seek peace – but not suicide.

There could have been no clearer statement from the Prime Minister before the Knesset forum on his intention to instruct the army to cross the border if the anarchic situation continued.

The state of Israel's security did not change – at all events not for the better – and the blockade of Eilat persisted. Ben Gurion had no doubts whatever that it was Israel's duty to safeguard the freedom of her shipping, and that to do so she would have to seize the Straits. Accordingly, at the beginning of November 1955, he raised the issue for consideration at a meeting of the Cabinet; but despite his plea and his explanations, the Government decided that the moment was not propitious. They added, however, that Israel should act 'in the place and at the time that she deems appropriate'.

This decision was transmitted to me, and I responded with the following letter to Ben Gurion on 5 December 1955:

To the Minister of Defence:
Subject: Israel–Egyptian Relations
1 Six weeks ago, the 'El Al' airline company stopped flying over the Straits of Tiran on its Israel–South Africa route. This was done after the Egyptian announcement that they would fire on planes passing without permission over this region which Egypt claims is Egyptian territory. The chapter on the Straits of Tiran is well known and I shall not recapitulate it here; but I consider that our present policy on this matter is incorrect and will, in effect, lead to the loss of our naval and aerial freedom through the Straits. Eilat will thereby become for us a coastal strip along a closed lake, exit from which will be conditional on Egyptian agreement.

There was a similar development, at the time, with freedom of access to Mount Scopus (in Jerusalem) and with the use of the Latrun road (between Jerusalem and Tel Aviv). The guarantee of both was decided on in principle in the Armistice Agreement, but owing to Jordan's refusal on the one hand and our failure to implement them by force on the other, they were never carried out.

The issue of the Straits of Tiran is very much graver, for:

(a) Egypt has no legal excuse to prevent our free passage;

(b) The importance of movement through the Straits is much greater than movement through Latrun and access to Mount Scopus;

(c) Blockade of the Straits is part of an overall plan to seize the Negev.

2 Following the Egyptian announcement, we have stopped our flights over this route; yet we continue to sit with the Egyptians on the Mixed Armistice Commission. This indicates that we do not regard their action as a cancellation of the Armistice Agreement. Rather does it suggest that we are reconciled, in practice, to their 'interpretation', and that we continue to view the Armistice Agreement as the basis of our relations with Egypt – even when they deny us passage through the Straits.

3 The formula that we shall act 'in the place and at the time' we deem appropriate is a realistic formula when indeed the place and time for such action are apparent. In practice, any action undertaken in any *place* other than the Straits – in order to lead indirectly to a lifting of the blockade of that waterway – would have to be aggressive, protracted and decisive. As to *time*, it does not seem to me that the moment for action – capture of the Straits – will be more favourable a few months hence. With the strengthening of the Egyptian forces, particularly in the air, our military prospects of succeeding in such an operation will be weakened. It may be, of course, that one of these days a situation will be created which makes military action possible, but this will be the fruit of chance and not the planned result of postponing it to a specific 'time' and 'place'.

4 I therefore see our failure to act now, and our continued recognition of the Israel–Egyptian Armistice Agreement in these circumstances, as a *de facto* surrender of our freedom of shipping and flight through the Straits of Tiran. Furthermore, the fact cannot be ignored that on this subject unequivocal declarations have been made by you and by your

predecessor as Prime Minister; and that you made known to the Prime Minister of Egypt, through General Burns (General E. L. M. Burns, a Canadian, Chief of Staff of the United Nations Truce Supervision Organization), the policy of the Government which holds that Israel will not agree to a one-sided adherence to the Armistice Agreements.

It is accordingly my view that we should undertake as soon as possible (within one month) *the capture of the Straits of Tiran.*

5 I must stress that if the Egyptian air force has MIG-15s while we possess no planes comparable in quality, our chance of success in capturing the Straits will be much reduced. This is a difficult and complicated operation which will depend decisively on freedom of action in the air.

Although my letter was addressed to Ben Gurion, it should not really have been directed to him, for he after all was the one who was anxious to instruct the army to break the blockade and it was the Government which decided that the time to do so had not yet come.

Postponement, however, did not solve the problem, and even a year later Israel was still confronted by the alternative of surrendering her freedom of movement to the Red Sea or achieving it by seizing the Straits.

7

The alternative to the use of force – settling controversial problems by negotiation – was denied to Israel because the Arabs refused to negotiate. This refusal was not accidental. It sprang from their opposition to the recognition of Israel and the establishment of peaceful relations with her. For the Arabs, the question was not one of finding a solution to this or that problem; the question, for them, was the very existence of Israel. Their aim was to annihilate Israel, and this cannot be done at a conference table.

The first war by the Arabs against the people of Israel did not go well for them, and in 1948 their attempt to conquer and destroy the Jewish community there ended in failure. The Iraqi army, which had participated in the attack, returned, after the defeat, to its country. But Egypt, Jordan, Lebanon and Syria were forced to sign Armistice Agreements with Israel, for otherwise the Israeli Army was likely to continue its advance right into their territories. (As a matter of fact, in the south and the north, Israeli forces *had* crossed the borders, pursuing the Egyptians into Sinai and the Lebanese up to the river Litani.)

The Armistice Agreements were reached under the chairmanship of United Nations representative Dr Ralph Bunche and were based on the decisions of the Security Council and on the UN Charter. The preamble to each agreement states: 'The Parties to the present Agreement, responding to the Security Council resolution of 16 November 1948, calling upon them as a further provisional measure under Article 40 of the Charter of the United Nations and in order to facilitate the transition from the present truce to permanent peace in Palestine, to negotiate an Armistice; having decided to enter into negotiations under United Nations Chairmanship concerning the implementation of the Security Council resolutions of 4 and 16 November 1948; and having appointed representatives empowered to negotiate and conclude an Armistice Agreement; . . . have agreed upon the following provisions . . .'

But negotiating, drafting and signing the Agreements were not the only activities carried out under the aegis of UN representatives. Supervision of their implementation was also entrusted to the United Nations and conducted by a special staff of military observers established for this purpose.

Small wonder, therefore, that the representatives of the UN, the Secretary-General and the Chief of Staff of the UN Truce Supervision Organization, were the mediators and the liaison officers between Israel and her Arab neighbours, dashing from capital to capital, particularly between Jerusalem and Cairo, trying to prevent border incidents and reduce tensions.

The activities of the Chief of Staff of the UNTSO (during 1954–6, this was General Burns) were largely of a technical nature, and he participated in political discussions only when he accompanied the Secretary-General, who at that time was Dag Hammarskjöld. The UNTSO occupied itself mostly with post-factum investigations. Following a complaint by one of the parties, it would make its examination and transmit a report of its findings to the Secretary-General, or, if the incident were sufficiently grave, to the Security Council. Neither side – neither the Arabs nor Israel – had much faith in the UNTSO knowing that it was little more than a letter-box, capable of receiving complaints but powerless to do anything about them. In 1955, at the height of the fedayun attacks, General Burns tried to get the Egyptian authorities to stop them, but he was turned down. In his book *Between Arab and Israeli* he writes: 'It was never possible to prove that the orders for the fedayeen, or any other marauders, to enter Israel and commit terroristic acts came from Cairo. When challenged on this point privately by myself or the Secretary-General the most that would be admitted was that the raiding could be stopped by the authorities, not that it had initiated them' (page 89).

The activities of Secretary-General Dag Hammarskjöld were in the political sphere. His meetings were at a higher level, but he was equally unsuccessful. All his efforts to persuade Nasser to agree to or even promise to obey the decisions of the Security Council on the passage of Israeli vessels through the Suez Canal, freedom of shipping through the Straits of Tiran, and the cessation of fedayun attacks, proved fruitless.

At the end of 1955 and beginning of 1956, with the increasing strain in the region, the activities of UN representatives reached their peak. In December 1955, Prime Minister David Ben Gurion called General Burns and told him that the Israel Government had reliable information that the Government of Egypt was responsible for the fedayun operations. He asked him to demand of Nasser full compliance with the Armistice Agreement, and the fulfilment of two articles in particular: the one calling for absolute cease-fire and the prevention of attacks on the civilians of one State by her neighbour; and the other (Article 1) which contains four basic injunctions: Prohibition of 'resort to military force in the settlement of the Palestine question'; the obligation of both parties not to 'undertake, plan or threaten . . . aggressive action by the armed forces – land, sea or air – against the people or armed forces of the other'; the 'right of each party to its security and freedom from fear of attack by the armed forces of the other'; and the 'establishment of an armistice between the armed forces of the two parties as an indispensable step towards the liquidation of armed conflict and the restoration of peace'.

General Burns was unable to secure from Nasser the required undertaking; nor was Dag Hammarskjöld, who visited Cairo and saw Nasser a few weeks later.

Two months went by, and on 14 March 1956, Israel submitted

17

to the Security Council a sharp complaint on the breaches of peace along the Gaza Strip border. Attached to the complaint was a list of 180 Egyptian acts of hostility – mine-laying, shooting, murder – which had been carried out during the previous three months, from December 1955 to March 1956. The situation steadily worsened. The fedayun attacks, bringing in their wake the military reactions of the Israel Army, became more frequent and more violent, and the Secretary-General decided to return to the Middle East and try to resolve the crisis. On 10 April he arrived in Israel. After talks there, he flew to Cairo; then back to Jerusalem; then on to Amman; again back to Jerusalem; and again on to Cairo. He did all this in seven days, and it seemed that this time his efforts might be successful.

On 17 April he received the following letter from Ben Gurion:

I write this to confirm, in the name of the Government of Israel, that in accordance with Article 2, paragraph 2, of the Israel–Egypt General Armistice Agreement, orders again go into effect as from 6 p.m. (Israel time) on 18 April 1956 for the scrupulous implementation of the instructions prohibiting all units of the Israel Defence Forces from firing across the armistice lines, and prohibiting all crossing of the border by military or para-military forces, including non-regular forces, for any purpose whatsoever. This undertaking is given subject to full reciprocity on the part of Egypt.

Two days later, on 19 April, Hammarskjöld – who was then in Cairo – notified Ben Gurion that the Government of Egypt had given a similar undertaking and that the cease-fire orders went into effect on 18 April at 6 p.m.

Hammarskjöld believed that he had really succeeded in putting out the fire and prevented a flare-up; but on 29 April, while the Secretary-General was still in the Middle East, the gifted leader of kibbutz Nahal Oz, Roi Rutenberg, was shot by an Egyptian border patrol who fired at him from across the frontier of the Gaza Strip. On the same day, an army command-car went up on a mine near Nir Yitzhak, on the southern border of the Strip. Israel did not react to these two incidents, hoping that they were not committed with the knowledge of Cairo; but within a few days her illusions were shattered. The fedayun went back to work with full vigour, entering Israel both from the Gaza Strip and Jordan, mining roads, murdering labourers, tossing hand-grenades into houses, firing at buses on the highways. This became the habitual pattern.

Hammarskjöld did not take the initiative this time to return to the Middle East; nor did Israel's Prime Minister invite him to do so.

At a session of the Knesset on 15 October 1956, Ben Gurion, reviewing the political situation, said:

In his report to the Security Council on 9 May 1956, the Secretary-General of the UN condemned these 'reprisal actions'. Even if the UN Charter had not specifically guaranteed the right of self-defence to every nation, this right exists on its own. The apparatus of the UN has demonstrated its incapacity – I do not say its unwillingness – to prevent the continued and systematic murder of citizens of Israel. As far as I know, this is the only country where the lives of its inhabitants are endangered by bands of murderers sent in by the rulers of the neighbouring states. I cannot imagine any other country reconciling herself to a situation in which her citizens were at the mercy of assassins organized by neighbouring Governments. The UN truce observers and the UN Secretary-General well know that these bands act on behalf of their Governments, and that Egypt is the prime and central mover in their organization, equipment and training, and in the planning of their operations. Members of the fedayun who have been captured by us have admitted this at their trials; and the Egyptian Waqf Minister, Hassan al Bakuri, said in a broadcast on 11 April this year over the 'Voice of Cairo' ('Sa'ut al Arab') which is subordinate to the Egyptian dictator: 'There is no reason why the fedayun who hate their enemies should not penetrate deep into Israel and turn the lives of her people into a living hell.'

The Government of Israel will not allow the country to be turned into a living hell, and the assassins and their masters will not go unpunished.

Fourteen days later, on 29 October 1956, the Sinai Campaign was launched.

CHAPTER TWO

*

PRELUDE TO SINAI

1 September 1956

There was a full meeting of the General Staff this morning, with the participation of the Prime Minister and Minister of Defence, David Ben Gurion, to review our employment of armour. In the middle of the discussion, a 'Most Immediate' signal from our Military Attaché in Paris was brought in to me, with information on the Anglo-French plan to seize the Suez Canal. It said that the purpose of the Anglo-French move was the occupation of the Canal Zone and the annulment of the nationalization order. (Nasser had announced the nationalization of the Suez Canal on 27 July 1956.) The signal added that the operation had been given the code name of 'Musketeer' and that it would be commanded by the British general Sir Charles Keightley, with the French vice-admiral Pierre Barjot as his deputy.

In the last few days we have had intelligence also from other sources indicating that the political situation was likely to become more grave.

During our lunch break, we held brief consultations on these developments and we decided that, at all events, we had to prepare for the possibility of war in our area. I accordingly ordered my staff to cut down the office meetings which had been scheduled for me over the next two weeks and to arrange instead a series of visits to our operational units.

If indeed Britain and France capture the Suez Canal and restore its international status by force of arms, the political implications for us will be of the highest importance. Not only will the Canal be open (I hope) to Israeli shipping, but Britain will be engaged in a military conflict with Egypt over interests which serve us too. I well remember what King Abdullah of Jordan told me not long before he was murdered. He said he

20

was prepared to reach an agreement with us, but the British representative Kirkbride (Sir Alexander Kirkbride, British Minister in Amman) was opposed to it, for he felt that this would harm the friendly relations between Britain and Egypt. At that time – the late 1940's – Britain was supporting and encouraging Arab nationalism, and saw her association with Egypt as the basis of support for her position in the Middle East. It would be interesting to know if Britain's Prime Minister, Anthony Eden, still feels that it was worth preventing peace between Jordan and Israel only in order that Britain should not appear pro-Israeli in the eyes of Egypt (the Egypt of King Farouk!).

This evening, Cairo Radio announced that heavy losses were inflicted on Israeli patrols along the border of the Gaza Strip. The truth is that not a man of ours was hurt and none is missing. I wonder whether the people in Gaza really believe what they hear on Cairo Radio, or whether they have already come to realize that its announcements on Israel offer propaganda rather than information.

7 September 1956

Yesterday I visited the headquarters of the Armoured Corps, accompanied by heads of the various branches of the General Staff, to see what could be done to speed up the training of crews to man the additional tanks we have received.

Today I visited Air Force Headquarters to review their situation and their training programme in the light of what we may expect in the near future. I emphasized that our political circumstances obliged us to be capable of going into action and operating all our aircraft – including our new acquisitions – and not to be caught in a position in which we would have to pass up favourable political opportunities to strike at Egypt, or go into battle with old planes for lack of pilots for the new ones.

I am confident that the Air Force is alive to the urgencies and will do all they can to hasten the 'pilot producing' process. They plan to train propeller aircraft pilots directly on jets without putting them through the customary intermediate stage. They will go from Harvards straight to Meteors, and cut out the training phase on Mustangs.

21

As usual the chronic problems were raised – shortage of manpower and limited budget. We have to scratch around for additions to the operational budget from every corner. Among other things I did today was cancel the departure of nine officers who were scheduled to leave for courses overseas. True this will save $70,000, but I doubt whether I would have done this in other circumstances.

The day after tomorrow I shall inspect the Golani infantry brigade to check their state of readiness on the spot. I shall do the same on the 19th with the paratroop brigade.

17 September 1956

A week ago I ordered the branches of the General Staff to examine the various operational plans on the Egyptian front, from the capture of the whole of the Sinai Peninsula to such partial actions as securing control of the Straits of Tiran (at the southern end of the Gulf of Akaba) or of the Gaza Strip. I followed it up with a meeting today of the full Operations Branch of the General Staff, including senior officers of the Air Force and the Navy.

I outlined the political and strategic background, distinguishing, in accordance with the Defence Minister's guidance, between international problems and our own special problems. The operation which is likely to be launched will have been prompted by the abrogation of the international status of the Suez Canal. This is not a specific Israeli problem, even though it is naturally of close concern to us. We have no aspirations to reach Suez and become an involved party in this dispute. This, however, is not the case with the Straits of Tiran (the narrow passage between the islands of Tiran and Sanapir and Sharm e-Sheikh) and the Gaza Strip. These are problems specific to us. The one is used by Egypt to blockade shipping to Eilat, the other as a base for Egyptian terrorist raids on Israel.

Military action against these targets may be taken by us at our own initiative, either in association with the forces operating against Egypt or without any contact with them, whenever the Government of Israel decides that the situation warrants it.

24 September 1956

Ben Gurion called a special meeting of the Cabinet today to approve military retaliatory action against Jordan's Arab Legion. With all our wish not to aggravate the Arab–Israel conflict at a time when the West is in dispute with the Arabs over Suez, and not to give the British a pretext to condemn Israel and thereby cover up their own ineffectiveness in the Suez affair, we cannot avoid taking vigorous military steps against Jordan. The Arab public regard terrorism against Israel as part of an obligatory national war. It helps satisfy their yearning for vengeance and restores something of their honour, tarnished by the defeat of the Arab armies in Israel's war of independence. The Arab Government leaders, including Jordan's King Hussein, claim – for overseas consumption – that they are powerless to prevent acts of terror which, they say, are the deeds of Palestinian refugees. Among their own people, however, they applaud the terrorism, which is carried out by personnel of the special army unit, fedayun, sent from Gaza to operate in Jordan, Syria and Lebanon (where they are supplied with arms and wages by the Egyptian embassies in these countries). There can be no doubt that in the present circumstances the only means we have to bring about a stoppage of their attacks on Israeli civilians is sharp army action against Arab military objectives. We hope that these operations will convince the Arab Governments that it is in their own interests to prevent fedayun activity, for in the end the weakness of the Arab armies will be demonstrated and they will be shown up as incapable of meeting the Israel Army in the field. The consequence to the Arab leaders can only be a loss of standing and prestige.

From the political point of view, it is by no means simple to send armed forces into action in peace-time, and to order them to attack targets across the border; but the past week has seen a marked increase in the acts of terror from Jordan – way beyond the point where we can permit ourselves restraint.

On the 22nd of the month – two days ago – Arab Legion positions just north of Bethlehem opened up with machine-gun fire on a group of our archaeologists who were visiting the excavations at Ramat Rachel, on the southern outskirts of Jerusalem. The Arab post is close to the Mar Elias Monastery, and the Israeli archaeologists were standing in full view of them, exposed, without shelter. Within a few moments, four of them were killed and sixteen wounded.

There were two more incidents yesterday, one also in the vicinity of Jerusalem, at the new immigrants' farm settlement of Aminadav, close to the Jordan border. Two women, a mother and daughter, were out gathering wood when they were fired on by Arab legionaries from Kafr Beitir, just across the frontier. Both were wounded, but the mother managed to dash back to Aminadav for help. When she returned with several of the villagers, they found the daughter dead from stab-wounds. The Arab soldiers had crossed into Israel, murdered her, and cut off and taken one of her hands.

The second incident occurred at kibbutz Maoz Haim in the Bet She'an valley. In this area, the Jordan river forms the boundary between Israel and Jordan. Here, Arab soldiers crossed the river, shot a young tractor-driver who was out ploughing, and dragged his body over to Jordan.

In all three cases, the Arab attackers could have been in no doubt that their victims were civilians going innocently about their business, and in no doubt that they were doing so on the Israeli side of the border.

25 September 1956

I met Ben Gurion at about 08.30 today at the military airfield in Ramla. He came in a Piper Cub from Sde Boker. Though he is no longer young – he will be sixty-eight this year – he insists on making the bumpy drive by car every Friday from Jerusalem or Tel-Aviv to his desert hut in kibbutz Sde Boker in the Negev, and returning by Piper – a highly uncomfortable flight – on Sunday morning. For Ben Gurion, settlement in the Negev is the supreme expression of Israel reborn, an Israel turning the wilderness into a source of life through the dedication of her new immigrants and young, locally born, men and women who have given up the comforts of city life to join in the pioneer venture. As the antithesis of this he sees the city of Tel-Aviv, and I have heard him mutter as we walked through its crowded streets – 'Nineveh'!

Shimon Peres (Director General of the Ministry of Defence) was also at the airfield and the three of us drove to Jerusalem. As a reply to the murders of the last few days I suggested to Ben

Gurion action against any of four possible targets: Dahariah, in the Hebron hills: Jenin, in Samaria: Husan, or Tzurif, both in the Jerusalem hills. There are Jordanian armed forces stationed in all these places, and the aim is to strike at them and not to harm the civilians.

Ben Gurion is inclined to authorize limited action in the Jerusalem area so as to underline the link between this operation and the region from which the Jordanian attacks were launched.

Continuing our journey, we then reviewed the results of Peres' visit to France, from which he has just returned. It appears that Christian Pineau, the French Foreign Minister, left the second London Conference (on 21 September) gravely disappointed. This was to have been the founding conference of the Suez Canal Users' Conference, suggested by John Foster Dulles, the United States Secretary of State, but it became clear to Pineau that in fact the American design was to nullify any attempt to void the Egyptian nationalization of the Suez Canal. He also believes that the British will not initiate military action against Nasser. Britain's Prime Minister, Anthony Eden, is in favour of such action, but he has encountered strong opposition even inside his own party. On the other hand, the feeling in French Ministry of Defence circles is that military operations against Egypt are essential and that France should launch them – even if she has to act alone. If she does, they believe that Britain, in the end, will join in the campaign. They do not think the United States will interfere; as for the Soviet Union, they just cannot guess what the reaction will be.

26 September 1956

Last night we carried out a retaliatory action against the Arab Legion position at the Tegart police fortress of Husan. ('Tegart fortress' was the name given to the strongly built police posts erected in key spots throughout the country by the British Mandatory Administration in the late 1930's on the recommendation of Sir Charles Tegart, who had been brought in as an adviser on security.) During such engagements I like to be at the forward command post of the fighting unit; battle, even on a limited scale, is after all the Army's basic business. I do not know if the unit commander 'enjoys' finding me at his elbow, but I prefer, whenever possible, to follow the action – and if necessary even intervene in its direction – close to the scene and while it is happening, rather than read about it in a dispatch the following morning and reveal the wisdom of hindsight.

Rear HQ of this unit was at the farm settlement Mevuot-Betar. I left my car there and went on foot to the brigade command post which was on a hill a few hundred yards from the enemy positions. When I returned shortly before dawn, I found that several of our men who had remained at rear HQ had been wounded when the settlement was mortared by the Arab Legion. Among them was my driver, Noam. His wounds were not serious and he had not lost his sense of humour. He was paying, he explained, for not heeding my suggestion that during battle you should stay out in the open, and not beneath some shelter which hides you from your star up on high, for how then can it keep a protective eye on you . . . ?

The objective was gained. The police fort was completely demolished, and all the Arab positions were overrun. But we paid a heavy price – ten killed and sixteen wounded. Enemy casualties known so far are thirty-nine killed and twelve wounded. The Legion tried to rush reinforcements to their unit under attack, but our men ambushed them *en route*, and prevented them from joining the battle.

Most of our casualties occurred when they stormed the enemy positions entrenched in the side of the hill. The Arab legionaries here put up a very determined fight, possibly because they had been left no means of retreat. Then came another obstacle – our vehicles were held up by a deep anti-tank ditch. There was nothing for it but to use a fighting company to fill the ditch with stones and earth.

The overriding difficulty of such night actions springs from the limited time in which they must be conducted. In the few hours of utter darkness, over terrain marked by steep hills covered by boulders and thorn-bush, our fighters have to capture the enemy's entrenched border posts, move on to storm the police fort, clear a path across the trackless ground for the vehicles carrying explosives to be moved up to the fort buildings, blow them up, and then return with all our men – including killed and wounded – before first light.

In these actions, our commanders go in with the advance

troops of their units, and in every battle some of the best of them become casualties. In our last action at the beginning of the month, against the Jordanian police fort at Rahawah (on the Hebron–Beersheba highway) the finest of our commando soldiers was hit. He is Captain Meir Har-Zion, a twenty-one-year-old, whose fighting skill and extraordinary courage are legendary in the Army. He was gravely wounded, the bullet striking his windpipe, but his life was saved by the medical officer of the unit, who crawled to him under fire and performed a tracheotomy with his pocket-knife. I do not think there is a single veteran officer in the paratroopers who has not been wounded in one of their actions.

The unit arrived back in Israel territory before dawn, bearing their casualties. Ambulances awaited them at the assembly point and rushed the wounded to hospital. In one section of the dining-room at Mevuot-Betar the returning troops were being given tea and sandwiches, while in another, the early-rising farmers of the kibbutz were snatching a hasty breakfast before going out to the fields.

After hearing details of the battle from the officers – and, according to them, the errors in the operational planning – I returned to GHQ. Travelling with me in the car was paratroop officer U. who was lightly wounded and who refused to be taken to hospital. The pre-dawn chill and the swaying over tortuous roads kept us from sleep, and so we just chatted. Among other things told me by U. was the story of two young officers of his unit who were bitten by the spiritualist bug and who, on the nights when they are not in action, 'converse' with their fallen comrades. The 'conversation' proceeds by their asking questions of the spirit of the deceased and receiving answers in taps and other signs. When U. mentioned their names, I could scarcely believe my ears. I cannot imagine any young men more intelligent and sober than they. I said this to U. and to my astonishment he replied with the utmost gravity that to anyone who spends two years in action, seeing dear friends killed at his side almost every week, intelligence and sobriety are of no help, and the borderline between life and death becomes inevitably blurred. I tried to press him further, but he preferred to change the subject.

27 September 1956

Most of today's meeting with Ben Gurion was taken up with his analysis of our political and security situation. The question of where the United States and Britain stand continues to disturb him. He is apprehensive of America and suspicious of Britain. He feels that Britain may wish to demonstrate her friendship for the Arabs by employing her forces against us in going to the help of Jordan. A full-scale engagement between us and Jordan could occur in any of three circumstances:

1 If Jordan goes to the aid of Egypt in the event that Egypt finds herself at war with us.
2 If terrorist activity from Jordanian territory and our military reactions to it develop into serious battles.
3 If the Iraqi Army enters Jordan and, in particular, if it is stationed on the Israeli border.

Jordan–Iraqi relations are not at all clear at the moment. Jordan wavers between a pro-Egyptian and a pro-Iraqi orientation, or rather between reliance on Egypt or on Iraq. At present, though, it seems that she is trying to strengthen her ties with Iraq within a royal Hashemite framework.

The Jordanian Chief of Staff, Ali Abu Nawar, visited Iraq in June, and the result of his trip was the setting up of a joint committee consisting of the Chiefs of Staff and Defence Ministers of both countries, with the task of determining the ways in which Iraq could come to the help of Jordan.

The committee decided that in the first phase, Iraq would station a reinforced division on the Iraqi–Jordan border ready to go to Jordan's aid when called.

More recently, with the sharpening of issues between Jordan and Israel, King Hussein flew to Iraq and met with King Feisal on the airfield at Habbaniyah. The subject of their special meeting was the transfer of the Iraqi division *into* Jordan.

Ben Gurion takes a very grave view of the possible stationing of Iraqi troops on the Israel border and declares openly that if this should happen Israel would move her forces to the west bank of the river Jordan. I am not sure whether he is absolutely determined to take such action or whether he hopes this threat will be enough to discourage such a move. At all events, the Israel–Jordan situation is very tense at this moment, on account both of the border incidents and of the Jordanian intention to open her doors to the Iraqi Army, and the question of Britain's behaviour if war should start between us and Jordan is not hypothetical.

28 September 1956

A meeting of the General Staff was held at 10.00. We leave tonight for Paris, and we must complete the listing of military equipment we shall try to get from the French. A check of our logistic *matériel* makes us more aware than ever what paupers we are. Nevertheless we have cut down the list to only the most urgent and essential items. For one thing, we do not wish to exaggerate, or even give the impression that we are exaggerating, in our demands. For another, we do not want to saddle our army with the complication of having to absorb at the last moment more new equipment than is absolutely necessary. Nor do we wish to clutter up the comparatively few roads which will be serving the fronts.

Despite this, the list is quite formidable. It includes tanks, tank-transporters, half-track vehicles, bazookas and transport planes.

We took off at 19.00 this evening from a military airfield, making for Paris via Bizerta. We were to have embarked at airfield L, but we left from airfield D through faulty navigation but correct judgement on the part of the crew of the French plane which had come for us at midday. Their flight plan called for their landing at airfield L, but for some reason they could not spot it. Suddenly, they noticed another airfield with French planes on the ground – Mystères and Ouragans. It happened to be Airfield D. 'Whichever airfield it is, it must be friendly, for those planes are ours,' the captain decided, and called the tower for permission to land. The commander of the airfield, E.W., had no warning that such a plane was expected, but he, too, when he identified its markings, decided that 'whatever it is, it's one of ours', and invited it down.

The flight to Bizerta took seven and a half hours. The crew were happy to share their food with us *en route*. We each received a giant bottle of red wine, a French loaf, cheese and yards of sausage. I do not know how this trip will end, but so far the gastronomic co-operation has been perfect.

Arrived in Bizerta, we were awaited by a major of the French General Staff who brought us to the base-commander, an admiral, and we were his guests for dinner. A few hours sleep, and at 5.00 tomorrow, the 29th, we take off for Paris.

1 October 1956

This morning we met with the French Chief of Staff, General Ely. The meeting was held at the home of our friend Louis Mangin, political adviser to the French Minister of Defence, Maurice Bourges-Maunoury. Participants from the Israel delegation were myself and officers of our Military Attaché's staff. With General Ely were his deputy for Air Force affairs, General Maurice Challe; General Martin, second-in-command to Challe; Colonel Simon, of Operations Branch of the General Staff; a Naval officer; and Louis Mangin.

General Ely spoke of Israel with friendliness and warmth. In style, manner and speech, he is very different from his predecessor, General Guillaume, whom I knew, and from Generals Challe and Martin. He is tall, lean and grey-haired, and he looks and talks like an intellectual. He has lost the use of one hand.

The purpose of our meeting was an exchange of information and the clarification of technical matters. General Ely opened by asking the strength of Egypt's forces, and we told him what we knew. Our information seems to tally with his own intelligence reports. He then turned to our security problems, asking me how I saw developments in the Middle East and in what way France could help us.

His initial questions were already indicative of his attitude. General Ely was anxious to be helpful to us but he was not disposed to talk about French plans for the Suez Canal. My efforts to get him to discuss these plans proved fruitless.

Towards the end of our meeting, General Ely asked what equipment we wanted from France. I handed him the list, which included 100 tanks (Super Shermans), 300 half-track vehicles, 50 tank-transporters, 300 trucks with four-wheel drive, 1,000 bazookas, and a squadron of transport planes. I do not know whether or not he had been briefed before our talk on the size and equipment of the Israel Defence Forces, but I saw his surprise when I told him that the military establishment of our units is roughly one quarter that of their counterparts in the French Army; that our ammunition supplies, spare parts and fuel are enough only for twenty to thirty days of battle; that we have only one squadron of transport planes; and that our armour consists of obsolete tanks – Sherman Mark 3s. I added my conviction that even with the equipment that we had – or rather despite the equipment that we did not have – we could, if war broke out between us and Egypt, defeat their Army and capture the Sinai Peninsula within a fortnight. If we do not get additional tanks, we shall use bazookas mounted on jeeps and command-cars. Our primary problem is vehicles that can move across desert. I do not know how tough will be the opposition from Egyptian armour; but I do know how tough an obstacle is the desert, and to overcome it and get our troops, ammunition and other supplies to Sharm e-Sheikh, we need suitable transport.

General Ely looked through the list and said that he would try and satisfy our request; but he has difficulties: the Army in Algeria puts up a constant cry for more equipment; and he is also reluctant to reduce the quantities earmarked for his units in Cyprus assigned to the Suez operations.

Incidentally, during the meeting, I explained to General Ely that the Israel Army was largely an army of reservists. When I told him that there was not sufficient equipment for them, so that they had to use civilian vehicles and wear their own civilian overcoats in winter, I could sense that he was conjuring up a picture of a civilian army of the eighteenth century, capable perhaps of mounting the barricades with their flags, but not of conducting a desert campaign with armoured vehicles and coping with the maintenance of long supply lines.

Tonight we fly back to Israel. Despite the pouring rain, we decided to spend the few hours before take-off wandering through the streets of Paris. But first we stepped into the Coq Hardi for a good French meal, and for coffee we moved on to one of the Champs Elysées cafés. On leaving, as we pushed our way between the crowded tables, we heard a startled voice exclaim in Sabra Hebrew: 'Hey, fellows, did you see who just passed? Moshe Dayan and Shimon Peres. Must be something up, something secret, for Moshe Dayan was wearing dark glasses to avoid recognition!'

2 October 1956

At 20.00 this evening I called a meeting of the General Staff to give them an Early Warning order. I told them of the likelihood

31

– although the Government has not yet taken a decision – of a campaign against Nasser. The estimated date of the opening of hostilities is 20 October 1956 and my reckoning is that the campaign will last about three weeks. I explained that as a consequence of British and French reactions to the nationalization of the Suez Canal, a situation might emerge in which Israel could take military action against the Egyptian blockade of the Gulf of Akaba. To do this we would have to capture the Sinai Peninsula. We had to be prepared for the possibility that other Arab States would join in the fighting against us and we had therefore to secure the Jordanian and Syrian fronts. At this stage, it was not yet necessary to mobilize our reserves, but all the preparations for doing so should be started. To avoid disclosure of our plans, such preparations should be explained in terms of the possible entry of Iraqi forces into Jordan, a move which would oblige the Israel Army to capture the west bank of the river Jordan.

I ordered that all our officers on training courses overseas should be recalled. Their participation in the campaign will give them more experience and teach them more than anything they can learn at a military school. Moreover, they are our comrades, and none will forgive us if, while there is fighting going on here, we let them sit in the classrooms of their staff colleges in France or Britain pursuing their studies – not for that did they volunteer to become officers of the Israel Army.

My news that we had to prepare for battle electrified the meeting. Though all present tried to hide their excitement behind an outward expression of calm, one could sense the tension in the room. It was as if, for them, the campaign had already begun.

Round the table sat the top men of the Israel Defence Forces – the Regional Commanders and the heads of the Armoured Corps, the Air Force and the Navy. Most of them were in their thirties. Yet it was not only their comparative youth which evoked their response; it was also their character. In the last few years, officers selected to command fighting units have been men whose natural reaction to a tough assignment was never 'But . . .' These young commanders well knew, from a wealth of personal experience, what fighting was, having fought as section and platoon commanders and gone right up to brigade and divisional command. They understood the full significance of

my early warning order. Yet they did not shrink from its implications: rather they welcomed them. The heightened Arab
terrorism of the past year and our military reactions produced in
them correspondingly heightened psychological tensions. What
was most burdensome was the feeling that despite these actions,
which cost the blood of our finest soldiers, the overriding
problem still remained unsolved.

Tonight, at last, they were given warning of a decisive cam-
paign, one which aims at driving the Egyptian Army from El
Arish in the north and from Sharm e-Sheikh in the south, a
campaign whose success will secure freedom of shipping to
Eilat and remove Egyptian military and terrorist bases from the
Gaza Strip and Sinai Peninsula.

My briefing was followed by several questions, most of them
of a technical nature relating to mobilization, the prospects of
additional manpower and spare parts, and the distribution of
ammunition from GHQ emergency stores to units. There was
also one non-technical question. Brigadier-General Y. asked
what were the chances of 'volunteers' from Russia or one of the
Soviet bloc countries being sent to the help of Egypt?

This was a question we had often asked ourselves, but so far
it had been raised within the framework of our political and
overall strategic reviews. Tonight, however, in this forum, it had
a very personal relevance. Our army has fought and planned its
actions so far against Arab fighters, and our commanders are
confident that they can defeat this enemy even though out-
matched in numbers and equipment because they feel they have
the advantage in quality. But what if they have to face Polish,
Czech or Russian fighters? For reply, I gave it as my judgement
that:

1 The shorter the campaign, the greater the chances that no
'volunteers' will come.

2 If they do come, they are likely to be Czechs or Poles but
not Russians.

3 Such 'volunteers' are likely to be not infantry units or tank
crews but pilots, so that we shall meet them only in the air. I
have no doubt that this will be less pleasant than facing
Egyptian pilots, but after all, Poles and Czechs are no more
than Poles and Czechs.

The meeting ended. During the course of it, each of the participants had signalled his staff officers to stand by, and now they all raced off to their HQs. The wheels are beginning to turn.

We have seventeen days left before the 20th – not much time for all our preparations, particularly when, to preserve secrecy, we cannot start mobilizing our reserves. But I do not regret this. For despite the imperfections and deficiencies entailed by the rush, we shall gain one major advantage – surprise. If we succeed in masking our plans so that the Egyptians remain unaware right up to the opening day of battle that our objective is the capture of Sinai, this will be a tremendous military gain. I know well the risk we are taking in postponing reserve mobilization until four or five days before D-Day – pulling our men out of their civilian jobs in field, workshop and office and, almost without preparation, flinging them into battle. I know the difficulties of going into action in this way. But it is worth doing.

3 October 1956

A meeting in my office of the inner General Staff. The first part was given over to problems of *matériel*, and there were no basic disagreements. We shall apparently be getting help on equipment for our infantry and armoured units, though not on the scale we requested. A signal has come in from Paris that there is approval for the dispatch of 200 half-tracks, 100 Super-Sherman tanks, 20 tank-transporters, and 300 6 × 6 trucks.

The second part of the meeting was devoted to the operational side of the campaign, and this was less agreeable. We started with the operational plan of the Air Force. It is clear that the Air Force is assuming a very heavy burden, stretching itself to the limit of its capacity, and if we do not succeed at the very outset in surprising the Egyptians and knocking out their planes while they are still on the ground, our plan will fail.

We went on to review the plan of our land forces – infantry, armour and paratroopers – and I stressed the point that speed was the key factor. We must end the campaign in the shortest possible time. The longer it lasts, the greater will be the political complications – pressure from the United States, the dispatch of 'volunteers' to aid Egypt, and so on. It must take no longer than two weeks, at the outside, and within this period we must complete the conquest of the whole of the Sinai Peninsula.

It is, however, not only political considerations that call for speed. From the operational point of view, rapidity in advance is of supreme importance to us, for it will enable us to profit fully from our basic advantage over the Egyptian Army. I do not mean the advantage in quality of the individual soldier – pilot for pilot, tank crew for tank crew – but in the handling and behaviour of our entire Army and its operational formations, brigade-groups, brigades and battalions, as against those of their Egyptian counterparts. The Egyptians are what I would call schematic in their operations, and their command headquarters are in the rear, far from the front. Any change in the disposition of their units, such as forming a new defence line, switching targets of attack, moving forces not in accordance with the original plan, takes them time – time to think, time to receive reports through all the channels of command, time to secure a decision after due consideration from supreme headquarters, time for the orders then to filter down from the rear to the fighting fronts.

We on the other hand are used to acting with greater flexibility and less military routine. We can base our operations on units which are not interdependent, and whose commanders, receiving reports and giving the necessary orders, are right on the spot, together with their fighting men. This advantage, if we can exploit it, will enable us, after the initial breakthrough, to press on before the Egyptians can manage to adjust to the changes in their front. I am confident that we can run the campaign in such a way that the enemy will be given no time to reorganize after the assault and that there will be no pause in the fighting. This is the basis of our plans. We shall organize separate forces for each of the main military objectives, and it will be the task of each force to get there in one continuous battle, one long breath, to fight and push on, fight and push on, until the objective is gained.

I know that this approach may not be appropriate for every campaign; but to my mind it is correct and feasible in the present circumstances – when the objective is the Sinai Peninsula and the enemy is the Egyptian Army. It also suits the character of our Army and of our officers. To the commander of an Israel unit, I can point on a map to the Suez Canal and say: 'There's your target and this is your axis of advance. Don't signal me during the fighting for more men, arms or vehicles. All that we could allocate you've already got, and there isn't more. Keep signalling your advances. You must reach Suez in forty-eight hours.' I can give this kind of order to commanders of our units because I know they are ready to assume such tasks and are capable of carrying them out.

I explained that in my view we should open the campaign with a paratroop drop in the vicinity of our final objectives, to seal the routes against Egyptian reinforcements and to capture dominant positions of tactical importance. The paratroopers will have to hold their ground until our main forces catch up with them, which I estimate should be not much more than forty-eight hours later.

Those at the meeting who had reservations about my presentation said that the problem was not the conception of the plan but the ability to implement it, and we had to examine its feasibility, particularly its logistics. They thought the plan was very ambitious and did not take into account the chance of anything going wrong. The discussion ended with the feeling that our plans are not yet ripe enough to be transmitted to the units. We fixed another meeting for next week. I, too, am not happy with the plan. I feel it leans too heavily on the frontal attack and gradual advance. Operations Branch had designated key positions on the northern axis as the area of the paratroop landing. This must be changed, and by H-hour there should be a sizeable paratroop drop close to the Suez Canal.

7 October 1956

I met this morning with the Ordnance Corps. The commander unburdened himself of a heap of technical problems which must be settled before we start. (Where, oh where, are the good old days of the simple wars, when, as the hour of battle approached, the commander got on his white horse, someone blew the trumpet, and off he charged towards the enemy!) To keep our half-track vehicles functioning throughout the campaign, we need at least 500 spare tracks – in addition to the hundred which have arrived from overseas and the seventy we have prepared locally. Track vehicles are the only ones that can cross desert and dunes and in many areas our movement will be dependent on them alone. Many of our Willys jeeps and trucks are stuck in workshops with faulty engines or in need of spare parts which we lack. The local Kaiser-Fraser plant which assembles them has hit some snags and awaits the arrival of experts from the parent company in the United States.

Then there are the tanks. To install the turret and new gun on the Shermans, we will apparently have to cannibalize some of our old Mark 3s, but this will give us fewer tanks for battle. The light French tanks, the AMXs, are equipped with a filter that does not answer the problem of dust and sand that will be encountered in the Negev, and they will have to be replaced by a special oil filter that is more suitable for desert conditions.

We have trouble with rifles. Our ordnance experts who flew to the F.N. Works in Belgium found that the rifles they were manufacturing for us do not accord with our specifications and refused to accept them. This does not worry the F.N. people, as they have an order for the same type of rifle from the Syrians!

Equipment for our paratroopers is inadequate – and some of it is unsuitable – for the heavy tasks they have been given in Sinai. We must get them more chains, pulleys, parachute harnesses and drop-sacks.

We decided that, on rifles, the ordnance commander would himself fly to Belgium and come to an arrangement with the F.N. Works; we must have those rifles. On spare parts needed for our Sherman tanks, Shimon Peres has promised to have them flown in. Air freight is indeed expensive, but we have no choice. As to parachute equipment, we shall try and borrow some from the French, and in the meantime we shall allocate IL.30,000 out of the IL.250,000 required and manufacture the most essential items locally. We just have not got enough money. I also ordered my staff to examine the possibility of using cinemas in army camps as emergency ordnance depots. We have neither the time nor money to build the additional storage structures required for the campaign, and we must use existing buildings. We decided that south of Beersheba, ammunition will be stored in the open.

At a staff meeting this afternoon, we dealt with the mobilization of the reserves. Here we are torn between our desire to postpone the call-up almost to the last moment before the opening of the campaign, and our need to give the units time to get organized, do maintenance on their tanks, carry out advance patrols, and make the numerous other preparations necessary before battle. The suggestion brought before me recommended the following time-table: Units assigned to cope with possible attack from the Jordanian and Syrian fronts to be mobilized on

D-day and D-day plus 1. The same for GHQ reservists. This suggestion is based on the assumption that even if Jordan and Syria will wish to go to the aid of Egypt and attack us, they will not be able to do so without prior preparation, which will take time. Units assigned to the capture of the Gaza Strip to be called up on D-day minus 4; all armoured corps units – D-day minus 8; units to operate along the southern axes of Sharm e-Sheikh and Nakhl – D-day minus 7.

Under no circumstances could I accept this recommendation. It would mean a general mobilization throughout the country about a week before the start of the campaign, nullifying our plan to surprise the Egyptians. We finally decided that only the officers would be called up a few days before D-day, and that armoured units would be mobilized D-day minus 3. All other units – D-day minus 2.

Last night I received a letter from the Prime Minister and Minister of Defence. In it Ben Gurion writes that he thinks it best at the moment not to take retaliatory military action for the provocative incident at S'dom in which some of our workers were murdered. (On 4 October, a truck carrying workers to the salt pans of the Potash Works at S'dom was ambushed and five were killed. The attackers escaped to Jordan.) Ben Gurion considers that it is of particular importance at this time to preserve our position in world public opinion as accusers and not accused, and that we should try as far as possible not to give Eden and Hammarskjöld any pretext to create difficulties for us.

8 October 1956

This morning I held an Orders Group on the Sinai Campaign. Its code name is to be Operation 'Kadesh', and the first planning order is marked 'Kadesh'-1 (Appendix 1). (Kadesh was the Biblical site where the Israelites sojourned long – probably organizing themselves before taking on their enemies – during their wanderings through the wilderness *en route* to the 'Promised Land'.) After reading the order, I answered questions and explained some of the points which required elaboration. I ended by underlining the following principles which will serve as directives in this campaign:

Our task is to bring about as quickly as possible the collapse of the enemy forces and to achieve complete control of the Sinai

Peninsula. We should try and capture what we can of the enemy's weapons and equipment, but we have no interest in killing a maximum number of his troops. Even if Egypt suffered thousands of casualties, she could replace them fairly quickly. Manpower for the forces is not a problem either to Nasser or to the other Arab rulers, and any advantage we can gain over the Arab armies will not be secured through numerical superiority.

Our units must stick to 'maintenance of aim', and continue to advance until their objective is gained. They must therefore be self-contained, carrying with them all they will need to reach their final target, and not be dependent on outside supplies. Once the roads are clear, they must press forward and not stop to clean up isolated enemy positions. There is no need to fear that Egyptian units who will be by-passed will launch a counter-attack or cut our supply lines. We should avoid analogies whereby Egyptian units would be expected to behave as European armies would in similar circumstances.

To make tangible my intention, I set the following order of priorities to our operations:

First, paratroop drops or landings; second, advance through by-passing the enemy positions; third, breakthrough. The point about this 'order of priorities' is that, if at all possible, it is preferable to capture the objectives deep in enemy territory right away, by landings and paratroop drops, than to reach them by frontal and gradual advance after head-on attacks on every Egyptian position starting from the Israeli border and slogging it out all the way to Suez. By the same token, our infantry and armoured forces should advance, wherever they can, by going round the enemy emplacements, leaving them in the rear and pressing on. They should resort to the assault and breakthrough of enemy posts only when there is no way to by-pass them, or, at a later stage in the campaign, when these posts are isolated and cut off from their bases in Egypt.

In accordance with this approach, I stressed that our first task is to capture the enemy heights in the vicinity of the Suez Canal, which is our final most westward objective. This of course can be done only by a paratroop drop. Then we must go for El Arish; after that, Abu Ageila and Sharm e-Sheikh; and only towards the end of the campaign should we deal with Gaza, which is right on the Israel border.

Under this plan, our paratroopers will have to carry out two operations within a very short time: dropping near Suez and capturing their assigned objective; and then, when the infantry column reaches them, reorganizing and making another parachute landing behind the enemy lines on the route to Sharm e-Sheikh, the most distant of our targets geographically and the most important of the campaign. The capture of Sharm e-Sheikh will in fact mark the completion of our control of Sinai.

I also underlined the need to plan the operations of each force in such a way that none is dependent on others, so that if one gets stuck, it will not hold up the advance of the rest.

9 October 1956

A meeting this morning on emergency officer-appointments. Some of our finest fighting commanders hold positions at present on the General Staff and in Training Command, or are on study leave. I feel they should be posted to formations which will be taking part in the Sinai campaign, and some should even be appointed commanders of units in place of the present ones, where this is justified. I know that this will not be easy. For one thing, unit commanders will be very hurt if they are replaced on the eve of battle; for another such personnel changes will leave gaps in the General Staff and Training Command. Nevertheless, it will have to be done. It might be different if we were in for an extended war; but with a campaign of only a few weeks, it is justifiable to concentrate our energies within the fighting arena at the expense of other areas, even if these should be weakened thereby for the duration of the operations. As to the personal feelings of displaced commanders, these must be weighed against the decisive criterion of military success. The plan of Operation 'Kadesh' is based on a huge measure of independence to commanders in the field. It is they who will be taking vital decisions on the spot in the midst of battle. Their action and their powers of leadership will determine the success or failure of the campaign.

I hope that this decision of emergency appointments will be understood and accepted in the proper spirit by the officers likely to be adversely affected by it. At all events, after signing the new appointments, I felt we had done our best to ensure that the team we shall be sending into Sinai will be 'Israel's Selected'.

At noon, a request came in from Southern Command for authorization to carry out patrols in the Rafah region to examine the possibility of tank movement in the area of the dunes. I am afraid that such patrols may be spotted and will arouse attention and suspicion. I therefore authorized one patrol alone, and even that only after I was assured that it would move along the pebbled bed of the wadi and not more than two men would actually walk on the dunes – and that these would wear Bedouin sandals made in Hebron so that their footprints would not be different from those of ordinary Arab smugglers.

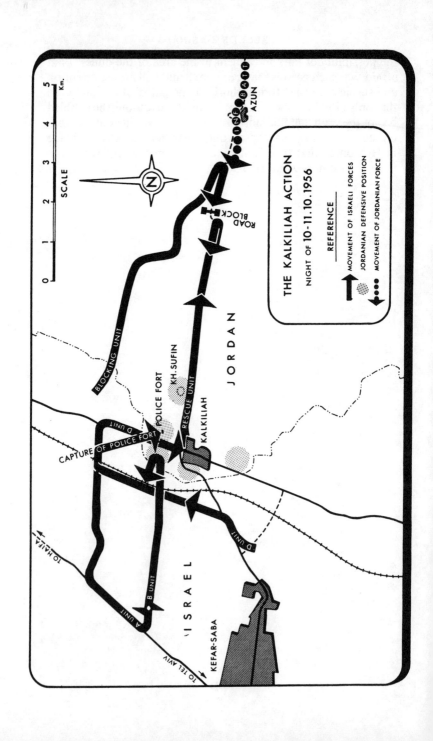

CHAPTER THREE

*

KALKILIAH

12 October 1956

Last night (10/11 October) we carried out a retaliatory action against the Jordanians. The target was the police fort situated at the northern edge of the townlet of Kalkiliah. The scale of operations was larger than any we have employed in previous reprisal engagements, and we suffered heavy losses: eighteen killed, of whom eight were officers, and more than fifty wounded, fourteen of them officers. The figures we have so far of enemy losses are about a hundred killed.

After the wave of murders last month and our reaction raid on the Husan police fort on 25 September 1956, we were anxious to avoid further military action, and we had hoped to be able to do so at least until the end of the Security Council meetings – when France and Britain are to take a final decision about their operations against Egypt.

But the provocation three days ago, on 9 October 1956, was too flagrant to be ignored. In full daylight, two farm-labourers were murdered while working in an orange-grove near Tel-Mond. The victims were shot and their ears cut off and taken by the terrorists to serve them as evidence that they had fulfilled their mission.

This region, the Vale of Sharon, is the easiest one to cross from Jordan into Israel. The border here is free of natural obstacles, and the distance from Kalkiliah, which is just inside the Jordanian boundary, to our railroad and main highway linking Haifa to Tel Aviv, is less than six and a half miles; to the suburbs of Tel Aviv itself it is less than twelve and a half. We cannot prevent the infiltration of terrorists by technical means or by reinforcing our guards; and if border villages in central Jordan are indeed to become the bases for hit-and-run raids on Israel, then terror units will be able to attack our most dynamic and sensitive region – the area of Tel Aviv. Small wonder that this time, when the terrorism was directed at the heart of Israel, we were given cause for concern.

To this highly provocative action must be added the intolerable policy of King Hussein of Jordan. In the past, whenever we demanded of the Jordanian Government that they prevent the activity of terrorists from their territory, the reply has come, through the representatives of Britain, the United States and the United Nations, that they were doing all they could but that they were powerless to control the infiltrators.

Even though we knew that they did not take the required measures, we decided after the murder at Ein Ofarim of the three Israeli Druzes a month ago (12 September 1956), to transmit to King Hussein information we received on the identity of the murderers. We hoped that at least at this highest level of the Jordanian régime there would be dissociation from the murders and instructions to proceed against the guilty. But our move had the reverse effect. As soon as he got our message, the King sent a special runner with a release order for the terrorist band, who had in the meantime been arrested by the Jordanian police for smuggling, and who had boasted that they had killed not only the three Israelis at Ein Ofarim but also the five workers at S'dom on 4 October.

This behaviour of Hussein, giving royal backing to the terror against Israel, heightened the gravity of the situation. It was clear that our restraint was interpreted by them as weakness, and if we continue in this way, the terrorism will be intensified. There seems to be no alternative to a firm reaction on our part which will make the Jordanian rulers realize the serious consequences they can expect if they persist in this policy.

Military action was set for after dark on the 10th. A few hours earlier, Ben Gurion had issued the following statement to the Press and to General E. L. M. Burns:

On 12 September 1956, as is known, three Israeli Druzes were murdered at Ein Ofarim by an armed band from Jordan. We were informed at the time by the Jordanian authorities that the murderers had been arrested by Jordanian police at Kafr Dahel. The arrested men admitted that they had killed the Israeli Druzes and among their possessions were found the weapons they had removed from the victims. Yet only a few days ago, King Hussein gave his personal order to release the murderers without trial and punishment. It is impossible to interpret this order, given by the King himself, as anything but direct encouragement for a continuation of acts of murder. We deem it necessary to underline the seriousness of this matter, particularly since murders by armed infiltrators are on the increase.

The Kalkiliah police fort was chosen as the target of our action because it is close to a well-populated townlet, numbering some 20,000, and its demolition would therefore have a wide public impact. But this very feature of proximity put limitations on the manner of the operation and created special difficulties. In order to avoid harming civilians, the unit going into action. was ordered not to enter the city – not even to pass through it to reach its objective. Moreover, we feared that there might be families of policemen living in the building, and our troops were therefore instructed to search the fort and evacuate any civilians who might be found there before blowing it up.

The purpose of such military action is political, and to achieve it, we must react as near as possible to the place and time of the Arab act of violence. Only in this way can Arab, Israeli and world public opinion recognize our operation as a reply to terrorism. Otherwise, even if there is a delay of only a few days, our action is seen not as a response but as the initiation by Israel of a military attack. Because of this, as soon as I received news of the murder of the Tel-Mond farm-labourers, I ordered Operations Branch to prepare that very night a plan of action against the Kalkiliah fort to be carried out within twenty-four hours. Next day, 10 October 1956, I went to Jerusalem and at 10.00 I brought before the Minister of Defence for his approval the following draft plan which I had received from Operations:

A Aim: Capture and demolition of Kalkiliah police fort by Paratroop Brigade.

B Method: 1 The target will be lit up by searchlights (stationed two miles away).

2 The attack will be carried out with supporting fire from a tank detachment.

3 After the softening-up by this support unit, two companies will storm the police building and blow it up.

4 Road-blocks will be set between Khirbet Sufin and Nebi Elias; between the police fort and the town; and on the road leading into the town from the south-east.

5 An artillery detachment will go into position opposite Kalkiliah to give counter-battery fire should our settlements be shelled.

6 Flat-trajectory weapons will open fire on the town if automatic fire from there is directed against our forces.

7 H-hour is between 19.00 and 20.00 hours.

Ben Gurion questioned me on several details, and urged me particularly to ensure that the action against the police post did not spill over to the town of Kalkiliah and cause the death of Arab civilians.

After agreeing to the plan, he called a meeting of the Cabinet for 11.00 hours and the Government approved it.

On the assumption that such approval would be forthcoming, the commander of the Paratroop Brigade had been summoned to GHQ at midnight on 9 October and been given instructions on the operation. In the hours that remained until the start of the action, the brigade had to gather its men from opposite ends of the country. Two half-track companies were somewhere south of Beersheba, and another paratroop company was up north in the Galilee mountains. Commanders of the units assigned for the action were called at 09.00 hours to a Planning Group. After that, they had to study the terrain of the action from maps and air-photographs and to examine the police fort of our own Kefar Saba which is more or less identical with that of Kalkiliah. Both were built by the British during the Mandatory period according to the Tegart plan.

The Orders Group was called at 16.45 hours, where they were given final instructions, and the action was launched at 21.00 hours.

At GHQ I was sharply criticized for the pace at which we had proceeded during the twenty-four hours between the murders and the start of our action. It was too fast to permit adequate preparation, and neither officers nor men had been given time to rest before the battle; this was likely to cost us dear. As an objective argument, this is no doubt sound, and I agree that scrupulous preparation and rest for the men before going into action are essential. But I feel that my critics do not pay enough attention to the other considerations. We must remember that military action is not an end in itself; it is taken to achieve a political end, and we, the Army, must suit ourselves to the conditions prescribed for us by the political circumstances. Otherwise, we may well reap military victories but they will turn into political defeats. Moreover, if we do not learn to organize outselves at this speed for battle against one enemy position situated close to the border, how can we undertake fast action in an overall campaign where the organizational difficulties will be infinitely greater and the political factors certainly no less limiting?

At 21.50 hours, as the spearhead of the assault unit got to within about 200 yards of the police fort fence, the Jordanians opened fire on them. The building was illuminated by our search-lights and it was subjected to direct artillery fire from our 25-pounders. Despite the accurate hits by our guns, the Jordanians showed tough opposition in the battle that followed, possibly because the assault unit had requested a cessation of the supporting fire too soon, and stormed the fort. In the forecourt of the building, well-prepared for defence, was a company of Jordanians, about one hundred men, with another company in positions near by. The battle was stiff, with hand-to-hand fighting, and eight of our men were killed, among them the company commander and his second in command, and twenty-nine wounded, most of them lightly. At 23.30, after the entire area had been combed and cleared, the building was blown up.

The first part of the action of our second unit, the road-blocking group, proceeded without mishap. They penetrated to a depth of about six miles inside Jordan territory and set up an ambush at the sides of the road leading from the Arab Legion camp at Khirbet Azun to Kalkiliah. And, indeed, immediately after the opening of the attack on the police fort, two companies of the Legion's 9th Battalion – the Bedouin battalion – set off in the direction of Kalkiliah aboard fifteen trucks. Our blocking unit opened fire and knocked out the first four vehicles of the convoy. The remaining vehicles stopped, about-turned and went back. Our unit moved its position, establishing itself on another hill that also commands the road, and about an hour later, Arab Legion reinforcements again came through on their way to

Kalkiliah, and also ran into our ambush. Two of their vehicles and a number of their men were hit and the convoy retired.

At midnight, our blocking unit received the order to return. Up to then, they had suffered no casualties, but as soon as they started moving towards the frontier, they came under heavy fire. The Legion troops who had not managed to advance by vehicle had dismounted and taken up positions in the rear of our unit, so that our men who had blocked the road against the Jordanian reinforcements now found their own route back to Israel blocked. The Jordanians quickly went over to the attack, and in a short time, out of our fifty-four men, there were eleven wounded and one killed. Among the first to be hit were the company commander and his second in command, and shortly afterwards the medical orderly and two of the three platoon commanders were wounded, so that of the officers, only two were left, one of them a platoon commander.

The unit was in a very bad way indeed, and the men were so tired they could hardly move. Only that morning they had been on a tough march in the Galilee mountains, and the same night, in utter darkness, they had done another six miles, clambering up terraces and over slippery boulders, wet from the night dew. They now tried to beat out an escape route and to evade the Legionaries who were rushing them with machine-guns and hand-grenades. They had only three stretchers with them, so that they had to carry most of the wounded on their backs.

The senior officer who was unhurt, a major, was in a state of shock, and to all our radio signals he just replied 'yes, yes'; it was clear that he was dazed and could not grasp what he was being told. The brigade commander thereupon had the other unwounded officer, a twenty-one-year-old, called to the receiver, and he entrusted responsibility for the unit to him. This young platoon commander collected his men and, firing as they moved to keep their assailants at bay and dragging their wounded and their dead comrade, they managed to reach a hill-top vantage point and organized themselves for defence.

At our advance command post, we were aware of the general situation of the unit. Communications worked well. It was clear that this unit was unable under its own power to break through the Legion's lines and get back to Israel, and it was certainly unable to do so bringing back its casualties. Three essential steps had to be taken. The first and most urgent was to enable the unit to hold out. Its ammunition was dwindling rapidly, and the Jordanians already had a marked advantage in fire-power. The second was to send an additional force which would try and reach the beleaguered unit and help to extricate it during the hours of darkness. The third – to get ready a strong force capable of breaking through and reaching the unit in daylight, if the night action failed.

During the last two years, paratroop units have on numerous occasions gone out on actions across the border, and only once was one of their wounded left behind in enemy territory. Now there was an entire unit, more than fifty men, in desperate straits, their ammunition spent, their officers out of action, cut off, and surrounded by the Legion's Bedouin troops.

The only immediate help they could be given was artillery fire.

Their embattled hill position was a distance of eight and a half miles from the 155-mm. battery which could give them support. With them was an artillery liaison officer as gunnery spotter. It was to him that the Chief Artillery Officer of the Army, who never moved from the battery throughout the entire night, now spoke by radio and explained what he intended to do. He was going to use his field guns as machine-guns, and pour intensive shell-fire on the slopes of their hill and on the road being used by the Legionaries. It might be hours before reinforcements would reach them, and in the meantime, using artillery was the only way in which we could help them. The beleaguered men were accordingly to be instructed to dig themselves in, so that our shell-fire could be directed almost to the very edge of their positions.

The gunnery liaison officer with the unit needed no elaboration. He knew they could not budge, and that they were without ammunition. Within a few minutes, their hill position was ringed by bursting shells which crept up to only fifty yards from them – even though the radius of burst of a 155-mm. shell is 100 yards.

Such artillery help, however, could only ease the situation, not solve it. Without the arrival of an additional force, the unit could not be saved. First to speed to their assistance was a paratroop company, with the battalion commander in charge. This was the company which earlier in the evening had covered the assault unit on the police fort and whose casualties had been light. It was now 01.30 hours, and the prospects were dim that this company would manage to reach the besieged unit and get it back before daylight; but its support would enable them to hold out until the arrival of further reinforcements.

This company was quickly followed by an additional force – two companies on half-tracks. Under normal circumstances, I would on no account have permitted this. A convoy of such vehicles moving through a black night on a paved road is more a vulnerable target than a breakthrough force. And it is that much worse in hilly country where there is no room for manœuvre; if one vehicle overturns, the whole convoy is held up. But in the situation we were in, there was no alternative. We had no other mobile force capable of reaching the surrounded unit in a short time and getting it back, with its wounded. The convoy dashed off along the main highway, and, driving at high speed and with lights full on, broke through the Jordanian positions at Kalkiliah and Khirbet Sufin. Though it was fired on from Kalkiliah and particularly from Sufin, it succeeded in reaching the beleaguered men without casualties. It got to them at 02.30 hours. Actually, only half the convoy made it – nine vehicles. The others lost their way in the alleys of Kalkiliah and did not manage to catch up. (They returned to base.)

With the approach of the half-tracks the pressure of the Legionaries on the besieged unit slackened. This was possibly due also to the two Harvards and two Mustangs which the commander of the Air Force had sent up to circle the battle area and so give the impression of a large attack being carried out by a mobile column with air support.

At 03.00 hours, the column began moving home. The wounded lay on the floors of the vehicles and the other troops had to sit on the sides, fully exposed, without cover. In the meantime, the Legion positions at Khirbet Sufin had been reinforced, and, as the convoy passed by on its way back, it came under heavy fire from machine-guns, anti-tank weapons, and grenades, which added five killed and some twenty wounded to our list of casualties.

But even this did not mark the end of the fighting. When the convoy had moved beyond the area of fire and assembled in the forecourt of the demolished police fort, it was found that one vehicle was missing. It had been put out of action and remained stuck in a ditch close to the Legion position at Khirbet Sufin. Four half-tracks thereupon went back to get it out. They did in fact succeed eventually in attaching a cable and towing it out, but they had to do it with their headlights on and under murderous fire from the Legion troops, and we lost another two killed.

By first light, the firing died down. The bodies of the two men killed while extricating the vehicle at Sufin had been left behind.

The troops were now back on our side of the border, and I could cancel the orders I had given during the night to prepare a force comprising two tank squadrons, one infantry battalion and fighter aircraft, with the task, at dawn, of breaking through to the beleaguered unit if we had not managed to get it out before.

Early in the evening, I had joined the commander of the operation at his command post, which was on a hill overlooking the Kalkiliah police fort; but when things began to go wrong, I returned to GHQ. News of the desperate position of the blocking unit had spread rapidly, and when I reached my office, I found various Army commanders and their Operations officers already waiting for me in case I should need emergency action. Now I could go back to the command post to meet the men returning from the engagement. From the paratroop brigade commander I learned that the last two men killed at Khirbet Sufin were the brigade's Operations officer, who had been with the blocking unit, and Lieutenant Yirmeyahu Burdanov, or, as he was known to all, Yirmi.

Yirmi had been demobilized long before, but they used to call him from time to time to take part in actions. He was an experienced officer, an excellent sapper, and a commando soldier whose courage knew no bounds. To this operation he came without being asked. Soon after the start of the action, when the Jordanians opened fire on our advance command post, we had jumped for cover into a trench and he and I had bumped into each other – literally. Seeing him there was unexpected; but I was not surprised. I knew that many paratroop officers after leaving the Army usually turn up whenever there is an action in order 'to give the youngsters a hand'. When the assault unit had started moving towards the police fort, Yirmi had sneaked out of the command post and joined them. When news came through of the grave plight of the blocking unit, Yirmi had climbed aboard the first half-track of the rescue force and had led the convoy to it. On their return, when it was discovered that one vehicle was stuck at Sufin, Yirmi had ordered the driver of his carrier to turn back. And it was he, still dressed in his civilian clothes, who got down and tied the tow-cable to the damaged half-track. His white shirt had attracted the Legionaries' fire, and a machine-gun burst had caught him in the belly.

15 October 1956

The Kalkiliah action created a greater stir than any other retaliatory operation on the Jordanian front, and above all it acutely strained our relations with the British. Apparently, the possibility of armed British intervention on the side of the Arab Legion was not very remote. The British Consul in Jerusalem found it fitting to contact our Foreign Ministry on the very night of the battle to inform us of a request from Jordan. He said that during the fighting King Hussein made contact with General Charles Keightley, Commander of the British Forces in the Middle East, and demanded that he implement the Anglo–Jordanian Defence Treaty. Hussein asked that Britain's Royal Air Force should go into action in support of Jordan's troops.

The implication of the transmission of this 'information' to us, in the middle of the night, was a warning to Israel of Britain's readiness to respond to Jordan's call. Next day, the 12th, the range of the dispute was widened. The British chargé d'affaires in Tel Aviv, Mr Peter Westlake, requested an interview with the Prime Minister at which he told Ben Gurion that an Iraqi division was about to enter Jordan, and if Israel took military action, Britain would go to Jordan's aid. Ben Gurion answered that Israel objected to the entry of the Iraqis and reserved to herself freedom of action if, despite her opposition, the Iraqis moved.

As a matter of fact, a week ago, following the murder of the archaeologists at Ramat Rachel and our reprisal action against the Husan police fort, the British chargé d'affaires told the UN's General Burns that one more Israeli reprisal action would bring into operation the Anglo–Jordan Defence Treaty. We heard of this conversation, and it may be taken as reflecting the British attitude to the present situation.

I do not know if the Royal Air Force would in fact have attacked our planes if the battle had continued after daylight; but the general view among us is that since the Jordanians sacked Glubb, Britain is anxious to show them that this was a mistake, and that she is their only faithful prop upon whom they can depend for defence against Israel. At all events, twice within twenty-four hours have British representatives informed the Israel Government that Britain proposes to go to the help of Jordan with military force. This iciness has been a feature of Britain's relations with Israel for some time, but now, with the intrusion of the Iraqi plan, it has reached a peak.

The plan was put forward last week by Nuri Said, Prime Minister of Iraq, who went on a visit to London. Before leaving Baghdad, he said in an interview with the correspondent of *The Times* that the Arab–Israel dispute must be settled on the basis of the UN Partition Resolution of 1947, according to which the Arabs should be given the Negev and Galilee. The next day, a spokesman of the British Foreign Office hastened to announce that Her Majesty's Government welcomed Nuri Said's statement and was willing and ready to mediate between the two parties. The spokesman went on to recall the words of Britain's Prime Minister in his Guildhall speech of 9 November 1955 in which he suggested that Israel should make concessions to the territorial demands of the Arab States and that the parties should agree to a compromise over Israel's frontiers between the existing ones and those set out in the UN Resolution of November 1947.

Anthony Eden's Guildhall speech of last year was considered hostile to us and caused great resentment in Israel. The British Government knows very well that land is not what the Arab States lack, and their territorial demands have as their purpose not the satisfaction of their needs but only the sabotaging of Israel, whose area and borders even now are limited enough.

Now, with the British spokesman's resurrection of the Guild-hall speech, and his linking of Eden's suggestion with Nuri Said's announcement, official backing is given to Britain's support of Arab territorial demands at the expense of Israel under the title 'The Iraqi Plan'. When the British Consul and then the chargé d'affaires transmitted their messages after Kalkiliah, the Israel Government naturally set them in the context of Nuri Said's announcement and his plan.

Foreign Minister Golda Meir reacted sharply to the British messages, issuing an official declaration that Israel would regard the entry of the Iraqi Army into Jordan as part of the Nuri Said plan which sought to force upon Israel an arrangement endangering her existence, and this would be resisted. Prime Minister Ben Gurion, too, in a statement on foreign and defence policy in the Knesset today, said that Israel was opposed to the entry of Iraqi forces into Jordan – even into eastern Jordan – and that 'the Israel Government reserves freedom of action if there is any violation of the status quo and a foreign military force moves into Jordan'.

Declarations, of course, are not one-sided, and today's *Times* again publishes an article explaining that Britain will go to the aid of Jordan if Israel continues to carry out reprisal actions against her.

Whatever Britain's intentions, to the credit of Jordan be it said that she does not limit herself to negotiations for Iraqi troops and to requests for British intervention. She is also taking practical steps to prevent infiltration into Israel. She has added a battalion to guard the central border – the Kalkiliah region – and Jordan's Prime Minister, Ibrahim el Hashem, with the approval of King Hussein, yesterday issued a defence regulation granting District Commissioners special powers against all who disturb security – including infiltrators. What is most revealing is that this regulation was issued at the suggestion of Zaim (General) Fauzi Mirad, commander of the Kalkiliah region. He urged an extension of the hours of curfew along the borders and a widening to five miles of the frontier strip in which movement should be prohibited during curfew. Orders were also given to Arab Legion units to carry out intensive patrols all along the border and to fire on anyone trying to cross the frontier 'since it is essential to prevent Arab infiltration which serves Israel as a pretext to launch cruel attacks on the soil of Jordan'.

On the morning of the 11th, after the units who had taken part in the Kalkiliah engagement had returned to their bases, I drove to Jerusalem to report to the Minister of Defence. I was accompanied by the commander of the Paratroop Brigade, who had been in charge of the operation. Ben Gurion, like all of us, was grieved and very concerned over our heavy casualties. Nor did the Consul's message about Jordan's request for British help make him feel any easier. Though he uttered no word of criticism of the action, he kept questioning us on one issue: were our high casualties absolutely unavoidable? Neither the brigade commander nor I could defend without reservation the manner in which the operation had been handled, for we each – or at least I – had certain hesitations on this score. In general, it was an abrasive meeting of three people with heavy hearts. Next day, the 12th, I reported to the Foreign Affairs and Security Committee of the Knesset, and was subjected – justifiably – to vigorous cross-examination. Yesterday, the 14th, I convened a meeting at GHQ to analyse the operation and draw the appropriate conclusions for the future.

Here, criticism was directed – mostly by paratroop officers who had taken part in the fighting – against the General Staff, i.e. against me, for having ordered them, against their view, to limit the scale of the action and refrain from seizing the enemy salient of Khirbet Sufin. Even now, after the battle, I think they are wrong. The capture of Sufin was not necessary for the execution of their prescribed task – the blowing up of the police fort – but only for the rescue of the blocking unit. The mistake, therefore, to my mind, lay in the siting of the road-block. It was too deep inside the Jordanian border, and it was thus possible for the Legion to cut off the unit's return route at Khirbet Sufin or at any other salient commanding the Azun–Kalkiliah road. On the other hand, I consider that the action was carried out in routine fashion, and not sufficient advantage was taken of the specially heavy artillery support which was made available on this occasion. It had not been possible in previous operations to illuminate the target by searchlight and riddle it with fire from tanks and field pieces at point-blank range. Here we had been able to do this, but the assaulting unit, out of habit, hastened to storm the objective before the opportunities of this support had been fully exploited.

Such behaviour is of course prompted by the best of motives. The paratroopers have developed a fighting spirit and a technique of warfare based on the unhesitating assault, daring and speed in action. It is almost an automatic reflex for paratroop commanders, when fired upon, to charge and capture the attacking position. The drive to rush upon the enemy springs not only from well-conceived military principle and battle technique. This unit has experienced a lot of action in the last two years, and every one of its men has seen many of his best friends and commanders struck down. When he goes into battle, he feels it his duty not to fall short of them in courage, but to jump to the assault without hesitation.

The Paratroop Brigade consists of volunteers, and it attracts the finest and most idealistic of our youth. Their toughness in battle – and in physique – are often misleading, masking integrity and a limitless dedication – dedication to the fulfilment of their assignment and devotion to their comrades. This is why they are most careful, even under the most trying battle conditions, to carry back their dead and wounded and not leave them on enemy soil. This has become almost an article of faith with them. There are no doubt rational grounds for such conduct, but the true reason is the depth of feeling each has for his comrades, facing danger together, as they do, time and again. But their magnificent fighting qualities and their utter disregard of peril should not absolve their commanders – of all ranks – from the need to seek ways of gaining their objective with the fewest possible risks. In my talks with the senior officers of the brigade, I therefore expressed the view that failure to take full advantage of artillery support in attacking the police fort was not only a tactical error, but, far worse, evidence of insufficient effort to exploit the special circumstances encountered in each military engagement.

However, the chief purpose of the meeting was not to air differences of opinion on this or that detail, but to consider the whole problem of retaliatory actions. There was general agreement that the present system needs revision. The gravity of Kalkiliah lay not only in what happened but mainly in what could have happened – and almost did.

We almost failed to rescue the blocking unit during the hours of darkness. The ammunition of the beleaguered men was practically exhausted – a factor which would have decided their fate even before daybreak. And if we had been compelled to send in an armoured rescue force with air support during the day, the possibility cannot be ruled out that we would have clashed with the Royal Air Force; and that is something which Ben Gurion has been apprehensive about, guarded against and been most careful to avoid ever since the establishment of the State.

The principal cause of the situation produced at Kalkiliah, which was not a feature of the early engagements, was our continued resort to the reprisal method. At first, it was the standard experience that our actions against the Egyptians and the Jordanians took them by surprise and found them unprepared. Now, after every murder committed in Israel by the fedayun, the Arabs know that they can expect an attack on one of their military installations, so that when our units go into action against an army camp or a police fort, they find the enemy well-prepared and well-organized for defence.

In all our discussions this week, in the Knesset Foreign Affairs and Security Committee, with the Prime Minister and Minister of Defence, and at GHQ, the question was asked 'What now?' I expressed the view that we cannot continue in this state of no-peace and no-war, and that we must compel our Arab neighbours to choose between stopping the terrorism and meeting us in a full-scale war. We can do this in two ways. One is to inflict our reprisal blows in daylight, using tanks and aircraft. This would not only reduce our casualties, but the Arab states, primarily Egypt but also Jordan and Syria, would be unable to ignore the shock to their prestige. No state could afford to overlook such action, and to states with a military régime, the challenge would be particularly grave. The second way would be to cross the border, capture the key positions commanding the enemy's territory, and make our evacuation conditional upon a stoppage of Arab terror. This would apply to the Gaza Strip, where the fedayun headquarters are located. Egypt is not now linked to any European ally who is obliged to go to her help. We could therefore seize the border positions along the Strip and announce that so long as Egypt fails to stop her terrorist activities against us, so long shall we remain in occupation of these positions and thus prevent the fedayun units from penetrating into Israel.

Neither at GHQ, nor in the Knesset Committee, nor in the talks with the Prime Minister, was anything definite decided about the future; but it is clear to all of us that we have reached the end of the chapter of night reprisal actions.

CHAPTER FOUR

*

ON THE EVE

16 October 1956

Today we learned that on 14 October 1956, less than forty-eight hours ago, advance units of the Iraqi Army entered Jordan. If we intend to react by military operations, we should do this soon, before their presence in Jordan becomes a recognized and accepted fact. It will be very difficult for us to allocate the required forces and perhaps fight a simultaneous war on two fronts, the Jordanian and the Egyptian. But I see no escape. What is happening now beyond each of these borders, the east and west, is likely to determine our future, and with all the hardship it will entail, we must deal with both.

The British, of course, can spare us this second front; but they are happy at the opportunity – and are perhaps creating it – to show the Arabs that their being with us on the same side of one political front, the Egyptian, is not due to their love of Israel, and does not mean their abandonment of the Arabs on the other fronts of the Arab–Israel conflict.

Even though we do not know whether the campaign over Suez will indeed be launched, we must make all the necessary preparations. This morning I visited Southern Command for an operational review of 'Kadesh'. The plan prepared by this Command is on the whole satisfactory. The main changes I introduced are designed to increase the independence of each force, so that one does not hold up the others. I also ordered a reduction in the number of vehicles assigned to the formation that will be operating along the southern axis – through Nakhl. It is not only that we have not enough – particularly those with front-wheel drive – but too many vehicles encumber the convoy and choke movement, and the luxury of abundance becomes a burden.

21 October 1956

This morning the French Military Attaché called at my office to clarify some of the points on equipment we are acquiring for the fuelling of planes. Before getting down to business, we exchanged views on the entry of Iraqi troops into Jordan. The Attaché said that in a talk with his people in London, the British told them that not only was Jordan not interested in having the Iraqi Army but even Nuri Said did not favour it, and the initiative was wholly British. They are convinced that the presence of the Iraqi Army in Jordan during the Jordanian parliamentary elections will strengthen the anti-Nasser forces there.

I must confess to the feeling that, save for the Almighty, only the British are capable of complicating affairs to such a degree. At the very moment when they are preparing to topple Nasser, who is a common enemy of theirs and Israel's, they insist on getting the Iraqi Army into Jordan, even if such action leads to war between Israel and Jordan in which they, the British, will take part against Israel. The result will be that instead of bringing down Nasser and safeguarding Britain's position in the Middle East as a power that stands firmly on her rights in the Suez Canal, they will leave Nasser gobbling his prey while they rush off to start a new Israel–Britain–Jordan conflict. I doubt whether anyone can explain why Britain does not hold off her Iraqi plan until after the Suez campaign.

The most ironic feature of the affair, however, is that while the Attaché was explaining to me with such gravity how the French representatives were utterly unable to persuade the British to abandon their Iraqi project, I already knew that the whole scheme was no longer practicable. The Jordanian parliamentary elections ended yesterday with a resounding victory for Nasser's supporters, and the Jordan Government, seeing what was happening, hastened to cancel its military agreements with Iraq. Nasser, on his part, has announced that he will extend military help to Jordan. Moreover, it appears that the Jordan Government has been negotiating for some time now to join the Egypt–Syria joint military command.

I do not know which is better – or rather which is worse – for us: the Iraqi Army in Jordan or a closer association between Jordan and Egypt; but for Britain, the election results in Jordan constitute a bitter defeat. This wave of nationalism in Jordan started mounting already at the beginning of the year. The Britisher Glubb, Commander of the Arab Legion from the day it was established, was summarily dismissed and ordered to leave Jordan within forty-eight hours. In his place came Radi Eynab. Eynab, though a Jordanian Arab, was not sufficiently anti-British in his nationalism and he was replaced by Ali Abu-Nawar. Meanwhile the web was spun wider and the demand was raised in the Jordanian parliament to annul the Anglo–Jordanian Treaty. The Government opposed it, and suffered a parliamentary vote of no confidence on 25 June 1956. King Hussein thereupon dissolved parliament and announced new elections in October, hoping that in the intervening three months he would be able to organize affairs so that the new legislature would boast a majority favouring the treaty with Britain. Now, with the elections over, it transpires that the position is unchanged, and even the new parliament will oppose an alliance with the pro-British Nuri Said and will demand closer contact with Nasser.

As for us, we can stop worrying about the Iraqi plan. Jordanian nationalism, aware of its 'Made in Britain' hallmark, has put paid to it. So there goes another of the Foreign Office's Middle East schemes – and with it another heavy boulder from our path!

25 October 1956

After numerous internal conferences, and contacts and clarifications with people overseas, which started about two months ago, we can sum up the situation today as follows:

1 The Prime Minister and Minister of Defence, David Ben Gurion, has given approval in principle to the campaign and its aims.
2 Our forces will go into action at dusk on 29 October 1956, and we must complete the capture of the Sinai Peninsula within seven to ten days.
3 The decision on the campaign and its planning are based on the assumption that British and French forces are about to take action against Egypt.
4 According to information in our possession, the Anglo–French forces propose to launch their operations on 31

October 1956. Their aim is to secure control of the Suez Canal Zone, and for this they will need to effect a sea landing or an air drop with, no doubt, suitable air cover.

At 13.45 I met with the senior officers of Operation Branch. For this meeting I prepared directives for the operational order (Appendix 2) which replaces those in the previous order, 'Kadesh'-1 (Appendix 1) of 5 October 1956. Apart from the time-table, which lays down the day and hour of the start of the action, today's order contains several changes from the previous order. The first occurs in the paragraph on aims. Stress is now placed on the creation of a threat to the Suez Canal, and only after that come the basic purposes of the campaign – capture of the Straits of Tiran (Sharm e-Sheikh and the islands of Tiran and Sanapir) and defeat of the Egyptian forces.

On this question of the defeat of Egypt's forces I have had several talks with Ben Gurion. It is clear that we have no interest in 'destroying the enemy's forces', the customary directive in the framing of war aims, and it is better that as little blood as possible should be shed. I therefore used the formula 'to confound the organization of the Egyptian forces and bring about their collapse'. In other words, we should seize the cross-roads and key military positions which will give us control of the area and force their surrender.

The second change in the operational order affects the phases of our action, and the third concerns the employment of the Air Force.

I hope these are the final changes. Only four days remain to the opening of the campaign.

At the beginning of the meeting I transmitted what I could of the political conditions within the framework of which we would be conducting our campaign. From the operational point of view we had to distinguish between the period up to the start of the Anglo–French action and the period after. It may be assumed that with the launching of their attack, the Egyptian Air Force will cease its activity against us. Egyptian Army units in Sinai will almost certainly be ordered to withdraw into Egypt, and those remaining in their positions will find their morale lowered. Therefore what it may be possible to do after the Anglo–French assault we need not try to do before.

I stressed that the Minister of Defence is worried about the heavy casualties we may suffer in the opening phase of the campaign, before the Anglo–French action, which, we hope, will indeed take place. He believes that as soon as we start our offensive, the Egyptian Air Force will attack Tel Aviv and Haifa with their Ilyushin bombers and cause considerable destruction to our civilian population. I do not share this apprehension. Of course we may not be able to 'pass between the raindrops' and emerge completely dry, but I think we can manage to avoid getting too wet. I believe that in the early phases we can give our operation the character of a reprisal action, and even though we shall have quite a strong force close to the Suez Canal, the Egyptians are not likely to recognize it as the opening of a comprehensive campaign, and will not rush to bomb civilian targets in Israel.

I explained that it was in conformity with this intention that I had introduced changes in our original plan. Our first action will therefore not now be the capture of objectives on the northern axis, but the landing of a paratroop battalion at the Mitla Pass (Jebel Heitan). The earlier plan called for the opening of the campaign with the seizure of objectives which dominate the main route between Israel and Egypt. This route extends across the northern edge of Sinai, running along the Mediterranean coast, and is served by a railroad, an asphalt highway, an airfield, and sources of sweet water. The surrounding area of course holds concentrations of the principal Egyptian forces assigned to the Israeli front.

The Mitla Pass, on the other hand, is close to the southern end of the Suez Canal, and its geographic link with Israel is an unpaved desert track which bisects the Sinai wilderness. This track is defended by small units of the Egyptian Army, and the pass itself is quite uninhabited. I hope therefore that the Egyptian military staff will interpret our paratroop drop at Mitla as just a raid. I do not believe the possibility will occur to them that a campaign to conquer Sinai can start in any way other than an attempt to secure control of the two northern axes, those of El Arish and Bir Gafgafa. Moreover, I assume that even next day, when the forces of our mobile brigade capture Thamad and Nakhl, points of defence on the Mitla axis, the Egyptian High Command will think we are doing so to rush reinforcements to our unit cut off at Mitla, and that our intention is to enable it to withdraw and return to Israel.

The second change I made, concerning the employment of the Air Force, is that it will not open the campaign with the bombing of Egyptian airfields but will confine itself in the first two days to providing air support to our ground forces and protection to Israel's skies. This change is also designed to strengthen the impression at Egyptian GHQ that we are engaged in a limited reprisal action and not a full-scale war.

There is naturally some risk in basing ourselves on my assumptions, and if they should prove wrong and the Egyptian Air Force reacts to our seizure of Mitla by bombing Israel's cities, we shall pay dearly for having passed up the opportunity of surprise and failing to knock out the Egyptian planes while they are still on the ground.

But I think this can happen only if the Egyptians secure intelligence of our plans. In the normal course of developments, I doubt that the Egyptian General Staff, on the first night of our action, will have any precise idea of what has happened. True, they will receive information from the units under attack on the Israel border; but these units report the presence of Israeli battalions and brigades even when they are faced only by sections and platoons, and Egyptian GHQ is already used to false alarms. Only next morning when the alarms will be found to have been valid will the Egyptian High Command consider how to react. They will certainly not hesitate to throw all their forces into action against the Israel units which penetrated into Egyptian territory; but I do not believe they will hasten to send their planes to bomb Tel Aviv.

It is almost certain that the first day of the fighting, the battles will be confined to the Nakhl–Mitla axis, the location of our units who will have broken into Sinai. A day later, at dawn, it is expected that the British and French forces will launch their campaign. If this really happens, we shall then be able to develop our operations in two directions – continue our advance to the south, to Sharm e-Sheikh, and open an attack on the north, on Rafah and El Arish. If, however, things go wrong and for some reason or other we have to halt the campaign, we shall evacuate our unit at Mitla through the Nakhl-Thamad axis, which will then be under our control, and claim that this was only a reprisal action and with its completion, our forces were returned to Israel.

26 October 1965

A meeting last night of the full General Staff. If all goes according to plan, this will be our last session before the opening of the campaign.

The orders have already been given to each unit by Operations Branch at individual meetings, and this wider forum was called together principally for a briefing on the political background and its implications.

The subject was somewhat complicated. Not all the information known to me was I able to transmit; and not all I transmitted was I able to explain. However, the general spirit of the meeting was good, and we all tried to restrain our excitement and apprehensions.

When I explained our relationship to the Anglo–French forces, I said that if our assessment is confirmed and they do indeed attack Egypt, we should behave like the cyclist who is riding uphill when a truck chances by and he grabs hold. We should get what help we can, hanging on to their vehicle and exploiting its movement as much as possible, and only when our routes fork should we break off and proceed along our separate way with our own force alone.

This illustration of getting a 'lift' from the Anglo-French truck evoked the not unexpected comments on the possibility of being crushed beneath their wheels, or of finding ourselves dragged to where we may not wish to go. I may not have chosen the most apt analogy, but anyway they well understood our situation.

Someone asked whether it was our intention to remain in Sinai or eventually to withdraw? All I could say was that in any event our first job was to capture the whole of Sinai 'so that if we had to retire, we would have somewhere to retire from'.

At the end of the meeting, I took advantage of their general good spirits to touch on the relationship between GHQ and the fighting units. I said we should all try to avoid giving these units the feeling that GHQ saddles them with tasks beyond their capacity, and through the callousness of officers sitting in comfort in Tel Aviv, does not bother to keep them supplied with the necessary means to fight. I stressed that such complaints are largely a reflection of the commanders. In the last year, the Army has achieved a very high fighting spirit. My experience of complaints from unit commanders to GHQ has been not that their tasks have been too heavy, but that they have been too light. Units have felt themselves discriminated against not because they had not been given enough vehicles or reinforcements but because they had not been called upon to take part in some action. This spirit was a tremendous asset which should be nurtured and strengthened. In Operation 'Kadesh' the units will be given tough missions, and there are bound to be some reverses. In such cases there may be a few officers who will 'naturally' seek to shift the blame on to the inevitable scapegoat – GHQ! If they do, it will be a grave error. There is nothing easier than 'passing the buck', but the commander who does so destroys with his own hands his capacity to demand and secure from his men a supreme effort to carry out their assigned objective.

In my presentation I offered no concrete examples, though we all knew that the problem was not theoretical, and none disagreed with my basic point. If we had to produce illustrations, they could be found from the war of independence right up to the action of Kalkiliah.

We are about to embark on the Sinai campaign after numerous reprisal actions, in which the Army registered a notable achievement – the ability and readiness of small units to carry out tough and daring missions. In Sinai we shall need to exploit this achievement to the full – though I am aware that most of the reprisal actions were carried out by a small group of picked officers and men, mostly the paratroopers, whereas now the entire Army will be facing the test. The most serious question is whether we may not be mistaken in expecting that Army regulars and reservists will attain the same fighting levels as those of our picked units in the reprisal operations. I hope they can, and I have no doubt that the key lies in the hands of their commanders.

*   *   *

This morning I met with the Commander of the Air Force, and later with the Commander of the Navy. At the end of the meetings the following directives were issued:

Directives by the Chief of Staff on the employment of the Air Force in Operation 'Kadesh'. 26 October 1956

1 In phase one, from D-day up to and including D-plus 2, the tasks of the Air Force will be basically defensive, and its action will be determined by the measures taken by the enemy in the air. During this phase, the intention is to limit the aerial warfare as much as possible while preventing Egyptian air action against bases and the civilian population in Israel. In the light of this, three functions may become necessary, in the following expected order of priority:

(a) Air cover and support for the ground forces in Sinai in the event that the enemy confines his air activity to the battle zone.

(b) Preparedness to defend Israel's skies and to activate the anti-aircraft system.

(c) Attack on the Egyptian Air Force and airfields in the event that the enemy widens the scope of operations and attacks targets in Israel.

2 In phase two, from D-plus 2 and onwards, our Air Force will concentrate on the following four functions:

(a) Support for ground forces.

(b) Interception.

(c) Protection of Israel's skies.

(d) Preparedness to act against other Arab States should they join in the campaign.

3 Throughout the entire period of the fighting, from H-hour on, the Air Force will play a major transportation role, dropping and landing troops, parachuting supplies to ground forces who are cut off, and assuming general duties of supply and evacuation.

Directives by the Chief of Staff on the employment of the Navy in Operation 'Kadesh'. 26 October 1956

1 Supply services and support on the coasts of the Red Sea (Gulf of Akaba).

2 Planning and preparedness to use the Navy in the event that Syria and Lebanon join in the fighting.

The Navy were disappointed that their tasks do not include operations in the Mediterranean; but it is our assumption that Anglo–French vessels will tie down the Egyptian Navy, and we must apply our naval strength to the Red Sea. Moreover, activity on our part in the Mediterranean without co-ordination with the Anglo–French forces is likely to lead to mishaps.

For our Navy to be able to act in the Gulf of Akaba, we must move landing craft overland to Eilat. This can be done only by special vehicles, and the operation requires special arrangements, starting with widening the angles of the sharp turns at the Scorpions Pass on the Beersheba–Eilat highway, and ending with the cutting of overhead telephone wires across the road where they are too low.

In the afternoon, I cleared my desk of all items which did not bear exclusively on the operational side of the campaign. I also delegated authority which in normal times I alone am empowered to exercise:

1 Permission to units to operate beyond the borders of Israel: delegated to General Officers Commanding Regional Commands.

2 Air photography and patrols across the borders: to Director of Military Intelligence.

3 Everything connected with Civil Defence: to the head of C.D.

4 Confirmation of court-martial sentences: to the Adjutant General.

5 Financial approval (unlimited): to the Financial Adviser.

In the evening, I met with Operations Branch. Code name for the operation to capture the Straits of Tiran will be 'Yotvat'.

The Intelligence Branch is spreading the rumour that the Iraqi Army has entered Jordan. This is part of the deception plan to produce the impression that our activity is aimed at Jordan and Iraq. (In Operations they claim that Intelligence is so successful that they have begun to believe their own rumours.)

As to whether Jordan will go to the aid of Egypt and join the war, most of us think she will. We cannot imagine that the new pro-Nasser Government of Jordan, with Nabulsi as Premier and Ali Abu Nawar as Chief of Staff, which has just joined the Egyptian–Syrian alliance, will wish to alienate Egypt. I at all events am proceeding on the assumption that Jordan will start operations against us on D-plus 2 or 3, and we have prepared our plans for the Jordanian front accordingly.

I looked into some of the neighbouring rooms when I left my office after midnight. In one of them they were busy preparing orders for sleepers for the stretch of railway that will need to be laid between Tel Aviv and Gaza – if and when we capture it. In another, they were drafting proclamations in Arabic for the inhabitants of Sinai. Only with jobs I never knew even existed can one keep a whole army fully occupied!

27 October 1956

The French shipment of 200 6 × 6 trucks with front-wheel drive came in today, and saved the situation. A hundred trucks were assigned to the Paratroop Brigade (202), which is to capture the Nakhl axis and move across this desert route to link up with those of its men who will have been dropped at Mitla. The other hundred were sent to 9th Brigade, which has to reach Sharm e-Sheikh through the wadi along the western shore of the Gulf of Akaba. After the poor crop of Israeli vehicles mobilized from civilian owners, I do not know what we would have done if these French trucks had not arrived.

We have decided that on the first night, the evening of 29 October 1956, we must capture the Egyptian posts on the border to enable us to open our principal routes of movement. These enemy positions are at Nitzana, Kusseima, Kuntilla and Ras en-Nakeb. I accordingly approved (after receiving the Defence Minister's agreement) the evacuation of UN Observers from Nitzana. Better that they complain of being ordered to move than that they should report the concentration of our forces preparing for action.

The Civil Defence chief suggests that we proclaim a black-out in our main cities on the night of D-day. I turned this down. It will only arouse needless suspicion and tension. I hold to the view that the Egyptians will not attack us in the first few days, accepting our version that our operation is only a somewhat stronger reprisal action. Nor did I agree to the Civil Defence request to exempt from the mobilization order those in what are designated as 'essential occupations'. The campaign will be so short that there is no danger of paralysis to the economy, and there is no need to introduce all the arrangements scheduled for a protracted war. This of course does not apply to such urgent services as electricity and water supply, and the problem of their personnel is being handled by various committees who are authorized to exempt those who are indispensable.

Two days left before the start of the campaign. Tomorrow I visit the Armoured Corps. To them falls the principal role in routing the Egyptian forces.

28 October 1956

A session this morning with the Adjutant-General's Branch to review the progress of reserve mobilization.

In the first two days of this mobilization, we avoided the method of emergency call-up, so as not to excite the public. But as a result, the response was less than satisfactory. Because of technical defects – wrong addresses, unrecorded change of abode – many reservists failed to receive their orders. This occurred particularly with men in the Armoured Corps. At first, in 27th Brigade, for example, only fifty per cent turned up. A large number of the reservists of this brigade are of Eastern European origin. Their addresses had been left in Hungarian, Rumanian and other such transcriptions, and army messengers who had gone to deliver call-up orders to their homes had difficulty in deciphering them. It was therefore decided the day before yesterday to go over to the emergency call-up system; and the situation has indeed vastly improved. The change is due not only to the technical advantages of this method but also – perhaps mainly – to its psychological impact. So long as there was no announcement of emergency, reservists thought this was just a routine test of the mobilization system; but when they realized that the call-up was for action, they streamed to their units – even those who had not received their orders. It was enough for some in each unit to get the order and present themselves, for the word to spread quickly to the others, who rushed immediately to their bases.

We now see that of the total of more than 100,000 men we propose to mobilize, ninety per cent will appear. The truth is that we did not expect such a handsome response. This high percentage reflects the volunteer spirit, and this is even more important than the numerical achievement.

On the other hand, I am not so pleased with the 'volunteer' spirit evinced by the G. O. C.'s Regional Commands who permitted themselves, despite instructions, to call up more men than they were allocated. Northern Command exceeded its quota by 2,000, Central Command by 1,500 and Southern Command by 1,000.

The main problems of mobilization, however, concern vehicles. The call-up went out for 13,013 vehicles. (It must have been a singularly unsuperstitious army clerk who contrived to get two thirteens in the total!) Apparently only some sixty per cent were brought in. It was thought at first that the vehicle-owners were reluctant to hand over their cars for army use and were evading the order, but the picture remained unchanged even after military and civilian police had been put on to them. The main reason for this 'drop-out' is the variety and poor technical condition of our civilian transport. I do not know if any army anywhere at any time went into action aboard so assorted an array of vehicles as we have, with such a variety of types, colours, shapes and sizes. Nathan Alterman (one of Israel's most distinguished poets who has a weekly newspaper column) could write a magnificent 'Column Seven' on laundry trucks and margarine vans reaching Suez (if they ever do). We can overlook a missing toolbox, or worn tyres; but when a truck turns up with a cracked cylinder-head or a faulty transmission shaft, it is just not worth mobilizing. I fear that in this matter our estimates were exaggerated, and in practice we shall find that we have less transport than we had planned on getting.

As the reason for their call-up, reservists were told that a clash was likely with Jordan because of the entry into its territory of Iraqi forces, and because of its joining the Egypt–Syria Command. This deceptive explanation ties in with the news and articles which have been appearing in the press in the last few days, and the prospects are good that we may succeed in camouflaging the true purpose of the mobilization.

With all the faults and defects, it will be an achievement of first-class importance if we manage to mobilize within one week the entire military array designated for action in Sinai; and from the latest reports today, it is clear that we shall. In the Air Force, for example the reservist mobilization was completed in forty-three hours.

At the end of the meeting with the Adjutant-General's staff, I asked for daily reports on the progress of the call-up in the following categories: infantry, armour, navy and service units. I still cannot find my way through the jungle of standard man-power reports, with their abbreviations, initials and endless figures on endless pages.

29 October 1956

Yesterday at 10.00 hours Ben Gurion brought before the Cabinet for consideration and decision the subject of the Sinai Campaign. The Government approved. Ben Gurion then met with representatives of the opposition parties and informed them of the Government's decision. This was followed by an official announcement explaining the necessity of the reservist mobilization.

It states that following the Arab military activity and its aggressive design, a number of reserve battalions have been mobilized 'so that we shall not have to face surprise attack from the south, the north or the east with inadequate defence'. The announcement ends on the old-fashioned note of pathos of our early settlers (taken from Psalms [121, 4]): 'Behold, he that keepeth Israel shall neither slumber nor sleep.'

This statement is intended primarily for the Israel public, and what is worth noting is not only what it says but what it omits: it contains no assurance that the mobilization is for a short period; and there is nothing in it to lessen the tension and the eve-of-war feeling in the country. As to its foreign affairs aspect, the announcement explains and condemns the aggressive intentions of the Arab States and the consequent need to mobilize additional army units. It masks the real purpose of the mobilization and, together with other means we have employed, is calculated to draw attention to the Jordan border as the source of tension and the likely scene of military conflict.

In the meantime we have received another cabled message from the President of the United States. In this as in the previous one (on 27 October 1956), Eisenhower expresses his anxiety over our mobilization. In both messages he links our call-up with the entry of the Iraqi Army into Jordan, and he explains that, in fact, according to his information, no Iraqi units have crossed into Jordan. Ben Gurion, in his reply, put the emphasis on the aggressive aims of Egypt, and he did not promise to satisfy the President's request to stop the mobilization of the reservists. When Ben Gurion was notified that a second cable was on its way, he was very apprehensive about its contents; but when it came in, and after he had studied it with great care, he felt easier. The terms of both messages were general, and could be 'swallowed'. In the second there was a stronger repetition of the

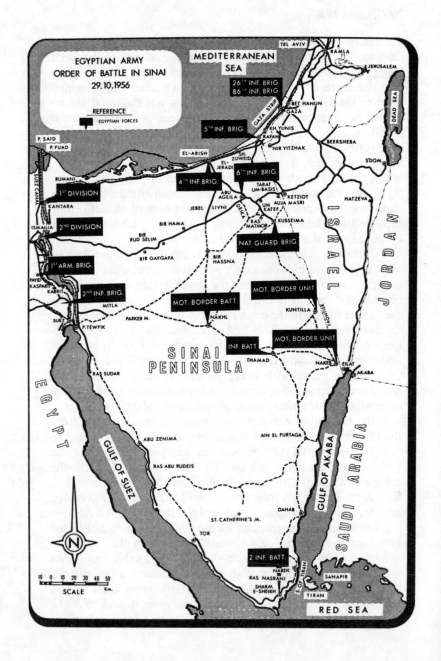

EGYPTIAN ARMY
ORDER OF BATTLE IN SINAI
29.10.1956

REFERENCE
EGYPTIAN FORCES

MEDITERRANEAN
SEA

TEL AVIV
RAMLA
JERUSALEM
DEAD SEA

26ᵀᴴ INF. BRIG.
86ᵀᴴ INF. BRIG.

BET HANUN
GAZA

5ᵀᴴ INF. BRIG.
KH. YUNIS
RAFAH
BEERSHEBA
NIR YITZHAK
S'DOM

P. SAID
P. FUAD

EL-ARISH
SH. ZUWEID
EL-JERADI
6ᵀᴴ INF. BRIG.
HATZEVA

RUMANI
4ᵀᴴ INF. BRIG.
TARAT UM-BASIS
ABU AGEILA
KETZIOT
UM AUJA MASRI

1ˢᵀ DIVISION
JEBEL LIVNI
KATEF
RAS MATMOR
KUSSEIMA

KANTARA

ISMAILIA
2ᴺᴰ DIVISION
BIR RUD SELIM
BIR HAMA

NAT. GUARD BRIG

BIR GAFGAFA
BIR HASSNA

1ˢᵀ ARM. BRIG.
FAYID
KASPARIT
KABRIT
2ᴺᴰ INF. BRIG.
MITLA

MOT. BORDER UNIT

MOT. BORDER BATT.
KUNTILLA

SUEZ
P. TEWFIK
PARKER M.
NAKHL

SINAI
PENINSULA

INF. BATT.
THAMAD

MOT. BORDER UNIT

RAS SUDAR

NAKEB
EILAT
AKABA

EGYPT

GULF OF SUEZ

ISRAEL

JORDAN

SAUDI ARABIA

ABU ZENIMA

AIN EL FURTAGA

RAS ABU RUDEIS

ST. CATHERINE'S M.
DAHAB

TOR

2 INF. BATT.
NABEK
RAS NASRANI
SHARM E-SHEIKH
SANAPIR
S. OF TIRAN
TIRAN

GULF OF AKABA

N

10 0 10 20 30 40 50
SCALE   Km.

RED SEA

SUEZ CANAL

warning contained in the first, urging 'that there be no forcible initiative on the part of your Government which would endanger the peace and the growing *friendship* between our two countries'.

In addition to these messages, the United States Ambassador announced that he had received instructions to evacuate immediately all American citizens in Israel (some 1,800 persons). We promised him our help. He said that similar instructions have been issued for United States citizens in Egypt, Jordan and Syria.

One of the politico-military items that needs attention is a statement by the Army spokesman. It is clear that this evening, immediately after the paratroop drop at Mitla, there must be an official announcement. This should be firm and threatening, but it must reveal nothing of our true intentions. After much drafting and redrafting, we brought to Ben Gurion for his approval the following suggested bulletin: 'The Army spokesman announces that Israel Defence Forces entered and engaged fedayun units in Ras en-Nakeb and Kuntilla, and seized positions west of the Nakhl cross-roads in the vicinity of the Suez Canal. This action follows the Egyptian military assaults on Israel transport on land and sea designed to cause destruction and the denial of peaceful life to Israel's citizens.'

We found Ben Gurion sick in bed, with a temperature of 103 degrees. He apparently has influenza. The weariness and tension of the last few weeks have also left their mark. But he continues with his work, and when I took my departure, hurrying back to my command post (to which we have moved from the GHQ buildings), there were still Foreign Ministry officials waiting to consult with him.

The situation with the United States is complicated, and not at all agreeable. Israel, wishing and needing to maintain close ties of friendship with the US, finds herself in the difficult position of having to keep from her – and even be evasive about – her real intentions. The alternative, however, is to forgo military action and just put up with the Arab acts of enmity – blockade of the Gulf of Akaba, fedayun terrorism, and military preparations for an attack on Israel. The United States is adamantly opposed to any military action on the part of Israel, yet she does not – perhaps she cannot – prevent anti-Israel action on the part of the Arabs. Moreover, the United States consistently refuses to grant or sell us arms, thereby exposing us to aggression by the Arabs who have open access to arms sources from the Soviet bloc.

The absurdity of the United States situation in these current Middle Eastern events is due also to her isolation from her allies, Britain and France, who have hidden from her their intention to attack Egypt. In his second signal to Ben Gurion, President Eisenhower says that on the basis of the joint responsibility of the signatories to the tripartite Declaration of 25 May 1950 (the declaration by the US, Britain and France guaranteeing the territorial integrity of the States of the Middle East), he will discuss the problem of Israel's security with Britain and France. From both his signals it is apparent that he thinks the imminent conflict is likely to erupt between Israel and Jordan and that Britain and France will co-operate with him in preventing this. How uninformed he is of the situation! In all its aspects, the reality is the reverse of his assumptions. The arena is not Jordan but Egypt, and Britain and France are likely to be found on the same front with Israel against United States opposition, and not with the US against Israel.

It seems to me, however, that this is not only a question of ignorance of the facts. The prime reason for the sterility in America's approaches to Israel is that she has no specific solutions to the problems which face us so acutely. I do not know whether this stems from political detachment, or what, but I was struck by the hollowness of the President's words in both cables that 'only a peaceful and moderate approach will genuinely improve the situation'; and also his notification, which is presumably expected to allay anxiety in Israel, that 'I have also directed that my concern be communicated to other Middle Eastern countries, urgently requesting that they refrain from any action which would lead to hostilities'. What content of reality is there to such well-worn phrases, and what is their practical impact on the terror acts of the fedayun, or the blockade of Israel shipping in Suez and the Gulf of Akaba, or the Egypt–Syria–Jordan military pact?

I am becoming more and more convinced that the principal force of the United States when she seeks to influence developments in the Middle East – short, of course, of the use of military power – lies in her pressure on us, but not in securing a solution to our problems with the neighbouring Arab States.

Back at the command post, there was an atmosphere of high

excitement. This did not express itself in shouting or raised voices. On the contrary, everyone spoke in subdued tones and they moved as if they were carrying piles of glass seven storeys high. But their expressions showed that all were thinking – tonight we launch the campaign!

In the measure in which I can judge, I have the feeling that the entire nation is in favour of this campaign, even though nothing is farther from them, nor more alien to their spirit, than militaristic ambitions. The lads who showed up at their units without being called are the very idealists who went out to found moshavim and kibbutzim with the purpose of building a just society based on the simple life of manual labour. For all who will be taking part in this campaign, the compelling motivating factors behind it are the same as those which inspired the major efforts of the last three generations to restore Jewish nationhood in Israel. The public senses that this 'Kadesh' campaign – though the name is not yet known – is directly linked to such episodes as the 'illegal' immigration operation to break the Bevin ban, and the drive to establish kibbutzim in the Negev in defiance of the 'White Paper' restrictions during the Mandatory period.

Among the senior officers of the Army there is the additional feeling that here is an opportunity to 'settle accounts', that 'the day we've been waiting for' has arrived, when at last there can be release for the pent-up bitterness they have harboured for the eight years since the establishment of the State of Israel, eight years of Arab threats to destroy Israel, accompanied by continuous terrorism and other acts of enmity. In the last few weeks, following the warning orders, there have been patrols and air reconnaissance and planning and a flurry of organizational activity; yet most of our officers did not really believe that we would indeed go ahead with the action. We have all had the thought that at the last moment, as usual, an instruction would come down from on high that the campaign was cancelled, or, in the accustomed phrase, that it was 'indefinitely postponed'.

I myself was not completely a party to this mood, and I often felt like someone who moves among well-dressed celebrants in his work-clothes. This was due not only to my matter-of-fact character. The truth is that the decisive moment for me has already passed, the moment when I knew that doubts had been resolved and the decision taken to launch the campaign. This occurred on the 25th, four days ago. Yet even now I am not certain that we shall not have to halt the action before its completion. I know well how complex are the political circumstances in which Israel embarks on Operation 'Kadesh', and I am aware that the Minister of Defence may call me any minute to inform me that a situation has arisen which makes it necessary to cease the engagement.

CHAPTER FIVE

*

THE CAMPAIGN OPENS

30 October 1956

Four actions were set for the opening night of the campaign (29/30 October 1956): Mitla, Ras en-Nakeb, Kuntilla and Kusseima. The first, the seizure of Mitla, started at 17.00 hours (16.59 to be precise) with the drop of 395 paratroopers at the Mitla Pass.

Apart from its direct operational part in the campaign – control of the Nakhl–Suez and Ismailia–Tor cross-roads – this action was also a test of our plan to deceive and surprise the Egyptian Military Staff.

The paratroop drop was carried out almost without incident – thirteen slightly injured. The unit took off at 15.20 in sixteen Dakota transports flying in four formations, each carrying a paratroop company.

Our main anxiety was that these transport planes might be discovered by the Egyptians and attacked by their fighters. The slow Dakotas, each loaded with twenty-five infantrymen with their personal equipment, would have been a pretty helpless target for the Egyptian Migs. Moreover, the dropping area was under the noses of the Egyptians – only about forty-five miles from their airfield at Kabrit – and hundreds of miles from our own air bases. In order to evade the Egyptian radar, the Dakotas flew close to the ground, sticking to a height of 500 feet, and only when they approached the jump area did they rise to 1,500 feet. Giving close escort to the transport planes were ten Meteors, while twelve Mystères patrolled the length of the Suez Canal to deal with any Egyptian plane that took off to attack our aircraft.

The Dakotas reached Mitla and dropped the battalion without encountering any Egyptian aircraft. But when our Mystères appeared over the Kabrit airfield, they were of course noticed; yet the sole Egyptian reaction was – to disperse their planes that

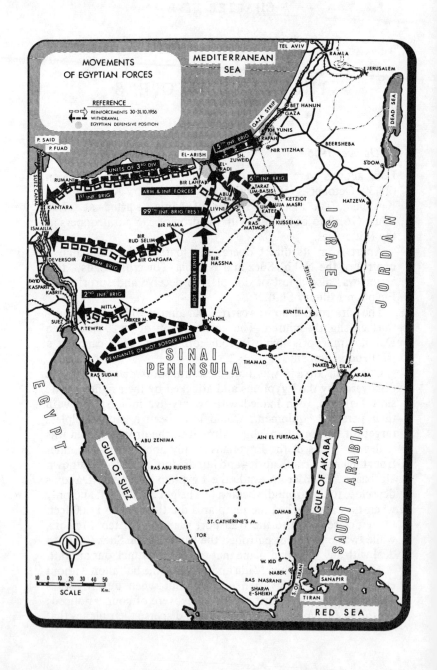

MOVEMENTS
OF EGYPTIAN FORCES

REFERENCE

REINFORCEMENTS 30-31.10.1956
WITHDRAWAL
EGYPTIAN DEFENSIVE POSITION

MEDITERRANEAN
SEA

TEL AVIV
RAMLA
JERUSALEM
DEAD SEA

P. SAID
P. FUAD

GAZA STRIP
BET HANUN
GAZA
KH. YUNIS
RAFAH
NIR YITZHAK
BEERSHEBA
S'DOM

EL-ARISH
5TH INF. BRIG
SH. ZUWEID
EL-RADI
BIR LAHFAN
6TH INF. BRIG
TARAT UM-BASIS)
KETZIOT
HATZEVA

UNITS OF 3RD DIV.
ARM. & INF. FORCES
ABU AGEILA
UM SHUJA MASRI
UM KATEF

RUMANI
1ST INF. BRIG.
KANTARA

99TH INF. BRIG. (RES.)
LIVNI
DUIKA
RAS MATMOR
KUSSEIMA

ISMAILIA
BIR HAMA

BIR RUD SELIM
BIR GAFGAFA
BIR HASSNA

DEVERSOIR
1ST ARM. BRIG.

FAYID
KASPARIT
KABRIT

2ND INF. BRIG.
MITLA
PARKER M.

SUEZ
P. TEWFIK
REMNANTS OF MOT. BORDER UNITS

NAKHL
KUNTILLA

SINAI
PENINSULA

THAMAD
NAKEL
EILAT
AKABA

RAS SUDAR

EGYPT

GULF OF SUEZ

ABU ZENIMA

AIN EL FURTAGA

RAS ABU RUDEIS

DAHAB

ST. CATHERINE'S M.

TOR

W. KID
NABEK
RAS NASRANI
SHARM
E-SHEIKH
TIRAN

SANAPIR

RED SEA

ISRAEL
JORDAN
SAUDI ARABIA
GULF OF AKABA
S. OF TIRAN

FRONTIER

BIR HANA

MOT. BORDER UNITS

N

10 0 10 20 30 40 50
SCALE   Km.

were on the ground. With our Dakotas safely back at base, we could breathe more easily. None of us could have been absolutely certain that no intelligence had reached the Egyptians, or that they suspected nothing of our real intentions; and we each conjured up a vision of our fleet of transport planes cumbrously writhing amidst a swarm of fighters sent up from airfields near Mitla and wreaking havoc on them.

It transpired from the reports that the pilots had erred and dropped our troops about three miles east of the designated landing spot. The paratroopers rectified this by a two-hours' march. By 19.30, the unit was in position at the proper place, the Parker Memorial (a monument to Colonel A. C. Parker, British Governor of Sinai from 1910 to 1923). At 21.00, additional supplies were parachuted to them as planned: eight jeeps, four 106-mm. recoilless guns, two 120-mm. mortars, ammunition and personal equipment.

A little earlier, their prowler guards encountered two Egyptian military vehicles. One was destroyed but the other managed to escape and return in the direction of Nakhl.

It is not clear whether the salient where the paratroopers are entrenched is the most suitable. Our first plan was to drop them at the western end of the Mitla Pass. But air photographs taken on 6 October showed this site to be occupied by sixteen shacks, and further photographic reconnaissance on the eve of the drop, the 28th, revealed that there were now also twenty-three tents and several vehicles. Though we could not know for certain what this meant, we resolved to change the objective and, instead, to take the salient at the Parker Memorial, located at the eastern end of the Mitla Pass. Incidentally, for some unexplained reason, the results of the air photography on the 6th were not transmitted to the brigade, and only on the night of the 28th/29th, after the second photographic mission, did they learn about it, and it was then decided – on the very last night – to make the change in the landing site.

The unit is now dug in and fortified close to the Parker Memorial, and this evening I sent another signal ordering them not to move westward. At this stage we have no interest in further provoking the Egyptians and widening our military activity; we should try as far as possible to get through the next twenty-four hours without additional battles.

*　　*　　*

The key to our situation in the next twenty-four hours is the balance of air strength. A relative comparison of these forces is not simple. For one thing, the types of planes we possess are different from those flown by the Egyptians, and each type has its drawbacks and advantages in specific conditions. For another, the distance between airfield and battle area is of crucial importance, and this distance is much shorter for the Egyptians. Mitla is two to five minutes' flying time from their airfields; it is twenty-one minutes from our nearest air base. This means that our planes can stay in the air above this zone only ten minutes before running out of fuel.

To these considerations must be added the comparative skills of the pilots, radar coverage, maintenance of the aircraft, technical levels of ground crews and ground equipment, and several other factors which determine in no small measure the quality of Air Force action.

The Egyptian Air Force is composed exclusively of jets, whereas ours is still based on quite a few piston-engined aircraft. As far as we know the Egyptians have received from the Russians about 200 Mig-15 fighters and some fifty Ilyushin-28 bombers. The question is how many of these planes are organized in operational squadrons with trained pilots and ground crews. In following their flights, we have so far identified eight squadrons of jet fighters, four of Mig-15s and four of Meteors and Vampires, each squadron comprising fifteen to twenty-four planes.

Against these eight jet squadrons, we can put into action in Sinai five jet-fighter squadrons, totalling seventy-nine planes – thirty-seven Mystères and forty-two Meteors and Ouragans. As for bombers, we have two piston-engined B-17 planes against two Egyptian squadrons – thirty to sixty planes – of Ilyushin-28s.

I know that in all the European armies piston-engined aircraft have been assigned to the scrapyards; but we shall use ours. We have sixty-four of them – twenty-eight Mustangs, thirteen Mosquitos, twenty-one Harvards, and the two B-17s. Altogether, then, counting 'the rabbits and camels' together, we have at our disposal 143 planes – roughly half jet fighters and half piston-engined aircraft – as against the 150 to 250 Egyptian planes, all jets.

The commander of our Air Force argues that even these comparative figures are optimistic and do not reflect the true picture. According to him, of our thirty-seven Mystères, only fourteen are serviceable, and even they are armed only with 30-mm. cannon, as we have not yet received the rockets and bombs for them. Moreover, most of our pilots are still novices, have not yet been in action and have not even managed to complete their full training. Our best planes, the Mystères, we started getting in April of this year, and most of them arrived only in August – just two months ago. I am quite sure that his figures, his description and his estimates are accurate; but when you visit the air bases and talk to the men, you find no resemblance between the discouraging picture that emerges from the statistical analyses and the high spirits and self-confidence of the pilots. Anyway, the relative strengths of the two forces will be tested in the air, and not in comparisons of lists and figures at an office desk, and in combat the determining factors will be the spirit of dedication and the standard of professional skill.

*   *   *

Tonight at 22.30 the first battalion of the 202 Paratroop Brigade's mobile column reached the Parker Memorial and linked up with the battalion that was parachuted. The rest of the brigade's units will get there within the next few hours. Breaking open this axis route, which is about 190 miles long – 125 of it inside Egyptian territory – took them twenty-eight hours. Our plan called for it to be done in twenty-four to thirty-six hours.

This is the Nakhl axis, and the Egyptians protected it with three defended localities: Kuntilla, on the Israel border, Thamad and Nakhl. Kuntilla was found deserted, for its defenders, of platoon strength, had retired to Thamad as soon as they saw our men approaching. (The report I received put it this way: 'When the Egyptian troops at Kuntilla saw our column moving towards them, they immediately dispatched a report and themselves to the rear.') Actual fighting took place only at Thamad, for at Nakhl, too, the Egyptian soldiers fled with the first shots opened on them. It would seem that of all the difficulties encountered by the brigade in its advance, capturing the Egyptian defence positions was probably the least worrisome.

The principal problems were organizational and technical, and the outstanding one was shortage of suitable vehicles for movement across desert. The brigade had first been promised

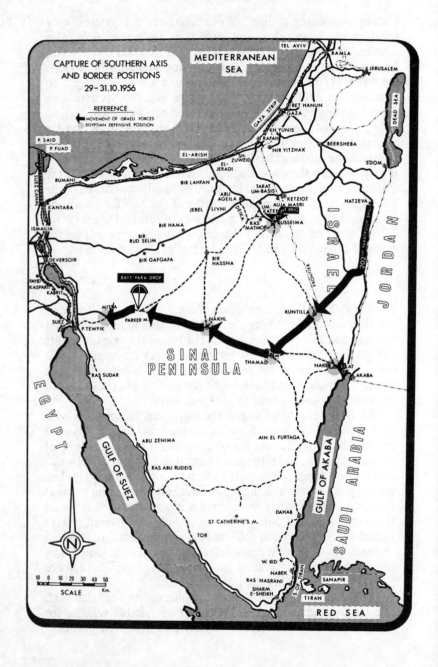

153 6 × 6 trucks. Twenty-four hours before H-hour they were notified that they would be receiving ninety. When they went into action it was with only forty-six.

Nor were they any better off with auxiliary equipment. Instead of the five ambulances they expected, they got only one; of four tow-trucks, only one. Their engineers had no netting and no steel slats for difficult stretches of the route. And in the entire column there was not a single spanner to fit the wheel nuts of the vehicles with front-wheel drive, so that any truck with a punctured tyre had to be abandoned.

In order not to show our hand, the brigade were given Ein-Hussub, on the Jordan border, as their concentration point. And it was from there that they set out, after a four-hours delay, while they were still far from being completely organized. But H-hour was approaching and they could afford to delay no longer. This distance of more than sixty desert miles across the Negev, from the eastern to the western border of Israel, was covered by the brigade column in nine hours, and they reached the jump-off point on the Egyptian border almost at the appointed time. (The delay was only half an hour.) This section of the route, however, already drew its toll of vehicles: some got stuck in the sand, others broke down, and many had to be abandoned, mostly those without front-wheel drive. As for the tanks, of the thirteen that set out from Ein-Hussub, only seven reached Kuntilla.

Nevertheless, the brigade command allowed none of these difficulties and unexpected mishaps to deflect it from its aim. With or without vehicles, the column maintained its advance. When its men found Kuntilla free of enemy troops, they pressed on to Thamad. Thamad was garrisoned by more than two enemy companies, and its topography, a rocky salient commanding the surrounding region, gave it natural defence. We launched our assault on it at 06.00 hours. Under direct covering fire from two tanks, our paratroopers aboard half-tracks broke right into this enemy position. (A typical illustration of the difficulties of movement over the stubborn tracks is the fact that of the thirteen tanks at the brigade's disposal – of which seven had reached Kuntilla – only three arrived in time to take part in the assault on the enemy's main defended locality along the route; and of these three, one overturned, so that only two managed to participate in the battle.)

The sun came to the help of our men. It was behind them and shone into the eyes of the Egyptian defenders, whose visibility was further confounded by the smoke and dust of our half-tracks and tanks which enveloped and screened our column. After forty minutes of fighting, the battle ended with the position in our hands. It is worthy of note that the defences of Thamad were well prepared with ditches and minefields, and equipped with heavy machine-guns and recoilless guns. Casualties suffered by our paratroopers were four killed and six wounded; the Egyptians lost more than fifty killed.

The attack on Nakhl began at 17.00 hours. The force designated to take this position by-passed Thamad even before it was captured and continued on to Nakhl. It consisted of two infantry companies supported by two troops of artillery, and two tanks which had managed to catch up with them. The fighting lasted twenty minutes. At 17.20, the two defending companies of Egyptian troops fled, leaving behind them a number of wounded and fifty-six killed.

A further report tells us that during the morning four Egyptian Mig fighters twice attacked Thamad after its capture, and three of our men were wounded.

We do not know yet the exact scale of the force which has already joined and will be joining up during the night with the unit at Mitla. The full brigade numbers 2,500 men, but part of this force will no doubt remain behind for the time being to protect the axis and to hold Kuntilla, Thamad and Nakhl. Nor is the vehicle situation clear. At the moment, some two-thirds of the brigade's trucks are stuck along the route, but I hope that most of them will be towed free and made serviceable quickly.

The real strength of the paratroop units lies not in their tanks, nor in their artillery nor in their vehicles, but in the men themselves, and so far only a few have become casualties. Moreover, their ranks keep expanding by additional arrivals, in all sorts of strange ways, of reservists who did not get their mobilization orders in time, and also by men who were in hospital or on courses and who managed to steal away and join their fighting comrades. Despite all the mishaps, mistakes and difficulties it encountered – some unavoidable, some unnecessary – the basic fact remains that the mobile column of the main force broke through the axis-route and succeeded in linking up with its parachuted unit. And this was effected within the designated time limit and with light casualties.

The southern border position, Ras en-Nakeb, was also captured last night, as planned. According to our intelligence, this post was held by two Egyptian mobile sections supported by patrols of a motorized border battalion. The capture of Ras en-Nakeb was entrusted to the Eilat Area command, to whom were attached three companies from 9th Brigade. Yesterday, at sundown, a reconnaissance company set out from Eilat, entered Sinai by a circuitous route through the 'Scouts' Ascent' and the 'Valley of the Moon', and seized the cross-roads Ras en-Nakeb–Thamad, Kuntilla–Sharm e-Sheikh.

At 21.00 hours, sappers cleared a passage through minefields and opened a path from Ein-Netafim to the Egyptian position. As our company approached the enemy post, they heard a single shot, and when they stormed into the police fort, they found it empty.

Before dawn, three Egyptian Land-Rovers were spotted moving towards the cross-roads. Our reconnaissance unit opened fire. One was knocked out and abandoned, but the other two got away.

I assume that when the commander of the action reported that 'it was fantastic', he was referring not to the behaviour of the Egyptians but to the scenery. In all the Negev desert, there is no region which boasts such majestic scenery as the area round the Gulf of Eilat. The most imaginative dream could not conjure up so felicitous a combination of sea, desert plain and granite promontories, splashed with Chagallian colour.

*   *   *

In the early hours of this morning Kusseima was also captured, by 4th Brigade. Our casualties were four killed and thirty-six wounded; the Egyptians lost forty-five killed and 370 captured, among them the wounded.

The Kusseima defended locality was held by two battalions of the National Guard and a reconnaissance company (probably of the motorized border formation). In addition, one company of the Egyptian 17th Battalion held the salient of Ras-Matmor which was part of the Kusseima defences.

Our 4th Brigade is composed of reservists, and they experienced all the difficulties that attend the hurried dispatch into battle of a hastily mobilized reservist unit. Their call-up orders got held up for some reason and reached the brigade late, so that they had only forty-eight hours to mobilize instead of the designated seventy-two. The number of messengers who turned up to distribute the mobilization orders was less than adequate, so that not all the orders reached the men in time; and even those that did were delivered at the wrong hour when quite a number of the reservists were not at home. In the end, it is true, between eighty and ninety per cent of those called presented themselves, but many of them were late.

The officers had insufficient time to study their expected tasks. The second-in-command of the brigade was appointed to this position on the day of mobilization, and the battalion commanders were given their objectives only twenty-four hours before the attack.

The main problem, as usual, was transport. The concentration area prescribed for them was at Bir Hafir, forty-three miles south of Beersheba and about twelve miles from Kusseima. Southern Command notified the brigade that it could be reached even with ordinary transport. This is normally true; but now, as tanks and other heavy vehicles began to move over the Bir Hafir track, they quickly churned up its top layer, turning it into powdery sand to a depth of ten cms. which could be negotiated only by vehicles with front-wheel drive. Pretty soon the dairy trucks and the ice trucks and the buses, which had been pressed into service to transport the troops, got stuck. In this predicament, the brigade commander had no other course but to transfer his men together with their light weapons on to the transport with front-wheel drive and to leave at the side of the track his auxiliary equipment, ammunition, mines, barbed wire and so on, in the hope that they could be picked up later.

This was not the only misadventure suffered by the brigade. In Beersheba there was a collision between two troop-carrying buses and thirteen men were injured. Traffic was blocked and the column had to by-pass the city, making the detour over a dirt road. The convoy guides were not familiar with the area and strayed into a wadi at the foot of an ominous hill, definitely not 'according to plan', and urgent time was wasted. The brigade Orders Group had lasted much longer than was necessary and precious hours were lost here too on detailed and superfluous explanation.

H-hour, which had been fixed for an hour before midnight –
23.00 on the 29th – had to be put off to 03.30 the next morning.
Only one unit, an infantry company whose objective was the
Sabha salient, operated at night. (Owing to a communications
breakdown, word of the postponement of H-hour did not get
through to them.) But they too, had a mischance. They took a
wrong track and went in to attack the site known as the Small
Sabha instead of the Big Sabha. They found the post deserted.
It transpired later that the emplacement they should have
attacked was also free of enemy troops, so their mistake made
no difference.

Finally, at 04.00 hours, the Israeli assault was launched on
Kusseima proper, and then it turned out that all that we had
done wrong had been put right by the Egyptians. They simply
ran. Only in one cluster of defence posts, the western salients,
did the Egyptians display serious opposition; but the brigade
reconnaissance unit – incidentally an excellent unit – which
arrived and joined in the battle tipped the scales. By 07.00 hours,
Kusseima fell to the brigade. At the same time, 7th Armoured
Brigade also entered Kusseima. It had been sent by the commander Southern Command who saw that the battle was
protracted and feared its outcome.

The capture of Kusseima completes the opening phase of
our plans. The four objectives designated for the first night of
the campaign, Mitla, Ras en-Nakeb, Kuntilla and Kusseima,
are in our hands. So is the Nakhl–Thamad axis; and the
paratroopers who jumped at Mitla are no longer cut off.

31 October 1956

On the ground, the Egyptian Army reactions in the first phase
accorded with our expectations. Most of their advance positions,
Ras en-Nakeb, Kuntilla and the Sabha, were given up without a
fight with the approach of our forces; and in the defended
localities designed to hold up an Israeli attack, Kusseima,
Thamad and Nakhl, there was initial resistance, but when they
saw that our forces continued to advance and their positions
were likely to be by-passed, they chose to flee rather than stick
to their posts and go on fighting, as their orders prescribed.
Moreover, in most cases, surrender came as soon as our men
broke into their strongholds, without the Egyptians' resorting

to hand-to-hand combat. As to the comparatively high number of enemy dead and small number of prisoners in the battles along the Kuntilla–Mitla axis, this is due to the way in which our paratroopers fight and not to tough resistance put up by the Egyptians holding this line.

In the air, too, our forecast of the Egyptian response in the opening phase of the campaign proved correct: if we would not attack their airfields, they would not extend their activity beyond the borders of Sinai.

The first attack by the Egyptian Air Force came in the morning of the 30th, between 07.30 and 09.30. Four Vampires flew a reconnaissance over our troops at Mitla and our column moving from Kuntilla to Nakhl. They were followed by two pairs of Mig 15s who strafed our units at Mitla and Thamad, hitting four of our men and a parked Piper Cub at Mitla, and three men at Thamad.

Action in the air went better for us in the latter part of the day. Our plans called for our aircraft to be in the air throughout the daylight hours to cover Mitla, and to give protection to our forces moving openly and fully exposed along the Nakhl axis. But for some reason, during the very hours of the Egyptian attack, none of our planes appeared. Later, however, patrols were kept up almost without a break, and from 10.30 onwards, after the Egyptian strafing, our Air Force was given permission to attack Egyptian ground targets, and also to head off Egyptian planes trying to take to the air from their bases near Mitla. And indeed in the afternoon an air battle developed over the Kabrit airfield between twelve Egyptian Migs and eight of our Mystères. Two Migs were shot down and two more were 'probables'; one of our Mystères was hit but it managed to return to base and land safely.

Though our air activity was largely limited to close support of 202nd Brigade at Mitla, our planes attacked many Egyptian ground targets, mostly convoys of vehicles and artillery moving from the Canal Zone towards Mitla. It certainly cannot be without design that in spite of this air action, and even though it took place very near to Egyptian airfields, their planes for the most part did not rush to the defence of their ground units; they sought to avoid meeting and doing battle with our fighters. After all, it is not the planes but the pilots who have to do the battling. On this point, the difference between Egyptian pilots and our own was given characteristic expression in our telephone line-cutting operation two days ago and in the Egyptian bombing attack last night.

On D-day, about two hours before the paratroop drop at Mitla, two pairs of our Mustangs flew off to cut the overhead Egyptian telephone wires along the Thamad–Mitla and Kusseima–Nakhl routes. The planes were fitted with tow-hooks so that as they flew, so it was expected, the hooks would grasp and wrench the wires. But this arrangement did not work. If the pilots had returned to their base and reported that the plan had failed, there would certainly have been no murmur against them. But after a brief radio consultation among themselves, the four pilots decided to take a risk and carry out their appointed task by cutting the Egyptian wires with their propellers and wings. It is pretty miraculous that they succeeded in doing this without crashing – the wires were only four yards from the ground – and without getting the wires entangled in their propellers.

As against this kind of behaviour, the Egyptian pilot who was sent in an Ilyushin-28 to bomb one of our airfields chose to 'play it safe' and dropped his bombs on a desolate hill near Jerusalem. It was only by chance that one of the farmers of Ramat Rachel village spotted the 'bombing'. He notified police, who went out to the site in the morning, and found fragments of Soviet bombs (type 100×11).

*   *   *

We do not know what the Egyptian Government's reaction will be to the Anglo–French ultimatum which was delivered last night at 18.00 hours (Israel time). It is possible that in view of the military threat contained therein, the Egyptians will change their instructions to their Army. In the meantime, we can sum up for ourselves the initial Arab response to our operations, even though our information so far is incomplete, and some of it is unchecked.

The first question is what the Arab States will do. Will they go to the help of Egypt, and if so in what way?

It is apparent that our deception plan was successful. Up to the last minute, that is, up to our paratroop drop at Mitla, the General Staffs of all the Arab armies believed that it was our intention to march on Jordan. Jordan accordingly reinforced her defence system along her border with Israel, and every defended locality which had formerly been manned by a company was now garrisoned by a battalion. Iraq, too, increased her forces designated to go to Jordan's aid and transferred an additional brigade to Habbaniyah. She now has a complete division on the Iraqi–Jordan border (at Habbaniyah and H–3) ready to join the Jordanian Army.

From the operational point of view, this move of Jordan is definitely defensive. If she were planning an assault, she should be concentrating her forces and not dispersing them battalion by battalion along the border. Nor does the Iraqi reinforcement show any deviation from the traditional Iraqi–Jordan plans, either in its scale or in the location of its concentration centres. It offers no signs of serious preparation for war.

Last night, however, after news reached Egyptian GHQ of our paratroop landing at Mitla, our attacks on Kusseima and Ras en-Nakeb, and the advance of our mobile column along the Kuntilla-Nakhl axis towards Suez, they began to recognize the true significance of our actions. We do not know yet whether the Egyptian General Staff have sent military orders to their allies, but the Egyptian Government has issued an open appeal (perhaps to mobilize the Arab public to bring pressure on their Governments) to the various Arab States, near and far, demanding that they make war on Israel.

In a military exercise, on a map or a sand-table or in manœuvres, nothing seems easier. The Jordanians simply have to cross less than twelve miles, as the crow flies, and the Syrians less than thirty, and – Israel is sliced in three! In fact, no appeal could be less realistic. There is not the slightest prospect that Syria and Jordan would even attempt to do so. These two countries can launch harassing action against us to add to our burdens and compel us to pin down some of our forces to cope with their fronts. They can perhaps shell our farm settlements and cities (Jerusalem) and interfere with our communications arteries, and so on. But the assumption that they can launch an all-out war on Israel within twenty-four hours is a mixture of hysteria and Don Quixotism.

Up to now, at all events, there is no indication of any attack from either Syria or Jordan. I must confess that so far it seems I was wrong in assuming that they would go to the aid of Egypt. Just as well.

The Egyptian Army itself was taken completely by surprise. Despite the news published several days now in the world press about our mobilization of reservists and our war preparations, the Egyptians never guessed that these moves were directed against them. Their Chief of Staff, Abd-el-Hakim Amer, left five days ago with a group of his senior officers on a visit to the Jordanian and Syrian armies, and he returned to Egypt only yesterday, as planned. I cannot imagine that he would not have hastened back sooner if he had suspected that something was likely to happen any day on his borders.

Prisoners captured by our paratroop brigade revealed that the first news on what was afoot was received by the Egyptian General Staff from a detachment of the 2nd Motorized Border unit based on Thamad. The men of this detachment saw the Dakotas parachuting our troops and later they saw the mobile column advancing in the direction of Suez, and they notified their command.

I do not know whether the Egyptians gathered the full import of our moves, but it must be said that they lost no time in reacting to them. They ordered a state of alert in the Army, Navy and Air Force. Ilyushin bomber crews were instructed to stand by for attack-missions on targets in Israel. 1st Brigade (GHQ reserves) were ordered to move to El Arish and 2nd Brigade to proceed immediately to engage our forces who were dropped at Mitla. All the other units on the 'Eastern Front' – the front bounded by Israel, which includes the Sinai Peninsula, the Gaza Strip and the Canal Zone – were directed to concentrate their forces, heighten their vigilance and stand ready to beat off an Israeli attack.

*   *   *

Yesterday I had a stiff contretemps with the GOC Southern Command who, contrary to GHQ orders, sent 7th Armoured Brigade into action before their appointed time.

Despite the specific orders that armoured forces were not to be employed before the 31st, and explanatory reasons for this, the commander Southern Command considered that not a moment should be wasted and immediately at the start of the operations initiative and surprise should be exploited to advance and capture whatever one could. He accordingly resolved to send into action, already on D-day, all the forces at his command. As for the instructions of the General Staff and the military-political considerations that called for a different approach, he, the GOC Southern Command, was not prepared to rely on the possibility that 'someone else' – i.e. Anglo–French forces – might go into action, and he therefore saw no justification for holding up our main attack for forty-eight hours. He felt that GHQ orders on this matter were a political and military mistake for which we would pay dearly.

Owing to last minute pressure of work, I was unable to leave my command post in the early hours of the morning, as I had hoped; and when I did get away, the drive south over narrow roads crowded with army vehicles and artillery units took longer than expected.

In Beersheba we looked in at Southern Command HQ but found no officers there. They were all out in the field at various advance HQs. We met up with the Commander at Beerotayim and together we proceeded immediately to Kusseima.

The village of Kusseima is in a valley and the battle that took place a few hours before our arrival was fought on the neighbouring hills where the Egyptians had set up their defences. Nevertheless the village too bore the marks of warfare. One miserable shop had been broken into, its shelves were bare, and the fragments of a shattered oil jug were strewn on the floor. At the side of the village well lay the carcasses of camels which had been needlessly killed. Among the thickets soldiers were chasing elusive chickens – who were proving too quick for them. I found the whole scene dreary and humiliating, the more so, perhaps, because of my anger at the action of the southern commander.

We found the head of 7th Armoured Brigade in the centre of the Ras Matmor chain of hills, twelve miles west of Kusseima. In the distance rose clouds of dust thrown up by the armoured vehicles streaming westwards. The brigade was already deployed some twenty-five miles inside Sinai, when according to plan it should still be twenty-five miles inside Israel at the concentration area of Nahal Ruth, silent, motionless, unobtrusive.

For a moment I recalled my childhood days when a herd of cows, stung to frenzy by summer flies, would go wild and bolt from my hands, while I, shamefaced and utterly at a loss, would watch them disappear into the distant fields, their tails high as a final act of defiance.

I had already heard, *en route*, the southern commander's explanation of why he had been moved to act against orders; and I managed to tell him what I thought of his behaviour before we met the brigade commander. The time had now come to issue instructions.

I had no doubt in my mind what the order should be, and I could already visualize the tanks turning round and going back on their tracks all the way to Nahal Ruth. From the point of view of discipline and good order, there is no question that this would be the correct course; but was it also correct in terms of advancing the success of the campaign?

Eight hours had already passed since the brigade entered Sinai. The southern commander said that the order he gave was for them to advance through Kusseima towards the defended localities of Um Katef and Um Shihan but to halt just before reaching them and not to attack. But, as happens in such cases, 'communications were faulty' and an armoured battalion team opened up on Um Katef.

Um Katef, however, did not fall. The attack met with strong resistance and accurate anti-tank fire from well-entrenched 'Archers'. One tank and one half-track were hit. A company commander and three men were wounded and the artillery liaison officer was killed as he got off his half-track to regulate his compass. In the meantime the brigade commander reached the spot, and it was his judgement that the battalion team had no chance of capturing the Egyptian position on its own. The battalion accordingly retired and the brigade commander started assembling additional forces for the attack.

What has been done is done. If indeed the advance of this armoured brigade into Sinai leads to increased Egyptian activity, particularly in the air, before the time expected on the basis of our original plans, there is nothing we can do now to prevent it. Better, then, at least to extract the maximum advantage from the brigade's having already joined in the fighting. I accordingly ordered that 7th Armoured Brigade should begin immediately to execute its assignment in Operation 'Kadesh' – to break through, capture and hold the central axis, Jebel Livni–Ismailia.

The brigade commander repeated that he was unable to take Um Katef with the force at his disposal without heavy casualties. I therefore told him to leave it for the time being, by-pass it from the south and advance westwards in the direction of Suez along two parallel axes, Bir Hassna and Jebel Livni. It is unlikely that all the Egyptian positions will put up strong opposition.

There are bound to be weak spots; and when the entire front opens up and the more resistant enemy posts find themselves surrounded and cut off, it will be less difficult to subdue even them. At all events, tomorrow at dawn the Anglo–French forces will start bombing Egyptian airfields and, presumably, after that we should be able to gain our objectives with greater ease.

Advancing the active entry of this armoured brigade means of course that we must advance the other actions planned for this front. I therefore ordered 10th Brigade also to put forward its start-time by twenty-four hours and already tonight, 30th/31st, to proceed with the capture of the forward Egyptian positions in the Nitzana region – Auja Masri and Tarat Um Basis.

We returned to Kusseima, and as soon as we entered the command post of 4th Brigade, news came through that the reconnaissance team of 7th Armoured Brigade had just captured the Deika defile. Deika is a narrow pass about twelve miles long lying some fifteen miles west of Kusseima. This pass links the Abu Ageila–Ismailia axis with its parallel axis Kusseima–Bir Hassna–Suez. At the southern entrance to the defile, the track crosses a bridge, and as our armoured reconnaissance unit approached it, the bridge was blown up. Three camel riders were seen racing off to the west. With the bridge knocked out, our unit skirted it and managed somehow to get across the wadi and continue along the defile, reaching the northern exit and organizing themselves there for defence. It would now be possible for the armoured brigade to attack Abu Ageila from the rear – from the west. Whatever problems this brigade will have tomorrow, they will not include a lack of targets for assault, routes for advance and space in which to spread themselves.

The commander of 4th Brigade set up his command post on a hill to the east of the village, far enough away to 'break contact' with the fleas in the thickets. I heard from him details of the capture of Kusseima and I informed him of the changes in our plans. We decided that, although his men were tired, he would immediately send the brigade reconnaissance unit to open the route to Nakhl and after them an infantry battalion to replace the paratroop unit holding Nakhl, since the paratroopers are required for additional engagements. 4th Brigade's reconnaissance unit is a picked force which is also equipped with suitable transport to cross the dunes. As for the follow-up infantry battalion, it is not clear who will carry whom – the buses the soldiers or the soldiers the buses. But we cannot wait. We must maintain the momentum of the advance and above all open fresh axes of movement. I hope that this Kusseima–Nakhl route will prove kinder to our vehicles than the one from Kusseima to Kuntilla, which is very poor. The problem of supplies will become very urgent as soon as the units run out of the food, ammunition and fuel they are carrying with them, and we must quickly secure lines of communication for a steady flow of supplies and equipment.

I left Kusseima with a memento – a flint arrow-head. Tank tracks had furrowed a hillock not far from the well and un-covered a heap of flint chips, blades and other artefacts. This was apparently the site, between 8,000 and 6,000 years ago, of a workshop manufacturing flint implements. There were remains of broken blades, arrow-heads worked into triangular shapes with a narrow base, and also blocks of flint from which the objects were fashioned. Who knows what wild tribe suddenly descended on this community thousands of years ago, scaring them into such panic flight that they left behind their implements, workshop and raw materials. Then came the storms of the desert and covered these ancient remains with layers of sand, preserv-ing them throughout the millennia until this morning, when a Sherman tank with a sharp turn of its treads brought them to light.

On my return to GHQ command post last night I set out anew the orders to the various brigades for the following day, 31 October 1956:

9th Brigade: To continue with its preparations for the march on Sharm e-Sheikh, but not to start moving as yet. (The 9th Brigade column will be the one most vulnerable to air attack, and on no account should it be moved until we can establish supremacy over the Egyptian Air Force.)

202nd Brigade: To reorganize in its present location and *not* to advance westwards to capture the Mitla Pass.

7th Armoured Brigade: To capture the defended localities of Abu Ageila, Bir Hassna, and Jebel Livni, and to continue advancing to Bir Hama and Bir Gafgafa.

10th Brigade: To capture the posts of Auja Masri and Tarat Um Basis on the night of 30th/31st, and on the following night, 31st/1st, to attack Um Katef and Um Shihan.

77th Formation: To capture the defended localities of Rafah on the night of 31st/1st.

27th Armoured Brigade: After the fall of Rafah, to advance towards El Arish and capture it quickly.

If all goes according to plan, these two days, 31 October and 1 November, will see the major battles in the northern sector where the principal Egyptian force is concentrated.

Late at night I went to see Ben Gurion who is still confined to bed with influenza. It became known that the Anglo–French forces had postponed their attack and would not be starting their bombing, as they had planned, at dawn next morning, the 31st. At this news, Ben Gurion was very worried about the position of our men at Mitla, and wanted them returned to Israel that very night. Deeply etched in his memory is the night of Kalkiliah and our grave fears for the desperate plight of our troops cut off deep in enemy territory. I too remembered that night, but I did not think we should bring back our unit from Mitla. Even if the Anglo–French invasion were cancelled, I was confident that we would be able to proceed with our campaign; and Mitla was of considerable importance also as a transit-site to reach Sharm e-Sheikh via Tor. I argued, therefore, that rather than withdraw our forces from there, we should strengthen them, and I hoped that we would be able to do so. With great reluctance, Ben Gurion abandoned the evacuation idea; but I could see that military logic did little to reduce his anxiety over the lives of our paratroopers.

After this, I did not dare tell him about the changes made on the Kusseima front and the entry into battle of 7th Armoured Brigade contrary to plan. As a matter of fact, for all my complaint both about the breach of discipline and the premature and poorly-planned action itself, I could not avoid a sympathetic feeling over the hastening of the brigade into combat even before they were required. Better to be engaged in restraining the noble stallion than in prodding the reluctant mule!

CHAPTER SIX

BREAKTHROUGH

31 October 1956

Last night at 18.00 hours (Israel time) the Governments of Britain and France delivered an ultimatum to Israel and Egypt. The ultimatum demands:

1 Stoppage of all warlike action on land, sea and in the air forthwith;
2 Withdrawal of all armed forces to a distance of ten miles from the Suez Canal;
3 Egyptian Government's agreement, 'in order to guarantee freedom of transit through the Canal by the ships of all nations and in order to separate the belligerents, to accept the temporary occupation by Anglo–French forces of key positions at Port Said, Ismailia and Suez'.

An answer is requested 'within twelve hours. If at the expiration of that time one or both Governments have not undertaken to comply with the above requirements, United Kingdom and French forces will intervene in whatever strength may be necessary to secure compliance'.

This ultimatum does not worry Israel. We are not within ten miles of the Canal and we have neither interest nor plan to come closer to it. It is clear that the whole purpose of the ultimatum is to give the British and French Governments a pretext to capture the Canal Zone by military force. Doubtless the Egyptians will not willingly agree to the conditions of the ultimatum, and particularly to the Anglo–French occupation of key positions in the Zone.

Simultaneously with the Anglo–French move, the United States is also active – but with the opposite intent. In addition to the two earlier signals, Ben Gurion today received another cable prompted by President Eisenhower suggesting that Israel withdraw her forces from Sinai since her aims – destruction of the fedayun bases – have been accomplished. If Israel would comply, the message continued, the President of the United States would immediately declare his deep appreciation of Israel.

When the US Government did not receive the desired reply from Israel, her representative at the UN, Henry Cabot Lodge, wrote to the President of the Security Council (who happened that month to be the French representative) urgently demanding a Council meeting to consider 'steps for the immediate cessation of the military action of Israel in Egypt'. Yesterday at 18.00 hours (Israel time), precisely the hour when Britain and France issued their ultimatum, the Security Council convened in special emergency session. The US representative moved the resolution calling 'upon Israel immediately to withdraw its armed forces behind the established armistice lines', and urging upon 'all members to refrain from the use of force or threat of force in the area in any manner inconsistent with the purposes of the United Nations . . . and to refrain from giving any military economic or financial assistance to Israel so long as it has not complied with this resolution . . .'

At the request of France, Britain and Israel, the session was adjourned for five hours (to 23.00 hours Israel time). When the Security Council resumed its meeting, news had already come through of the Anglo–French ultimatum, and the President of the United States regarded this as an act of fraud and treachery to himself on the part of his allies; he accordingly instructed his representatives to throw the full weight of the United States against the consummation of the Anglo–French plan.

Exercise of the veto by France and Britain prevented the adoption of resolutions unfavourable to them, and at 04.00 (Israel time) the Security Council dispersed.

In the meantime, at midnight (30 October 1956), Israel's Foreign Minister transmitted our reply to the ultimatum:

The Government of Israel has received the communication adressed jointly by the Governments of France and the United Kingdom to the Governments of Israel and Egypt for the cessation of hostilities and the withdrawal of their forces to a distance of ten miles from the Suez Canal.

In response to this communication the Government of Israel has the honour to state that it accepts the conditions both as to time and area and declares its willingness to take the necessary practical steps to this end.

In giving this undertaking it is assumed by the Government of Israel that a positive response will have been forthcoming also from the Egyptian side.

Egypt replied, as expected, that she was not prepared to accept the terms of the ultimatum. If this is what the British and French had in mind, they got what they wanted, and they can now move against an Egypt that refuses to comply with their demands.

1 November 1956

At 19.00 hours (Israel time) on 31 October 1956, Anglo–French forces began bombing Egyptian airfields in the Canal Zone.

This action started not twelve hours after the issue of the ultimatum – the time of expiry – but twenty-five. The time-table of events, then, has been: at 17.00 hours on 29 October, Israel paratroopers dropped at Mitla; twenty-five hours thereafter, at 18.00 on 30 October, Anglo–French ultimatum sent to Israel and Egypt; and twenty-five hours after that, at 19.00 on 31 October, Anglo–French forces launched military action against Egypt with the object of capturing the Suez Canal Zone.

Up to now – that is, not only after the ultimatum but even after the Anglo–French bombing – the Egyptian High Command has not yet changed its orders and has not yet instructed its units in Sinai to withdraw to the other side of the Canal. Yesterday, Egyptian infantry (1st and 2nd Brigades) and armoured forces (1st Armoured Brigade Team) continued to move from the Canal Zone, where they were held as GHQ reserves, and joined their units in Sinai. The Egyptian Naval Command, too, ordered three of its Soviet-supplied Motor Torpedo Boats and the destroyer 'Ibrahim el Awal' into action against Israel, and the frigate 'Domiat' to rush reinforcements to Egyptian forces at Sharm e-Sheikh.

In spite of this, I believe it is only a question of time, probably not many hours, before the Egyptian General Staff will order those of its units who can manage to withdraw to the Canal Zone to do so.

The battles today, apart from aerial engagements, took place in the region of Abu Ageila, where our armoured units were active, and at Mitla, in which the 202nd Paratroop Brigade were involved.

The battle at Mitla (the official name of the defile known as the Mitla Pass is Jebel Heitan) began at 12.30 yesterday (31 October). Even before then, in the small hours of the morning, immediately after the main force of the paratroop brigade moving through the Nakhl axis had linked up with the unit parachuted at the Parker Memorial, the brigade commander had wanted to advance and seize the Pass; but there was a specific order from GHQ forbidding this. He therefore requested and received permission to send out a patrol, and towards noon a 'patrol unit' set forth. This unit was in fact a full combat team, quite capable of capturing the Pass. It consisted of two infantry companies on half-tracks, a detachment of three tanks, the brigade reconnaissance unit on trucks, and a troop of heavy mortars in support. Commanding the unit was a battalion commander. The deputy commander of the brigade went along, too.

As soon as the convoy entered the defile, they were fired on from the hillocks flanking them on both sides. Permission for the patrol had been granted on the condition that they avoid involvement in serious combat, but they continued through the defile on the assumption that it was held by only light Egyptian forces. As the spearhead of the convoy penetrated deeper into the narrow pass, the firing grew in intensity, and the half-tracks – and the troops they were carrying – were hit. The commander of the unit rushed forward to rescue them but he too found himself trapped, unable to advance or to retire. Nevertheless, the forward portion of the convoy, totalling more than one company, despite the murderous fire poured into the defile, succeeded in breaking through and reaching the western end of the Pass; but the rest of the force remained pinned down, their casualties mounting under the continuous heavy fire from the heights above.

For seven hours – from 13.00 until 20.00 – the Israeli paratroopers fought an extremely tough and bitter battle until they finally overcame the Egyptian opposition and captured the Pass. This was a battle the like of which not even a veteran combat-hardened unit like this had ever experienced. Their casualties, too, were unprecedentedly heavy: thirty-eight killed and 120 wounded.

The Egyptian troops had taken up positions in natural and

artificial cavities in the slopes of the hills on either side of the Pass, covering the track beneath them with automatic weapons and anti-tank guns. Early in the morning of 30 October, the Egyptian 2nd Brigade sent its 5th Battalion, reinforced by a company from 6th Battalion, to occupy the Pass. These five Egyptian infantry companies were armed with fourteen medium machine-guns, twelve 57-mm. anti-tank guns, and about forty Czech recoilless guns. They were also given air support of four Meteors which were covered by six Migs from the Kabrit airfield. The Egyptian planes operated without interference. Actually, there were at the time six of our Ouragans in the vicinity of Mitla, but owing to faulty communications our men could not signal them for help.

At the very start of the battle the fuel truck of the paratroop unit went up in flames, to be followed by the ammunition truck and three other vehicles. The company commander who jumped from his half-track was killed on the spot. The 120-mm. heavy mortars which were to give support to the unit were knocked out of action. Four half-tracks, a tank, a jeep and an ambulance were also hit and immobilized.

The only course open to the paratroopers was to scramble up to the hillside caves of the Egyptians and in hand to hand fighting capture one position after another. This was their sole course not only to put an end to the battle as victors but also to make possible the extrication of the scores of wounded and killed who lay at the side of the track among the burning vehicles.

This, then, is precisely what they did. I doubt whether there is another unit in our army which could have managed in these conditions to get the better of the enemy. Those paratroopers who had succeeded in breaking through the trap, together with two additional companies who had arrived as reinforcements, worked their way round the Egyptian posts, climbing to the ridges of the hills, and then scrambled down and broke into the line of enemy cave-positions on the slopes. By the end of the battle, there were 150 Egyptian dead, and the rest of the enemy, the fit and the wounded, got away in the darkness and fled across the Suez Canal.

This bloody capture of the Heitan defile at Mitla might have been justified if the task of the brigade was to reach Suez and was prevented from doing so by the Egyptian force entrenched against her. But in the present circumstances, when our aim is to proceed southwards to capture Sharm e-Sheikh and not to get any nearer to Suez, there was no vital need to attack the Egyptian unit defending the approaches to the Canal. The valour, daring and fighting spirit of the paratroop commanders are qualities which should be applauded and encouraged, but this battle was not essential. Moreover, after capturing the Pass, the paratroopers continued to base themselves near the Parker Memorial. The Pass was therefore attacked, captured and abandoned.

Several officers of the General Staff observed to me, with disapproval, that my behaviour towards the paratroopers is too forgiving, when I know that they assaulted the Mitla defile against my orders and that their action had such murderous consequences. There is no need to say how much we all deplore their heavy casualties; but my complaint, a grave complaint, against the paratroop command is not over the battle itself so much as over their resort to terming their operation a 'patrol' in order to 'satisfy' the General Staff. I am saddened that they should do this, and I regret that I did not succeed in moulding such relations of mutual trust between us that if they wished to act contrary to my orders, they would do so directly and openly.

In analysing the action at Mitla, we should distinguish between the faults or errors and the breach of orders. I am angered by their decision to attack in defiance of orders, but I can understand them. It is only eight years since our war of independence when I was in charge of a jeep commando battalion, and I can imagine a situation where I would decide to seize a tactical position to give a secure base to my unit even if my action were contrary to GHQ orders. I can well believe that a commander could behave in this way quite innocently in the conviction that staff officers, who were not in the area, could not know the conditions nor the enemy positions, and that only the man on the spot was capable of appreciating the situation and taking a correct decision.

The principal mistake of the paratroopers in their assault was tactical. The unit command estimated that there would not be a strong Egyptian force at Mitla, and they therefore allowed themselves to proceed along an easy topographical route, through the wadi, with their men bunched together aboard vehicles in column formation. They thought that even if they encountered enemy forces, they would be able to deploy and ready themselves for attack in time.

These paratroopers have plenty of self-confidence, and they have developed battle procedures based on speedy organization and the dash into action. But the special topographical features of the Mitla Pass did not suit such procedures.

In other circumstances, the paratroop command would doubtless have reconnoitred the area, either on the ground or from the air, before going into action; but in the present conditions, with the brigade hundreds of kilometers inside enemy territory, cut off from the rest of our forces, and only a comparatively few kilometers away from the Egyptian tank and air bases, small wonder that they were anxious to consolidate their position quickly.

For their mistaken judgement and tactical errors, the paratroop unit paid heavily in blood. As for the breach of my orders and my forgiving attitude, the truth is that I regard the problem as grave when a unit fails to fulfil its battle task, not when it goes beyond the bounds of duty and does more than is demanded of it.

In the fighting by our ground forces, yesterday was the day of the 7th Armoured Brigade. Its units captured Abu Ageila, the Ruafa dam, Bir Hassna, Jebel Livni and Bir Hama. They too had their mishaps. During the day they were attacked several times by our own planes, which of course did not miss! A half-track of one unit was hit in the strafing, and at Jebel Livni a quartet of our Ouragans attacked a tank detachment, wounding seven of our men and damaging some of their vehicles. These misadventures were largely due to lack of contact between 7th Brigade and the Air Force. The air support signal instruments went out of action as soon as the brigade entered Kusseima, and for two days, the 30th and 31st, this had not been remedied, so that the brigade was unable to summon support or maintain any other contact with the Air Force.

On the previous night (30 October), after the capture of Deika, the armoured battalion teams crossed through the defile so as to be ready, at dawn, to attack their objectives just north of it. This move through the Deika Pass, with its bridge blown, was difficult and exacting. It took the whole night and left the men exhausted. Not only ordinary transport but even the 6 × 6 trucks were unable, despite all efforts, to move over the obdurate

103

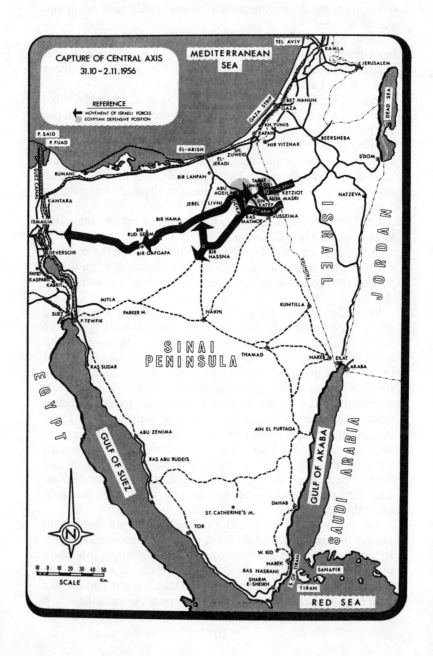

CAPTURE OF CENTRAL AXIS
31.10 - 2.11.1956

REFERENCE
← MOVEMENT OF ISRAELI FORCES
⬡ EGYPTIAN DEFENSIVE POSITION

MEDITERRANEAN
SEA

TEL AVIV
RAMLA
JERUSALEM

GAZA STRIP
BET HANUN
GAZA
KH. YUNIS
RAFAH
NIR YITZHAK
BEERSHEBA
S'DOM

DEAD SEA

P. SAID
P. FUAD

EL-ARISH
SH. ZUWEID
EL-JERADI

RUMANI

BIR LAHFAN
ABU AGEILA
JEBEL LIVNI
BIR HAMA

TARAT
UM-BASIS
10 INF. BRIG.
KETZIOT
UM KATEF
ALUJA MASRI
7 ARM. BRIG.
RAS MATMOR
KUSSEIMA

KANTARA

ISMAILIA
BIR RUD SALIM
BIR GAFGAFA
BIR HASSNA

DEVERSOIR

FAYID
KASPARIT
KABRIT

MITLA
PARKER M.
NAKHL
KUNTILLA

SUEZ
P. TEWFIK

SINAI
PENINSULA

THAMAD
NAKEB
EILAT
AKABA

RAS SUDAR

ISRAEL

JORDAN

EGYPT

SUEZ CANAL

GULF OF SUEZ

ABU ZENIMA

RAS ABU RUDEIS

AIN EL FURTAGA

SAUDI ARABIA

GULF OF AKABA

ST. CATHERINE'S M.
TOR

DAHAB

W. KID
NABEK
RAS NASRANI
SHARM
E-SHEIKH
TIRAN

SANAPIR

S. OF TIRAN

RED SEA

N

10 0 10 20 30 40 50
Km.
SCALE

course, and the fighting vehicles alone, half-tracks and tanks, managed to reach the other end of the defile by dawn.

At 05.30, an armoured team set forth to attack Abu Ageila. The defending Egyptian unit had heard and seen our armour moving near-by throughout the night, and awaited them with a well-planned reception, starting to shell them when they were still three kilometers away. This stopped our infantry, but our tanks and half-tracks continued to advance. When the first tanks got to within 200 to 300 yards of the Egyptian position, they were met with flat-trajectory fire from anti-tank guns and machine-guns. One detachment of tanks that tried to get round the position from the left found themselves stopped by a deep dry watercourse (Wadi El Arish); but from here, next to the wadi, they had a good field of fire, and with this support, the half-track unit was able to advance along the road and breach the Egyptian defences.

In the meantime, our right flank remained exposed, and the Egyptian commander, noticing this, sent an infantry company to this sector to attack our men from this direction. They managed to move out under covering fire from their base, but they were spotted and tackled by a half-track platoon who were in the rear of the armoured column and who moved to outflank the Egyptians, forcing them back into their defence posts. The battle was decided when tanks and half-tracks reached these posts, although some of the defenders continued to show great courage, even firing their bazookas while openly facing the tanks. By 06.30, an hour after it had started, the fighting was over. Our losses were light. What the Egyptian casualties were we do not know. Holding the position were an infantry company and support units, as well as the Egyptian forces who had retreated from Kusseima the day before. A group of Egyptian soldiers with an officer at their head came to our blocking unit to give themselves up, but the commander refused to take them prisoner. Instead, in accordance with the orders of the battalion commander, he sent them off to join their comrades who had fled into the sands, and no one even bothered to count them.

Soon after its capture, Abu Ageila was heavily shelled by Egyptian artillery positions at Um Shihan, and at the same time a mixed Egyptian unit, comprising motorized infantry, 'Archer' anti-tank guns and several tanks, began approaching from the direction of El Arish. Twice this unit tried to advance right up to the captured positions, and twice they were pushed back by tank-fire, retreating in a cloud of dust. On their third attempt, our forces were joined by aircraft, and the Egyptians finally disappeared, leaving behind them this time burning vehicles and columns of black smoke.

The heaviest fighting of the armoured brigade on this day was at the Ruafa dam, and the unit involved was the same armoured battalion team which had captured Abu Ageila in the morning.

The men of this unit have been fighting for three days without rest, and they are almost at the end of their tether, but their battalion commander keeps pressing them on, urging them to exploit to the full the momentum of their breakthrough. Last night, only the sappers got three hours' sleep: lack of *their* alertness when clearing minefields could have fatal results.

The Orders Group lasted three minutes. The battalion commander announced simply that the objective was the defended locality of Ruafa and he assigned each company its sector.

The assault was put in from the south-west, and facing our men on this sector were well-entrenched defence posts consisting of more than twenty anti-tank nests, including ten 'Archers', seven 57-mm. guns, two 30-mm. cannon, as well as six 25-pounders sited for direct laying.

The attack started after sunset. In the dim dust-laden twilight, the weary eyes of the tank crews could hardly see ahead. The Egyptians opened up their frontal fire with everything they had, and right away scored a direct hit on one of the half-tracks; all the men aboard became casualties. This stopped the rest of the half- racks, but they recovered in a few minutes and continued their advance. Soon darkness fell, and all that lit the black night were the illuminated flight-paths of the criss-crossing shells and the bursts of flame from exploding Egyptian ammunition stores which we had touched off. All the tanks of our assault unit were hit by anti-tank fire, but most of them managed to continue their advance. In the final stage of the battle, these tanks ran out of ammunition and their crews fought on with hand-grenades and sub-machine-guns. After clearing the Egyptian posts and their communications trenches from the last nests of resistance, the wounded were assembled, and bandaged by the light of jeep headlamps. If the Egyptians had counter-attacked at this moment, it is doubtful if our men would have stood up to it. Even the odd tank that was comparatively unscathed was now without fuel and without ammunition. But the Egyptian troops, too, needed a few hours to organize themselves for a counter-attack, and when it came, just after 21.00, our armoured unit had already managed to refuel its tanks and restock them with ammunition and was properly arrayed for defence. The Egyptian attack was supported by artillery from their posts at Um Katef and Um Shihan and close covering fire from mobile 'Archers'. But it failed, and the Egyptians retired to El Arish, leaving behind them four 'Archers' and an additional thirty-seven killed. Our unit's losses in the capture of the Ruafa dam were ten killed and thirty wounded.

We have not yet received detailed figures of the quantities and types of enemy weapons, ammunition and equipment seized by this brigade from captured Egyptian positions and abandoned camps, but the information is that they are considerable. As for prisoners, here, too, as at Abu Ageila, no one bothered to round them up. Our armoured troops have neither the technical means nor the time to do so. Immediately after the reduction of an enemy position, officers of armoured units see it as their first function to reorganize and continue their advance, and they are not prepared to spend time and men in dealing with the captured area and its problems. Moreover, the crews have to attend to their tanks. After the attack on the Ruafa dam, for example, when all our tanks were hit, the crews and teams of mechanics worked all night repairing them, and by morning, all except three were ready for action.

We are now in virtual control of the three southern routes: Nakhl–Mitla; Jebel Livni; and Bir Hassna. Bir Hassna was captured this morning without difficulty by an armoured team. At the same time, along a more northerly parallel route, a second armoured team advanced on the Jebel Livni cross-roads, which it captured at noon, and continued westwards, reaching Bir Hama at 16.00 hours and capturing that too without encountering strong opposition. Only the defended localities of Um Katef and Um Shihan are still in Egyptian hands, but they too are almost encircled – our forces are on three sides of them – and their sole contact with their base is through El Arish.

The biggest surprise to us is the Egyptian armoured force. According to our information, the Egyptians have two armoured units in Sinai. One is 3rd Armoured Battalion, which is under the command of 3rd Division whose headquarters are at El

Arish. The other is 1st Armoured Brigade Team, belonging to GHQ reserves in the Canal Zone. This brigade force was sent into Sinai on 30 October to join in the fighting against us, and it comprises two battalions of Soviet T-34 tanks, an artillery battery of Soviet SU-100 self-propelled guns, and a motorized infantry battalion on armoured troop carriers – also of Soviet make. Our 7th Armoured Brigade was on the look-out yesterday for this Egyptian brigade force, but did not manage to meet it. Our aircraft reported from time to time that they had attacked it, that it was moving to and fro along the route between Bir Gafgafa and Jebel Livni, and also that it had sent off a detachment in the direction of Mitla through Bir Hassna. At all events, our armoured units failed to make contact with it. True, after our capture of the Ruafa dam, our planes attacked several tanks which had opened fire from some distance on our forces there; but these probably belonged to the battalion of Shermans based at El Arish. Whatever the explanation, the fact is that our ground forces have not so far come across Egyptian tanks, and opposition to our assaults on enemy positions has come mainly from the static anti-tank weapons of the defended locality. These weapons, 57-mm. guns, 'Archers', bazookas, and also 25-pounders sited for direct laying, were effective. In other words, the Egyptian defence systems based on static weapons, with ranges pre-set, more'or less fulfil their function; but the operational units – tanks and mobile infantry – have so far fulfilled no function whatsoever and have taken no part in the fighting. This was the case with their 2nd Motorized Border Battalion on the Nakhl axis, and also with their 1st Infantry Brigade and 1st Armoured Brigade Team sent into Sinai as reinforcements by Egyptian GHQ. These reinforcements are apparently rushing around somewhere or other in the rear without succeeding – if indeed their commanders wish to succeed – in involving themselves in the campaign.

*   *   *

The Anglo–French bombing of Egyptian airfields which started last night has neutralized the capacity of the Egyptian Air Force to operate against us. Even before this, throughout the first night of the campaign (29 October) and the two days of fighting which preceded the Anglo–French action (30 and 31 October), Egyptian air activity did not extend beyond the boundaries of

Sinai. The neighbouring Arab States, Syria and Jordan, who were asked to attack Israel from the air and who promised to do so, in fact did nothing. Actually, the Egyptian Air Force did send over Ilyushin-28 bombers on two occasions, on the nights of the 30th and 31st, one bomber on each mission, but they dropped their bombs on open ground, far from city or village, without discrimination and without causing damage.

Apart from their Ilyushins, the Egyptians put into action Vampires, Meteors and Mig-15s. The Vampires and Meteors would usually fly with a protective escort of Migs, and their tasks were patrol and attack of Israeli ground targets, mainly in the Mitla area and along the Nakhl axis. The Migs, in addition to escort duty, were to give support to the 1st Armoured Brigade Team and protection against air attack by us.

Despite the closeness of the battlefield to Egypt's air bases, the Egyptian pilots did not overwork. On the first day (30th), they flew about forty sorties (less than one per plane) and on the next day ninety.

In general, it may be said that the pilots of the Mig-15s did not avoid battle, and at times they even set an ambush for our planes when these were returning from sorties with their fuel running low and their ammunition spent. But they were careful to appear in comparatively large formations of four to eight planes, and they sought to end an engagement quickly and steer clear of prolonged combat. Our planes, which flew low to score more accurate hits on Egyptian ground targets, were occasionally hit by anti-aircraft fire; but in air battles (fourteen), not a single one was brought down. On the other hand, at least four Migs and four Vampires were shot down by our pilots.

Egyptian air strikes against Israeli ground targets were grave on only one occasion – during the battle of the Heitan defile at Mitla. It is difficult to determine exactly how many casualties among our men and equipment were caused by enemy planes and how many by their ground troops. But it is estimated that their air attacks accounted for ten of our killed and twenty wounded, and also for our heavy mortars, ammunition truck and three other vehicles which were knocked out. On all the other occasions when Egyptian planes attacked our units – at Thamad, the Parker Memorial, and the column moving from Eilat to Nakhl – our casualties in men and vehicles were insignificant, and did not affect the course of the battle.

Though we cannot know what percentage of the damage inflicted on the enemy is attributable to our Air Force, there can be no doubt that in these few days it has had a decisive impact on the campaign. It is, I think, no exaggeration to say that our aircraft have accounted for at least half of the enemy casualties in men and equipment.

Their principal missions have been attacks on ground targets – enemy emplacements, the railroad from Egypt to Gaza, convoys and armoured columns. In the defence of these objectives against our attacks, the Egyptian Air Force has registered complete failure. Almost none of our air assaults has been frustrated by the intervention of Egyptian pilots. It is not improbable that the Egyptian 1st Armoured Brigade is not managing to move eastwards of Bir Gafgafa because of the attention it is receiving from our Air Force, and that the 3rd Armoured Battalion took no effective part in the defence of Abu Ageila and Ruafa because of the attacks on it by our planes. The fact is that in the first days of the fighting, only our Air Force has engaged Egyptian tank units – and has done so with much success.

*   *   *

Yesterday at dawn there was an Egyptian naval attack on Haifa. The results could not have been more dramatic. Within a few hours, the attacking vessel, the destroyer *Ibrahim el-Awal*, was hit by our forces, surrendered, and was brought together with her crew to Haifa.

It transpires that the day before, the 30th, when the *Ibrahim el-Awal* dropped anchor at Port Said, her commander, Lt Cdr Hassan Rushdi Tamzan, received a telephonic instruction from Egypt's naval chief, Admiral Sliman Azat, ordering him to get ready for an operation on which he would be embarking that night. The exact objective would be transmitted to him after leaving port.

The crew spent the day getting the vessel prepared and stocking up with fuel, ammunition and food, and after dusk they slipped silently out of the harbour.

According to the vessel's log book, the commander received the coded Operational Order at 19.30. It called on him to carry out a dawn attack on the port of Haifa, to shell its shipping, oil tanks and military bases.

He decided not to wait until dawn but to attack during the

110

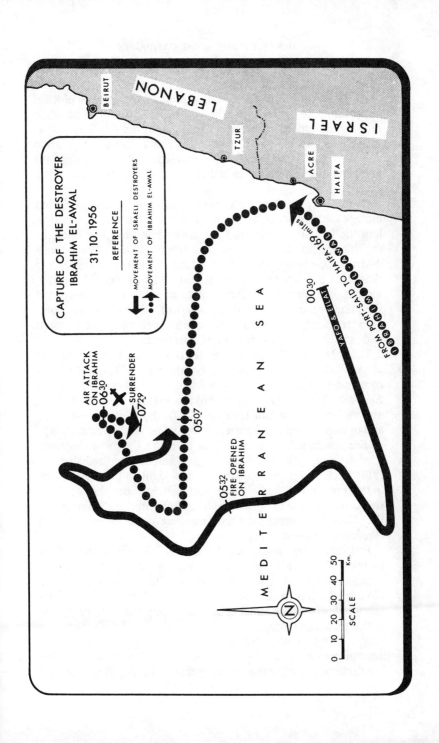

CAPTURE OF THE DESTROYER
IBRAHIM EL-AWAL

31. 10. 1956

REFERENCE

→ MOVEMENT OF ISRAELI DESTROYERS
••• MOVEMENT OF IBRAHIM EL-AWAL

BEIRUT

LEBANON

TZUR

ISRAEL

ACRE

HAIFA

FROM PORT-SAID TO HAIFA-169 miles

IBRAHIM EL-AWAL

YAFO & EILAT

00:30

MEDITERRANEAN SEA

05:07

05:32
FIRE OPENED
ON IBRAHIM

AIR ATTACK
ON IBRAHIM
06:30

SURRENDER
07:29

N

SCALE

0   10   20   30   40   50   Km.

hours of darkness so that by first light he could be well away from the zone of action.

At 03.30 (morning of the 31st), therefore, the *Ibrahim el-Awal* approached to within six miles of Haifa harbour, and while moving at a speed of twelve to fourteen knots she fired 220 4-inch shells into the port. Some of the shots were quite accurate and shells fell on the quay, the navy compound and the shipyard area, but there were no casualties and not much damage was caused.

Our radar picked up the vessel and marked her approach, but did not identify her as an enemy ship. Our own warships patrolling the Israeli coastline did not notice her, and only after the shelling began was the defence system alerted. The French destroyer *Crescent*, which was in the vicinity of Haifa at the time, was the first to spot her and at 03.38 opened fire on her, discharging sixty-four shells. But she did not pursue the Egyptian vessel and contact was lost. The *Ibrahim*'s commander, seeing that he had been spotted, promptly put on speed and withdrew in the direction of Port Said.

Israel Naval HQ signalled its destroyer squadron, which was at sea at the time some thirty-two miles west of Haifa, to intercept and engage the enemy vessel. The two destroyers *Jaffa* and *Eilat* set off immediately (at 03.56) towards the *Ibrahim el-Awal*, and an hour and a half later (at 05.27), they sighted, identified and opened fire on her from a range of 9,000 yards. The exchange of fire continued for a time, and then the Egyptian destroyer tried to escape the Israeli shelling. When she realized that her route back to Egypt was barred, she sought to flee northwards in the direction of the Lebanese port of Beirut. But she could not shake off the Israeli squadron. The *Jaffa* fired 242 rounds and the *Eilat* 194, some of them bursting close enough to the *Ibrahim* to cause damage.

Just before first light, Naval HQ called for air support. First to take off was a Dakota, and after identifying the Egyptian vessel (at 05.46), it was joined by two Ouragans. The Dakota directed the jets to the *Ibrahim el-Awal* which was now thirty-seven miles from the Israel coast. No enemy planes were sighted in the area. The Ouragans dived on the Egyptian destroyer – not even waiting for our own ships to stop firing – releasing their armour-piercing rockets (each plane carried sixteen) and strafing her decks with their cannon. Their rockets damaged the forward part of the vessel. When the Egyptian commander realized that his steering mechanism had been knocked out, the electrical system had stopped working, and the ammunition lifts had jammed, he ran up the white flag of surrender. The time was 07.10.

When the *Jaffa* and *Eilat* closed in on the *Ibrahim*, they saw that she had lowered a life-boat; but it had capsized – its bottom had been riddled – and they fished out of the water fifty-three members of the crew, two of them wounded. On the deck of the captured ship they found another six wounded and two killed, and the rest of the 153-man crew. The vessel was attached to the *Eilat* and towed into Haifa harbour.

The Egyptian mechanics had tried to sink the ship by opening the stop-cocks to the sea-water, but the valves were rusty and could not be turned.

The destroyer's log book recorded the final exchange of signals with Egyptian Naval HQ at Alexandria:

Alexandria:	06.31	You have Egyptian air cover above you, in addition to bombers rushing to your help from Syria.
Ibrahim el-Awal:	06.41	At the moment we are being engaged by three enemy planes and two of their vessels. Our help has not yet arrived.
Ibr. el-Awal:	06.50	I have been brought to a standstill.
Alexandria:	06.55	Help is on its way to you from Beirut. Continue firing your guns.
Ibr. el-Awal:	06.56	The vessel is out of action.
Ibr. el-Awal:	07.00	Our ammunition is spent.
Alexandria:	07.01	Abandon ship.
Alexandria:	07.03	Abandon ship after making all preparations to destroy all papers, books and instruments and ensure the sinking of the vessel.
Ibr. el-Awal:	07.25	Our Haifa operation was successful. Cannot determine number of enemy casualties. We have some wounded. We are sinking the ship.
Ibr. el-Awal:	07.32	We are all abandoning ship. We shall give ourselves up.

| Alexandria: | 07.37 | You have all fulfilled your mission and you should be proud of yourselves. We and the fatherland will always be proud of you. We shall look after your families. God be with you. |
| *Ibr. el-Awal*: | 07.50 | We have opened the valves to sink the ship. We are between two Israeli destroyers, *Jaffa* on our left and *Eilat* on our right. |

*   *   *

Immediately after the start of our action in Sinai, when the news reached the world, there were condemnatory outcries which increased with the British and French entry into the arena – first with their ultimatum and then with their aerial bombing of Egyptian air bases.

At the head of the campaign against the Suez–Sinai operations stands the Government of the United States, and a similar position against the military attack on Egypt is of course taken by the Soviet Union. These two 'soloists' are accompanied by an assorted choir of 'peace-at-any-price' enthusiasts – particularly when the price does not have to be paid by them.

Since, following the Anglo–French veto, the Security Council dispersed yesterday (31 October) without a decision, the Yugoslav representative proposed, with the ardent support of UN Secretary-General Dag Hammarskjöld, that the UN Assembly be convened immediately. Britain and France opposed this; Australia and Belgium abstained; but the seven other members of the Security Council voted in favour, and it was decided to call an emergency meeting of the Assembly for 17.00 today – midnight Israel time.

There were even graver reactions to the Anglo–French operation in Parliament and among wide circles in Britain. Criticism is directed primarily against their Prime Minister. There is no doubt that the bulk of his people and even the majority of his Cabinet are not behind Eden in his Suez action. Nor is his task made any easier by Britain's army commanders. They said they were persuaded that the Egyptian forces were strong; they had accordingly planned a complicated military operation, and set a later date for the landing of their ground forces.

114

From the political point of view, there is no doubt that time is working against us and the pressure on Britain and France – and certainly on us – to halt our military action will become more and more acute. Who knows how many more campaigning days are left to us? True we started only the day before yesterday, but we must finish quickly, otherwise we may be forced to stop before the task is completed, and then both the military and political gains will be wiped out.

Yesterday morning I visited the 10th Brigade's sector with the GOC Southern Command. We went through the advance Egyptian posts which had been captured by the brigade the night before, Auja Masri and Tarat Um Basis, and we inspected the brigade positions opposite Um Katef and Um Shihan. In spite of what had been called for in the plan of 'Kadesh', the battalion commanders had not made the necessary preparations for the attack on these two defended localities. The two battalions who were to take part in this action had not been moved until yesterday from their assembly area near Ketziot, and had not advanced, following the capture of Auja Masri and Tarat Um Basis, to the positions for the assault on Um Katef and Um Shihan.

I explained to the brigade command that Um Katef had to be captured as quickly as possible. Time was fast running out, and it was essential to open a favourable axis of movement for 7th Armoured and 202nd Paratroop Brigades. Um Katef commands the only asphalt road which can serve our forces who have penetrated to Jebel Livni and Bir Hassna. The dirt track through Kusseima is in such poor condition after its heavy use by our vehicles that it is now negotiable only by transport with four-wheel drive, and there is a bottleneck in our supply convoys; this may hold up our advance.

It appeared that the postponement of the attack, which was originally timed to take place on 30 October, was made at the order of the GOC Southern Command, and at his request, GHQ Operations authorized the attachment of 37th Armoured Brigade, which up to now has been kept as GHQ reserve, to Southern Command to join 10th Infantry Brigade in the capture of Um Katef and Um Shihan. I was promised that the attack would definitely be launched that night (last night) by the infantry and would be completed next morning (this morning) with the help of the armour. Despite all the arrangements,

orders and promises, I did not have the feeling that I had succeeded in injecting into the commanders on the spot a recognition
of the high urgency to make an all-out effort to capture these
two Egyptian positions without delay.

The meeting with these officers was tough and not at all
agreeable, and we all got rather angry. It was not only that I felt
I was not getting through to them in my efforts to rouse them to
action; it seemed clear that we were just not seeing things in the
same light. Here was I urging the brigade command to get into
combat, to advance and assault Um Katef, and they were just
not prepared for it. They said they had been told by Southern
Command that this assignment would be given to another unit.
They had a thousand and one good and understandable reasons
why they were unable that night to storm the Egyptian positions,
with their minefields and well-laid defences; but the fact is, in
all its brutality, that the sole purpose in bringing them here was
for them to capture these very positions, and it was vital for the
campaign that this should be done as soon as possible. I dealt
with them as if they were a regular unit of the paratroopers or
the armoured corps, when in fact 10th Brigade is a reservist
formation. It was apparent that the officers were not sure of the
capacities of their men, who are older than the average and not
sufficiently trained. It may also be that the Negev is strange to
them, a new kind of terrain for this brigade.

I know the feeling. Some years ago, when I was appointed
GOC Southern Command, I had the sense for quite a time that
I was in a new kind of world. My criteria of field-craft had to be
thrown overboard. Judgement of distances, orientation, identification of territory – all were different here. I had to learn
everything anew, adapting myself to spaces unmarked by a
single tree or house, and to flat stretches of black flint that looked
to me like burnt fields.

But I was impatient with them. I had no ear for the complaints,
problems and difficulties raised by the brigade command. Their
men are tired, supplies do not reach them on time, the nights
are cold, the days are hot, their dust-clogged rifles don't fire,
their vehicles get stuck in the sand. I know that all this is true,
but I have no solutions to such problems. The Negev I cannot
change, and the new axis *must* be opened.

*   *   *

Our two attacks on Um Katef last night and this morning by 10th Infantry Brigade and a unit from 37th Armoured Brigade failed. That they failed is certain. Less certain is whether the actions can be called attacks.

Egyptian defence of the Abu Ageila–Um Katef–Kusseima region is based on their 6th Infantry Brigade. It consists of three infantry battalions, the 12th, 17th and 18th, and also under its command are two infantry battalions of the National Guard. Um Katef itself, the central strongpoint of this defence area, whose orders from the Egyptian General Staff are 'to fight to the end', is manned by two infantry battalions, one troop of anti-tank guns (six 'Archers') and one field troop of six 25-pounders, and is also included in the general support provided by the divisional artillery regiment.

Although on the eve of the attack we captured the Egyptian positions of Abu Ageila and Ruafa and thereby exposed the west flank of the defended locality, neither Um Katef nor Um Shihan was evacuated by the Egyptians. They continued to hold and defend both. It is clear that sooner or later the 6th Brigade will have to abandon them and withdraw to El Arish – if it will still be in Egyptian hands – but the fact is that in the meantime they are there and putting up a vigorous fight.

Two days ago (30 October) our 10th Brigade received orders to capture, that day, Auja Masri and Tarat Um Basis. This task was entrusted to the brigade reconnaissance company reinforced by an infantry company and a tank detachment, and at 15.30 Auja Masri was in our hands. Apparently it had been held only by a reinforced infantry section, and as soon as our tanks opened fire, they left their posts and our men walked in without opposition. The reconnaissance unit continued to advance and at 17.00 captured Tarat Um Basis, which had also been evacuated with the approach of our troops.

The first luke-warm attempt to attack Um Katef took place, on the orders of GOC Southern Command, yesterday morning (31 October). Again the brigade reconnaissance unit was sent in, reinforced this time by ten half-tracks, several command cars and an infantry company. When this force reached the ridge opposite the Egyptian strongpoint, they were greeted by enemy artillery fire. They withdrew, and the unit commander signalled that he would be unable to capture Um Katef in daylight.

The brigade accordingly mounted another attack that night, this time with two infantry battalions who were sent to flank Um Katef from the south and the north. The first battalion missed its way, failed to find the main enemy position, lost contact with its companies, tramped about the hills all night, and in the end, next morning at 10.00, captured a subsidiary peripheral emplacement about a mile and a half from Um Katef.

The second battalion, too, had difficulty in finding their objective, and after an arduous night of slogging up and down the resistant sand dunes, they managed at 04.30 to get near the enemy position. One platoon reached the force of the strong-point and met with enemy fire. One man was killed and another wounded. That was the end of their attack. The battalion withdrew. The two casualties were left near the fence. Earlier, during their night movement, the battalion had suffered some thirty casualties, wounded by Egyptian artillery fire.

Our next attack, by the unit of 37th Armoured Brigade, was carried out at 04.00 (1 November). If the main cause of the failure of 10th Brigade was its inability to execute a real assault, the failure of 37th Brigade was due to the over-eagerness of its officers to rush the enemy defences.

According to the plan, the armoured unit was to join in the attack with the two battalions of 10th Brigade, and while these engaged Um Katef from the flanks, the armour was to break through in the centre. The composition of this unit was to have been a tank squadron – two troops of medium tanks (Shermans) and one of light tanks (AMXs) – two infantry companies on half-tracks and one motorized infantry battalion. The brigade left its concentration area near Rehovoth in the afternoon, and its first units reached Nitzana, after refuelling in Beersheba, close to midnight. It was here that they made their final preparations for action, and at 02.00, the two half-track companies were ready to attack. But the tanks had not yet arrived. The brigade commander, with the approval of the GOC Southern Command, decided to wait one hour for the tanks and after that, whether they arrived or not, to go into action. At 03.00, the tanks had still not shown up – they came an hour later – so the brigade commander went off to attack Um Katef with the two companies of half-tracks. It was still night, and the column moved with headlights full on. When they neared the Egyptian position, they deployed and began advancing in battle

118

formation. The Egyptians, who had heard and seen the approaching vehicles, opened up on them with anti-tank and heavy artillery fire. The first half-tracks went into the minefield that encircled the fence round the Egyptian salient and were put out of action, serving as an admirable target for the enemy guns. The command half-track was among the first to be hit. The brigade commander was killed and the officers with him were gravely wounded.

To continue the attack was impossible. Actually, one platoon of half-tracks did manage to breach the enemy's defences and hold on to its position, but there was no one at the unit command (who had all become casualties) in a position to receive its message to exploit this breach. The liaison officer, who was also wounded, was the only senior officer capable, physically, of taking any action. He organized help, and under covering artillery fire and with the support of the tanks who had in the meantime arrived, the casualties were extricated from the minefield and the force retired to base, carrying with them more than eighty wounded.

There is no doubt that the manner in which 37th Brigade command carried out its action was incorrect and ill-considered. To undertake a motorized attack at night, over mined and unknown terrain; to leave without waiting for tanks due to arrive shortly; and to crowd all the officers of the command into the same half-track – for all this there was no military justification. But it was not only mistaken judgement that led the command to act as it did. There were two other factors. One was faulty intelligence. For some reason, the information in the hands of the GOC Southern Command indicated that the Egyptian force at Um Katef was crumbling, its men in flight, and it would therefore be enough for our unit simply to approach and open fire for them to give up. The second factor was the pressure of the GOC Southern Command – following my pressure on him – to hasten the opening of the Um Katef–Abu Ageila axis. The southern commander told the brigade commander he had promised me that the axis would be opened by first light. My orders were indeed to speed its opening – though not specifically during the night but up to noon next day; I did not believe in the possibility of using armour at night – and I did indeed demand that this be done even if it meant a difficult frontal attack involving heavy casualties.

I gave the order to attack Um Katef at the earliest possible moment. On the face of it, the order was carried out. But Um Katef was not captured. Southern Command had all the force necessary to undertake this engagement successfully – infantry, armour, artillery and so on. But the required military action was not executed. The attack did not follow a sound operational plan which would give full battle expression to the entire strength allocated for this operation.

* * *

Tonight we start attacking the defended localities of Rafah, and the intention is to follow immediately with an advance on El Arish. These two places are the key to the Ismailia axis, and with their capture, northern Sinai will be in our hands.

From the military point of view, this will be the central action of the campaign, deciding the issue in the contest between our forces and the Egyptian Army.

In two battle-arenas, air and sea, the operations are over to all intents and purposes. With the commencement of action by Anglo–French air and naval units, it is unlikely that the Egyptian Navy and Air Force can continue activities. I must say, to the credit of our troops, particularly our Air Force, that even before the Anglo–French intervention, they had the upper hand, despite the many limitations we imposed on them, including the ban on bombing Egyptian airfields. It is my view that if we had had to go on fighting alone, our Air Force would have neutralized the Egyptian Air Force in a few days.

As for tank-warfare, we have not yet had a serious confrontation with the Egyptian Armoured Corps, nor is there any certainty that we shall. So far their units are moving around in the rear and evade contact with our armoured formation, 7th Brigade, even though this brigade is already more than half-way to the Canal. The Egyptian tanks are also steering clear even of our paratroop brigade at Mitla, though it is only about thirty miles from Suez, cut off from the rest of our forces and located in open ground very suitable for armour.

However, the main Egyptian military forces defending Sinai are their reinforced infantry divisions: 3rd Division, 8th Palestinian Division, and also 2nd Division which serves as a reserve for the eastern sector. The Egyptian protection of Sinai rests on four principal defence bases: El Arish, Rafah, Abu Ageila and Sharm e-Sheikh. One, Sharm e-Sheikh, is a self-contained and independent defended locality; but the other three have overlapping and interlocking defence provided by a single force, 3rd Division. The Gaza Strip, stretching north of Rafah and defended by the 8th Palestinian Division, is also linked to the military defence system of El Arish. If El Arish and Rafah fall to us, the Gaza Strip will be isolated and unable, alone, to hold out.

Now, forty-eight hours after the start of the campaign, the time has come to attack the core of the Egyptian forces in Sinai, at Rafah and El Arish, and this we must do with all the drive of our momentum. The preparatory phases we set for ourselves before this attack are already over. The Egyptians already recognize that our intention is not simply a local reprisal action. Along the southern axes, Nakhl–Mitla and Kusseima–Jebel Livni, our units have advanced and reached their objectives. And the Anglo–French Air Forces started bombing Egyptian airfields after dusk last night. It is also now certain that the strongest possible political pressure will be brought to bear upon us to halt our military activities immediately, and so we must endeavour to complete our conquest quickly.

It is for this reason, too, that I decided, against the recommendation of Southern Command, that Rafah would be assaulted from the north and not from the south. This will enable the maximum force of armour to be employed early in the operation. I know that this means a frontal attack on Rafah's emplacements in precisely the sector in which they are well arrayed for defence; but I fear that if we look for routes deep to the south in order to envelop them, we are liable to get stuck in the dunes and lose tanks and, what we have least of all, time.

It is my intention to join the units attacking Rafah and to stay with them until the capture of El Arish is completed. I have every confidence in entrusting the normal handling of the campaign to the reliable hands of officers (Operations Branch) with skill and judgement of the highest degree. Nevertheless, my absences are not viewed kindly by the General Staff. I spent the first two days of the campaign mostly in the field, the first day with 7th and 4th Brigades at Kusseima, and yesterday with 10th Brigade near Um Katef. True, I returned to GHQ command post each night, but of course my non-appearance during the day makes things difficult and upsets the ordered organization of the work.

In the field there is a radio transmitter with me all the time and I am in constant contact with GHQ, but my staff officers complain that this is not enough. They may be right; but I am unable, or unwilling, to behave otherwise.

3 November 1956

Our capacity for misadventure is limitless. Yesterday (2 November) at noon, one of 7th Brigade's tank squadrons opened up by mistake at a range of less than 1,100 yards on another of our tank squadrons, belonging to 37th Brigade, and in five minutes hit eight tanks and knocked them out of action. I have not yet been able to find out the number of casualties, but it seems that the squadron commander is among the killed.

The basic reason for these mishaps which afflict us is the speed, and inadequate preparation, with which we go into action. As a result, there is not always enough co-ordination between our various units. Moreover, in accordance with my orders, formations continue to operate even when there is a breakdown in communications and they lose contact with each other, or with our Air Force, and in such cases of course misunderstandings can occur which lead to one unit's opening fire on another. Nor is it always easy to distinguish between friendly and enemy forces. Our tanks are unmarked, and when they are also enveloped in clouds of dust, it is difficult to determine whether they are ours or Egyptian. In addition, when our troops capture equipment, particularly vehicles which are serviceable, they hasten to use them without bothering to repaint them and mark them with our army signs. Clearly, we must see to it that unit commanders make every effort to ensure recognition and identification of other units in the field. But even after yesterday's grave mishap, I am not prepared to make any change in the orders which is liable to slow down the rapidity of our advance or limit the initiative of our commanders. All our chances of success in this campaign depend on these two factors – speed and initiative.

What happened, yesterday was due to a special, and quite unnecessary, misunderstanding. The intelligence officer from Southern Command arrived early in the morning at 7th Brigade's sector and met with the commander of the armoured battalion which was near Abu Ageila at the time. It was apparent to the intelligence officer that the Egyptian prisoners were not being properly interrogated. He lost no time and on the spot began questioning an Egyptian soldier about what was happening in the 'pocket' (Um Katef and Um Shihan, which had not fallen).

In the light of the prisoner's reply, the intelligence officer, together with the battalion commander, decided to send a note to the commander of the Egyptian forces at Um Katef calling on him to surrender, and giving him the deadline of 14.00 hours. The note was written in Arabic and English and was dispatched, at 11.30 hours, through two Egyptian prisoners driving a captured jeep flying a white flag.

At just about this time, our pilots who had been sent to bomb Um Katef signalled that they could detect no enemy movement in the area, and that they believed the Egyptian forces had probably evacuated their emplacements during the night.

37th Brigade command decided thereupon to send in a squadron of tanks from the direction of Kusseima to investigate, and if in fact the positions were already, or in the process of being, evacuated, to press through and join up with 7th Armoured Brigade which was on the other side of the Egyptian posts.

It transpired that Um Katef and Um Shihan had indeed been abandoned during the night, and when the tank squadron entered the Egyptian camp, the first prisoners to surrender were the two Egyptian 'dispatch riders' who had been sent there in the jeep with the white flag. Sending back the 'ultimatum letter' with its bearers to Southern Command, the squadron continued westwards for its rendezvous with 7th Brigade. And as it began descending the Um Shihan ridge, it did indeed meet – with 7th Brigade's fire; for the latter thought it must be an Egyptian unit who, instead of surrendering and behaving in accordance with the ultimatum letter of the battalion commander, had no doubt decided with the power of its armour to break out of the ring.

The only ones who realized immediately what was happening were our pilots, who knew that both armoured columns were ours. They swooped low and with various signs got the unit to stop its fire. The firing stopped, but only one tank, the last in the column, had managed to retire behind the ridge and avoid being hit.

As to the withdrawal of the Egyptian forces from Um Katef and Um Shihan, it appears that the day before yesterday, 1 November, within the framework of a general withdrawal order

123

from Sinai issued by the Egyptian General Staff at noon on that day, orders reached the Egyptian 6th Brigade at 16.00 hours to retire to El Arish. According to their instructions, the soldiers were to move on foot, leaving behind their heavy equipment. The withdrawal began at dusk. A rear guard kept up artillery fire, and from time to time also fired other weapons to deceive our forces. They did not blow up their stores or installations lest we suspect their intention to retreat.

The beginning of their withdrawal was orderly. Company by company the Egyptian units left, proceeding northwards across the sand dunes. But after a time there was confusion. The troops lost contact with their commanding officers and the retreat turned into a panic flight. The men of 18th Battalion routed through Magdawa succeeded in reaching El Arish during the night. But the rest turned towards Bir Lahfan and there fell prisoner to our units.

The positions of Um Katef and Um Shihan – or, as the Egyptians call them, the defended localities of Abu Ageila – are the only sectors where, so far, the Egyptians fought extremely well and our forces extremely poorly.

The basic fault in our fighting here is that it was done in dribs and drabs. At first, on 30 October, a unit from 7th Brigade attacked Um Shihan; then came an attack on Um Katef by 10th and 37th Brigades. In neither action did the attacking unit concentrate and throw in its full strength. This criticism of course applies only to the eastern section of the Abu Ageila defence base, for its two western outposts, Abu Ageila proper and the Ruafa dam, were captured in two attacks carried out on the same day (31 October) by a battalion of 7th Brigade. Our mistake lay in not gathering for a combined and co-ordinated attack all the forces available to us on this front – and which could have been assigned to this task. The blame lies with those at a higher level than the combat units. It lies with Southern Command, with GHQ and with the Chief of Staff (myself).

The Egyptian forces fought well during the static phase of their combat. So long as they were required to use their weapons which had been dug into fixed positions in advance – anti-tank, field and anti-aircraft guns – they did so automatically, accurately and efficiently. But this was not the case when they had to leave their entrenched posts or make changes in their plans. They carried out almost no counter-attacks; and when they did, their action was pretty poor. Moreover, the Egyptians did not bring into combat the very tanks assigned to this sector – 3rd Armoured Battalion, stationed at El Arish – nor their reserve infantry units. Divisional HQ at El Arish did not make a single military move to influence developments on this front. The forces at its disposal were not committed. They did not even stir from their base.

As to the tactical value of the Abu Ageila defence base, the very fact that part of it was not captured by us offers confirmation of my assumptions about the fighting in this region.

I do not know whether the military doctrines followed by the Egyptians were taught them by their British, German or Russian instructors. At all events, in the reasoning of the Egyptian General Staff, Abu Ageila was intended as a barrier against an attempted breakthrough to Sinai in the central sector, the Kusseima–Nitzana sector. Their system of defence here was based on six major positions, Kusseima, Um Katef, Um Shihan, Abu Ageila, the Ruafa dam and Ras Matmor, which were held by a reinforced infantry brigade and various support units. The aim, as determined by the Egyptian High Command, was to neutralize Israel forces attacking from the east, and to wipe out enemy units who may have penetrated into the region by parachute or any other way.

This system of the Egyptians for the defence of Sinai was known to us, and I saw in it three basic errors. First of all, I was convinced that the Egyptians exaggerated the defensive power of such positions. Defended localities with similar functions which had been built in Europe in the last world war had been ringed by wide belts of minefields and formidable concrete fortifications, and had been equipped with vast quantities of anti-tank weapons, heavy artillery and anti-aircraft guns. But the countries of the Middle East cannot establish fortified zones of such a character. They have not the manpower, nor the weapons nor the large amount of money these require.

It is thus pure illusion to expect a defence position like Abu Ageila to hold out against serious attacks; and, indeed, the two posts, Abu Ageila itself and Ruafa, did not last even an hour against the assault of our armoured battalion team, which went in with two troops of tanks and one company of infantry aboard half-tracks.

The second error also stemmed from a false analogy with Europe. This was the assumption that by seizing key salients, it was possible to block and prevent the movement of sizeable military forces into Sinai and Egypt. This sort of thing may be possible in many regions in Europe where there are lots of rivers, marshes, forests and mountains. In Europe, defence barriers can be established 'from sea to sea', and so constructed and fortified as to make them extremely difficult to breach.

But this system cannot be duplicated in the Middle East, and certainly not in Sinai. The terrain in the Negev and the northern half of Sinai is such that it is possible to by-pass defence bases like Abu Ageila. Sand dunes are no substitute for powerfully fortified defence lines, and the Deika defile is no river Rhine. The armoured units of 7th Brigade were therefore able to advance westwards and northwards even after the Deika bridge was blown up; and in spite of the grave supply difficulties encountered by not having an asphalt road, our forces managed to by-pass Abu Ageila and continue towards Suez by using desert tracks.

The third Egyptian error, the main one, lay in their concept of warfare. Abu Ageila could play a decisive role in the defence of Sinai only if it served as a solid base for mobile forces who could go out and engage an enemy seeking to break through to the Canal. In desert terrain like Sinai there is no alternative to armour, aircraft, paratroopers and motorized infantry. The defending force must be able to meet such attacking units with its own counterpart mobile units. The Egyptians made a fatal assumption in thinking that their fortified defence positions of Abu Ageila, Rafah and El Arish would prevent our penetration into Sinai and would protect the Canal without requiring their armoured and air forces to join in blocking our breakthrough, and without their men having to go out and fight us beyond the perimeter of their posts.

These three Egyptian assumptions about defensive positions – their strength and ability to hold out for long; their effectiveness in sealing penetration routes; and their usefulness as a substitute for mobile warfare – proved unrealistic. The Abu Ageila base for some days remained in Egyptian hands, yet during that time it did not stop our advance.

There is an epilogue to this chapter on the fighting round Abu Ageila. After the defective employment of 10th Brigade, I was informed of the decision of the GOC Southern Command to transfer the brigade commander and to appoint another in his place. I confirmed this change. A military command is not a duty which every citizen must fulfil, nor is it a privilege to which everyone is entitled. The supreme function of a unit commander is to lead it in battle, and if he does not stand the test, he should not be punished, but he should be replaced by someone who does. I am not able and do not wish to enter into all the details of the action of 10th Brigade on the night of their attack. The failure of this brigade was not poor direction of the battle. Nor was it lack of skill, loss of control or tactical errors which brought about the débâcle. What happened there, from the military point of view, was more grave – the unit did not make the effort required to enter into effective combat.

*   *   *

Whatever the different estimates of the importance of resolutions of the United Nations General Assembly, there can be no question that the ring of demands the UN is making upon us, whatever their value, continues to tighten round our neck.

The emergency meeting of the Assembly opened two days ago, 1 November, at 17.00 hours. The British and French representatives argued against the legality of the session, basing themselves on technical points, but their opposition was overruled and the session continued. The principal demand of the various speakers was a decision calling for an immediate cease-fire. The representatives of the Arab States and their supporters went further, and urged that the Assembly should condemn Israel, Britain and France and decide on the imposition of sanctions.

The United States was represented by her Secretary of State, John Foster Dulles. After declarations of deep friendship for Britain and France – and, at a somewhat lower level, for Israel – he put the pill on the table: the United States' draft resolution for Assembly decision. Here is the full text:

THE GENERAL ASSEMBLY:
Noting the disregard on many occasions by parties to the Israel–Arab Armistice Agreements of 1948 of the terms of such agreements, and that the armed forces of Israel have penetrated deeply into Egyptian territory in violation of the General Armistice Agreement between Egypt and Israel,
Noting that armed forces of France and the United Kingdom are conducting military operations against Egyptian territory,

127

Noting that traffic through the Suez Canal is now interrupted to the serious prejudice of many nations,
Expressing its grave concern over these developments,
1 *Urges* as a matter of priority that all parties now involved in hostilities in the area agree to an immediate cease-fire and as part thereof halt the movement of military forces and arms into the area;
2 *Urges* the parties to the Armistice Agreements promptly to withdraw all forces behind the Armistice lines, to desist from raids across the Armistice lines into neighbouring territory, and to observe scrupulously the provisions of the Armistice Agreements;
3 *Recommends* that all Members refrain from introducing military goods into the area of hostilities and in general refrain from any acts which would delay or prevent the implementation of this resolution;
4 *Urges* that upon cease-fire being effective steps be taken to re-open the Suez Canal and restore secure freedom of navigation;
5 *Requests* the Secretary-General to observe and promptly report on the compliance with this resolution to the Security Council and to the General Assembly, for such further action as they may deem appropriate in accordance with the Charter;
6 *Decides* to remain in emergency session pending compliance with this resolution.

The provisions in the American draft resolution which call for action contain two demands of the combatants: immediate cease-fire, and withdrawal of forces behind the armistice lines. They also contain two recommendations: that UN Member States refrain from acts liable to disturb the implementation of the draft resolution; and that the blocked (by the Egyptians) Suez Canal should be cleared and opened quickly to free navigation.
The demand for an immediate cease-fire would mainly affect the operation of the Anglo–French forces. According to their time-table, they should continue bombing the airfields and other military installations in the Canal Zone and the Port Said area up to 6 November, and only then would their units land on Egyptian soil.
As for us, if we can succeed in dragging out the negotiations for a cease-fire another two or three days, we shall manage in the meantime to capture Sharm e-Sheikh, and since this will

mark the completion of the conquest of Sinai, we can agree to a cease-fire.

But this is not the case with the second demand – withdrawal behind the armistice lines. This is directed specifically against us, and we cannot satisfy it – unless we are prepared to retire completely from the campaign.

The UN Assembly session ended late, and, as expected, the American resolution was adopted. The next day, 2 November, the UN Secretary-General, Dag Hammarskjöld, handed the text of the resolution to the representatives of Britain, France and Israel, and asked to be informed as soon as possible about its implementation.

Israel's representative, Abba Eban, did not reply directly to Hammarskjöld's request, but, to gain time, sought clarification and made suggestions.

Incidentally, the blocking of the Canal by the Egyptians marks another military–political set-back for the British. They had known of Egypt's intentions to tow vessels into the Canal and sink them there, and Britain had therefore planned to bomb these ships before they could move to their destination and sink them at their anchorages at Port Said, Port Suez and in the Bitter Lake. I do not know why this plan went astray, whether the Egyptians stole a march on the British by advancing the movement of their ships to the Canal, or whether the British bombers missed their targets. All I know is that yesterday the Canal was already blocked.

The Arabs also succeeded, against British hopes, in carrying out their plan to sabotage the supply of Iraqi oil (along the Iraq Petroleum Company pipeline which also runs through Syria). The day before yesterday, 1 November, engineer units of the Syrian Army gained control of the three principal pumping stations of the IPC pipeline and blew them up. Apparently neither the British nor Nuri Said, Prime Minister of Iraq, has sufficient influence in Syria, and if the Syrian Army is not prepared to risk an attack on Israel, it can at least blow up British oil installations in its own territory.

These two actions, sealing the Canal and stopping the flow of oil from Iraq, will hardly strengthen Eden's standing in Britain or increase support for his policy. I do not know the real extent of Britain's dependence on Middle East oil, but according to the press it is a matter of economic life or death.

CHAPTER SEVEN

*

DECISION

3 November 1956

Unlike the centre and south of Sinai, which are rocky and mountainous, the northern part, close to the Mediterranean, is flat and sandy. The Egyptian defences of Rafah were therefore based, in the absence of more advantageous topographical features, upon a large number of emplacements exploiting slight rises in ground, each able to give its neighbour supporting fire, including flat-trajectory fire.

These were held by 5th Infantry Brigade, belonging to the Egyptian 3rd Division. The brigade normally comprised four infantry battalions; but after the start of our operations in Sinai, it was reinforced by two more, the 45th and 46th Battalions of the Palestinian National Guards' 87th Brigade.

To meet our attack, the Egyptian forces in the defended locality of Rafah thus consisted of six infantry battalions; two companies of the Motorized Border Battalion; one artillery regiment; one anti-tank battery (twelve 'Archers'); and one anti-aircraft battery. The tank squadron designated to support Rafah was at El Arish at Divisional HQ which decided to employ its 3rd Armoured Battalion (Sherman tanks) as a concentrated reserve and not to split it squadron by squadron among the infantry brigades.

Rafah's function was to prevent the breakthrough of Israeli forces into Sinai through the El Arish axis, and the Egyptian orders to the defenders of Rafah were 'to fight to the last'; but a few hours after the start of our attack, on 1 November, the divisional command ordered some of the units to withdraw to El Arish. These were the units in the area of Magrontin, which is in the rear, and they therefore managed to escape before our forces reached the El Arish–Rafah highway and sealed it.

We knew what Egyptian forces were ranged against us at

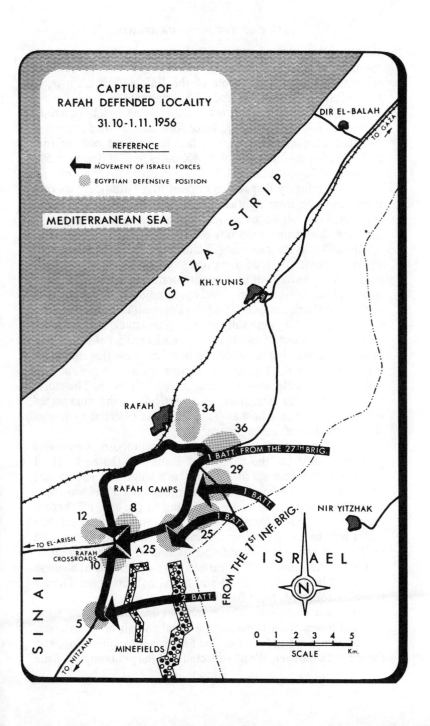

CAPTURE OF
RAFAH DEFENDED LOCALITY
31.10 - 1.11. 1956

REFERENCE

◄ MOVEMENT OF ISRAELI FORCES
EGYPTIAN DEFENSIVE POSITION

MEDITERRANEAN SEA

GAZA STRIP

DIR EL-BALAH

TO GAZA

KH. YUNIS

RAFAH   34

36

1 BATT. FROM THE 27TH BRIG.

29

RAFAH CAMPS   1 BATT.

8   NIR YITZHAK

12   1 BATT.

TO EL-ARISH   25   FROM THE 1ST INF. BRIG.

RAFAH   A 25   ISRAEL
CROSSROADS

10

N

2 BATT.

5

0 1 2 3 4 5
SINAI   SCALE   Km.

MINEFIELDS

TO NITZANA

Rafah, and we considered this to be a most difficult objective. We therefore assigned the task of capturing it, and thereafter of securing control of the whole of the Rafah–El Arish axis, to two brigades, 1st Infantry and 27th Armoured.

The armoured brigade, it is true, comprised, in addition to its motorized infantry battalion, three formations called armoured battalion combat teams; but in fact it consisted only of four tank squadrons – one of light AMX tanks, one of Sherman 50s, and two of Super-Shermans.

The 1st Infantry Brigade comprised four battalions: its own three, and one from another brigade which was put under its command for this action alone. Also attached to it was one of the Super-Sherman squadrons of 27th Brigade.

The difficulty in capturing Rafah was due not only to the heavy concentration of Egyptian forces and their carefully organized defences, but also to the conditions under which our men had to operate there. We could enjoy no advantage of surprise. Indeed, not only could the Egyptian units not be taken unawares, but they were fully expecting an attack, had prepared themselves to meet it, and had been reinforced for this purpose. In addition, the time available to our forces for this operation was very limited. Twenty-four hours earlier, we were still holding them back; now we were hurrying them up. The storm raised at the UN Assembly, and particularly the unexpected vigour of America's hostile stand, made it essential to hasten the completion of the campaign.

The operational factors also proved stubborn. Our early planning called for the capture of Rafah on the night of 31 October/1 November, so that by morning, the key points dominating the highway would be in our hands and we could proceed to the capture of El Arish. But in the end, all that remained of that night for action by our infantry was less than two and a half hours of darkness, from 03.05 to 05.30. The period before that was given over to naval and air bombardment to soften up the defences. For various reasons, the naval shelling could not begin before 02.00 and lasted half an hour. The air bombing followed, from 02.30 to 03.05.

It became clear after the event that in setting aside these precious hours of darkness for the naval and air bombardment, we had struck a bad bargain. The first was a complete flop, and the second a disaster. We all expected that the pounding from the destroyers would be carried out on a European scale, and we conjured up familiar scenes from war-films of powerful shells exploding on the coast on the eve of a landing. I myself hoped – and I said so to the officers in charge of the Rafah operation – that the naval action would bring about the collapse of the Egyptian defences, and the follow-up assault of our infantry would meet with weakish opposition.

But the leviathan gave forth a sprat. Altogether a total of one hundred and fifty 155-mm. shells from the naval vessels were fired on the Rafah camps – less than the number of rounds any self-respecting artillery battery of ours would have laid down for such an attack.

As to the Air Force, our pilots managed to drop their parachute flares right on to our own units, exposed them, and started bombing them. We immediately signalled them to stop, and the 'softening-up from the air' was called off before it caused damage to our men.

But what was done could not be undone, and only about 03.00 in the morning of 1 November could our ground forces go into action. The two brigades, 1st and 27th, ordered their units to cross the start line and attack the defence posts of Rafah.

The attack was carried out along three axes: the southern and centre by 1st Brigade, two infantry battalions to each axis, and the northern by the motorized infantry battalion of 27th Brigade. The plan was to capture not all but only the most important strongpoints of this defended locality, and also to open a path for the armour to enable it to reach the Gaza–Kantara highway and thus advance on El Arish.

The key to the Rafah defence base was the cross-roads where the highway from Gaza to El Arish cuts the road from Rafah to Nitzana. West of the cross-roads, in the direction of El Arish, there is only one road; but to its south, and north and north-east there are three: to the south is the road to Nitzana and Ketziot; to the north, the internal road through the camps of Rafah; and to the north-east, the road to Khan Yunis and Gaza. These roads prescribed the objectives given to our various units. The southern force was to open a gap through which armour could pass and get on to the Nitzana road. The force in the centre was to clear a way to the north-eastern road. The northern force was to create a passage to the road serving the Rafah camps. Though it was of course desirable to open all three roads, we took into account the possibility that in the first night's action only two might be opened, or even only one. But even then, the armour would immediately exploit the breach, get on to the Rafah–El Arish road and advance westwards.

The defence area of Rafah was a veritable labyrinth of numerous entrenched positions, well dug-in in the sand and set among orchards and hedges of prickly-pear. As the action proceeded, not a single one of our units failed to go wrong in identifying its target and in finding the way to it. Neither tracer-rounds nor directive artillery fire proved of help. The Egyptian positions were too close to each other. Bullets and shells, theirs and ours, flashed through the air in all directions, and it was impossible to determine whose was which. This structure of the enemy's defence system accordingly determined the character of our operation. Our attacking force, numbering close to three thousand men, split up into many small units and sub-units, and each had to beat out a path for itself through the minefields and barbed-wire fences, break through on its own to its target and fight an independent battle.

The capture of the southern axis was effected in two stages. In the first, one battalion had to seize the first three Egyptian posts, 6, 2 and 293, and then, the second stage, the other battalion was to follow in its wake and capture the remaining Egyptian posts on this axis.

The first battalion moved laboriously. The commander of D Company, who was supposed to capture the first post, Post 6, could not find it. As soon as the Egyptians opened fire, first with artillery and then also with machine-guns, the company commander requested permission to withdraw, and suggested the task be entrusted to another unit. Finally, when his appeals were turned down and he was given the categorical order by his battalion commander to press on with his mission, he signalled that he had completed it and that 'Post 6 is in my hands'. Only when dawn broke was it found that Post 6 had not been attacked and had not been captured; the Egyptians had abandoned it early in the night with the advent of our attack.

The second position, Post 2, was also abandoned without a battle, and C Company took it with no opposition. The third post, 293, was captured by B Company. This unit moved on half-tracks. As they approached the Egyptians, they deployed in line-formation and launched a frontal assault. They were met by fire, but they pressed forward, and as they did so, the firing stopped and the Egyptians fled. The post was taken. This marked the end of the first stage on this axis, the penetration stage. The battalion's casualties were two killed and eight wounded, caused by Egyptian artillery when the unit was about to cross the jump-off line. In the actual seizure of the enemy posts, there were no casualties. Even the half-tracks stormed through two rows of bakelite mines without their exploding.

Now came the main part of the action in this area – capture of the vital posts on this southern axis. The battalion that was given the assignment was a motorized unit, its men borne on 6 × 6 trucks and half-tracks. In support was a squadron of medium tanks (Super-Shermans) from 27th Brigade.

Although this motorized convoy followed the trail of the first battalion's half-tracks, as soon as it entered the mined zone its leading vehicle hit a mine. The command half-track tried to get round it from the right, but it too struck a mine and started burning. Egyptian artillery fire, which had been following the convoy all the time, now became more intensive, and more accurate, for the flames of the burning half-track lit up the targets for the Egyptian gunners. The Israeli sappers crawled between exploding shells and cleared a new path through the minefield, to the left of the knocked-out vehicles. The battalion commander assembled his men, who had taken cover behind sand hillocks and low bushes, and the convoy started moving again. Several half-tracks and two tanks successfully negotiated the new path, but the third tank struck a mine which for some reason had been missed and again they were held up. Again the engineers got out to clear a new trail, but the first tank that tried it hit a mine which tore off its tracks.

The battalion was stuck. The two tanks, half-track and 6 × 6 truck knocked out by exploding mines blocked the narrow paths through the minefield. And now the Egyptians opened up on the trapped battalion with all they had, artillery, mortars and heavy machine-guns. The time was 04.30. In another half-hour it would be light, and if the convoy remained where it was – and in the situation it was – it would be annihilated by the fire from the surrounding Egyptian posts. The battalion commander signalled his brigade commander suggesting that he get his undamaged vehicles away while there was still time, and dig-in in positions near by. To go on and advance to the cross-roads was just not possible.

The brigade commander rejected the suggestion, and was adamant in his demand that the battalion execute its task – capture of the posts dominating the cross-roads. If they could not proceed in their vehicles, they should get off and move immediately to their objective on foot.

It is possible that in other circumstances the battalion commander's suggestion would have been accepted; but not in these. Come what might, by morning the brigade had to open a way for the armour to get through and go on to take El Arish. There was no other unit which could have been given this battalion's assignment. The brigade had no reserves left. All its forces were taking part in the attacks; at this hour all were committed and engaged.

There was no point, however, in the trapped battalion's trying to reach their objective on foot. They were in no position to march the seven and a half miles to the cross-roads in time, and even if they were, their prospects of capturing the strong Egyptian posts without tank support were dim. There was only one thing to do: clear yet a new path through the minefield for their vehicles.

The last minutes of darkness sped by; but there is reward for those who try very hard. At 05.15, the battalion's sappers straightened their bent backs. The path they had cleared this time, north of the damaged vehicles, stood the test, and the last tank in the convoy went through without mishap. The battalion moved off, led by the reconnaissance unit, followed by the tank squadron, with C Company, on half-tracks, bringing up the rear. D Company, whose vehicles had been put out of action, jumped aboard the tanks and hung on to the manes of the war-horses – the Super-Shermans. Morale was high – among the men perhaps more than among the officers. The main thing was to be out of the mined and shelled inferno, to be on the move, to advance!

The convoy moved swiftly. By 05.50 they reached their first objective, Post 5. It was full daylight, and the Egyptians opened heavy fire. The jeeps of the reconnaissance unit returned the fire. The tanks did not wait for any order. They did what they had to do – deployed to the right and fired their guns by direct laying. The half-track company advanced in line formation, ground their way over the perimeter fences and stormed the enemy. At 05.55, five minutes after opening fire, the battalion commander signalled '5 is ours'. The way to the cross-roads was open. On the other side of the captured position glistened the black surface of the Rafah–Nitzana road.

At 06.30 the convoy set off to the cross-roads. Along the centre of the road moved the tanks, carrying the 'cavalrymen', D Company, and followed by the half-tracks. Flanking the tank column on either side, and controlling the convoy, drove the jeeps.

The cross-roads was defended by three posts, 8, 10 and 12. As the convoy approached, these opened fire with machine-guns and anti-tank guns. The convoy stopped. The commander signalled for artillery support. The exchange of fire continued for a while, and then the tanks began to storm the posts. As they did so, the Egyptians in the first post started to flee. Legs and vehicles were seen hurrying off westwards in the direction of El Arish. At 07.50 C Company, on half-tracks, seized Post 8, and D Company, the tank-riders, took Post 10. The last to be captured was Post 12, and the whole battalion descended upon it in almost ceremonial formation: A and C Companies moving in parallel, flanked by tanks on the left and jeeps on the right. At 09.00 came their signal: '12 is in our hands', and after an interval of a few seconds 'Cross-roads is ours, I repeat, cross-roads is ours'.

The battalion then organized itself most carefully for defence. The cross-roads was captured, but in the hands of the victors was only a thin wedge about nine miles long flanked on both sides by Egyptian positions. So long as the capture of the objectives along the central and northern axes still remained to be completed, the Egyptians could wipe out our success at the cross-roads. These fears, however, proved groundless. Not only did the enemy units not think of counter-attacking; they had not even been prepared stoutly to defend the positions they had held. In most of their posts, they fought only up to the close-combat stage, and as soon as our men started to rush them, they laid down their weapons and took off. Of the seven Egyptian posts along the southern axis, three were abandoned before our forces reached them (2, 6 and 8), and only at Posts 10 and 12 was resistance maintained until they were stormed.

For this reason, the casualties suffered by our battalion were not heavy: two killed and twenty-two wounded, caused mostly by artillery shelling and mines. The same was true of their vehicles. Four tanks, two half-tracks and one 6 × 6 truck were knocked out by mines, and only one tank was hit – and the commander and driver wounded – by an anti-tank shell.

Action along the central axis of the Rafah defence area was entrusted to the two veteran battalions of 1st Brigade. The task of one was to capture two Egyptian positions which were close to each other, Posts 25 and 25a. The battalion decided to attack them simultaneously, Post 25 to be taken by A Company and 25a by the Nahal Company. (Nahal is the Hebrew acronym for 'Fighting and Pioneer Youth', which is an army corps engaged, when not fighting, in founding and farming agricultural border settlements.) The two companies moved off from the start-line on foot. They had quite a distance to cover and they reached their objectives just before 05.00 in the morning. 'A' Company approached Post 25 and got ready for the assault. The Egyptians spotted them and opened fire, and they were immediately joined by their neighbouring posts. Our men had planned to breach the protective fence by bangalore-torpedo, but the long tube of the torpedo which was placed under the fence failed to explode. The company commander decided not to postpone the attack, and instructed his covering detachment to be prepared to pour concentrated machine-gun-fire into the Egyptian positions controlling the fence. As the order to fire was given, the company sprang to the fence, bent the barbed wire and pulled out the iron pickets with their bare hands, and scrambled across.

A surprise awaited them on the other side: a minefield encircled the post. While they were negotiating the fence, the Egyptians had marked their exact location, and they now directed heavy and accurate fire upon them. Retreat would have meant casualties, and would have solved nothing. The company had to get through the minefield, and get through fast, before daybreak. The sapper officer crawled forward and with a mattock began removing mines and clearing a path for walking. The company in single file followed in his wake. In this way they reached the slopes of the salient, clambered up and broke into the Egyptian defences with sub-machine-guns and hand-grenades. The sections split up in the communications trenches and advanced rapidly. When the enemy troops realized that the attackers were right inside their post, their resistance ceased. It looked as if all was going well; but when the first of our troops got to the centre of the salient, to their great surprise they saw coming towards them the Nahal Company which was supposed to be attacking neighbouring Post 25a. It seems that Nahal had made a mistake and broken through to Post 25 from the other side, thinking it was 25a. For several minutes the two company commanders were in a quandary. Their troops had intermingled and were scattered among the outposts and in the trenches which crisscrossed this large defence position. It was clear that Post 25a had now to be assaulted and captured, but the question was how, and by whom? In the meantime a communications trench was discovered linking the two posts. It was of course highly dangerous to use. If the enemy were waiting at the other end, it would be a trap for the assault force. After a brief review of the situation, the two commanders decided that in spite of the risks, it was worth trying, and a mixed unit drawn from both companies proceeded along the trench to 25a. No one awaited them in ambush at the exit, but they were greeted with stubborn fire from the enemy's heavy-weapons detachments. This resistance, however came too late, and by 05.30, already daylight, Post 25a was captured.

The battalion casualties in the seizure of both posts were six killed and twenty-eight wounded. The number of Egyptian dead were not counted, and at the orders of the battalion commander, no prisoners were taken; any Egyptian soldier who wished to flee was given the freedom of the dunes.

The other battalion's assignment was the capture of Post 29 and the near-by Post 27. Post 29 was considered to be the central and most vital post of the Rafah defence area, but, as it turned out later, its estimated strength had been exaggerated, and it was captured with less difficulty than had been expected.

The battalion crossed the start line at 03.30, advanced rapidly, and after an hour reached the vicinity of its objective. The companies deployed for the assault, but for the life of them the commanders could not identify in the dark which of the posts was which. The battalion commander signalled for artillery and tracer fire to be laid on Post 29. This was done, but it did not help. For the numerous Egyptian emplacements opened up, too, from several directions, and it was impossible to pick out our directive fire. 'A' Company suddenly found itself near a fence, broke through, and was faced by another fence. Rather than scrabble about between two fences – by now it was some distance from the original opening – it made a fresh breach, broke out into open ground again and continued the search for its objective. While it was doing so, the Egyptians intensified their fire from one of their posts, and this helped to identify it to our men as the sought-after Post 29.

It was now 05.00. The half-tracks spread out and directed bazooka fire at the enemy emplacements which covered the approach to their post with machine-gun and anti-tank fire. Nevertheless, two half-tracks managed to advance and at short range knocked out two Egyptian anti-tank guns. Fire from the post weakened, and the half-tracks plus a platoon from C Company broke through the fences and stormed the post. As day broke, A Company also found a winding path between the fences which bore fresh footprints, suggesting that it was used by the Egyptian soldiers themselves and was not mined. This judgement did not play them false, and the company used the path to penetrate the northern emplacements of the post without casualties.

At 05.30 the capture of Post 29 was complete, and the battalion commander organized his D and C Companies for the attack on near-by Post 27. At the same time, an armoured battalion team from 27th Brigade arrived, and agreed to his colleague's request for tank support. When the Egyptians saw tanks approaching, they began to flee, and when the two infantry companies broke through the defences of the enemy post, they found it empty. At 07.15 the signal went out '27 is ours'. The battalion casualties in the capture of both posts were three killed and forty-eight wounded.

The heaviest casualties in our capture of the Rafah defence area were suffered by the motorized infantry battalion of the 27th Armoured Brigade who operated along the third axis, the northern, and whose mission was the capture of Posts 34 and 36, the key positions on this axis.

The battalion consisted of four rifle companies, and attached to it was a troop of light AMX tanks. For some reason, permission to move to the attack was given late. The convoy set off at 03.45 and a quarter of an hour later ran into heavy and accurate artillery fire. The battalion commander was compelled to order his men to dismount and take cover. Casualties in this shelling were eleven killed and eighty-eight wounded, among them the commander of A Company and three platoon commanders.

Under this heavy fire, it was necessary to evacuate the wounded, get the convoy out of the vulnerable area, and reconstitute the assault forces. The commander of D Company took command of A Company, got together about two platoons, and moved off to attack Post 34. The commander of B Company reorganized his unit and set off for the other objective, Post 36. B Company were the first to reach their target. Under cover of the last minutes of darkness they deployed for attack, and at first light, 05.35, an infantry platoon on half-tracks and the light tank detachment broke into the Egyptian position. Following the tanks and half-tracks came the two other motorized platoons, and within a quarter of an hour, the company was in control of the post. This action cost the company three wounded.

A Company got close to their objective at about 05.45. Hidden by hedges, they advanced to within about 275 yards of the Egyptian anti-tank gun emplacements which protected the south-western flank of Post 34, and managed to silence the enemy guns with direct hits from their bazookas. The company was now joined by the light tanks which had come on after the fall of Post 36. The tanks supported them with direct fire and the company broke through and rushed the Egyptian defences. Meanwhile reinforcements arrived from D Company, which had been held in reserve, and by 06.30 the capture and clearance of Post 34 were over. Four of our men were wounded in this fighting.

This battalion was not the only unit that operated and suffered casualties in this northern attack. At 05.00, an armoured battalion team of 27th Brigade also arrived near the Egyptian Posts 34 and 36. This was the unit which had moved in the wake of the infantry battalion so as to get on to the Rafah road as soon as the breach was effected. It received orders from 27th Brigade commander to lend support to the infantry in the capture of the posts. The unit commander decided to attack Post 34 with some of his own forces, and he advanced upon it, personally leading a troop of tanks. When he got to within 450 yards of his target, it was already daylight, and the half-track in which he was travelling stood fully exposed to the Egyptians. (Owing to a breakdown in the signalling equipment in his command tank, he had transferred to a half-track where he could give visual signals.) The enemy opened concentrated fire, and their anti-tank guns scored three direct hits on his vehicle. He, the armoured battalion commander, was killed on the spot and the second-in-command of the brigade, who was with him in the half-track, was wounded in the eyes.

By 06.30, all the central and northern posts in the large defended locality of Rafah were in the hands of our forces. But two of the three armoured battalion teams who had been in action during the night and suffered casualties in men and vehicles needed a few hours to repair and refuel their vehicles and reorganize for continued combat. The third battalion team, which had been held in reserve, was accordingly ordered at 06.00 to move through the northern gap (Posts 34 and 36), clear the Gaza–Rafah road and join up with our forces at the cross-roads.

At 09.00, the leading tanks of this northern force approached the cross-roads. At first, our infantrymen there (from 1st Brigade) could not be certain of their identity; but after a few minutes, when the dust clouds had lifted, they saw clearly on the horizon the low hulls of our AMXs.

Though scattered shooting was still going on all around, and from time to time heads of Egyptian soldiers would pop up from behind the cactus hedges, officers and men of the battalion of 1st Brigade could not restrain their feelings; they came out of their posts and ran forward to greet the oncoming tanks. Within a few minutes, the cross-roads was full of tanks and half-tracks and joyous troops whose grins lit up their dust-covered faces. Even hardened veterans fell upon their comrades in spontaneous embrace. My particular victim – I had followed 27th Brigade throughout the attacks – was the second-in-command of 1st Brigade. We fell into each other's arms as in a classic Russian film.

The second phase of the operation opened at 10.30, when 27th Brigade started its advance on El Arish. Leading the brigade was an armoured battalion team consisting of a seven-jeep reconnaissance unit, a section of engineers, an infantry company on half-tracks, two troops of light tanks (six each), and an artillery troop of four 105-mm. self-propelled guns. This lead unit was followed by two other armoured battalion teams. The brigade command travelled right behind the lead unit, and I too pushed myself with 'the Chief of Staff's unit' among the brigade command vehicles. My 'unit' comprised two 6×6 trucks, one a radio truck through which I could maintain constant contact with GHQ command post and with the Air Force, and the other in which I travelled. With me was the head of the Southern Command Staff, the head of my office, and two signalmen.

As soon as we left Rafah, the excitement and tension suddenly vanished, giving way to the same serenity I used to feel after a jump during my parachute-training days. Once out of the plane there was sudden silence; gone was the ear-rending roar of the engines; gone was the air pressure; forgotten the blow of the jump; and for the few moments before the landing, one floated gently down, relaxed, calm, freed of all tightness.

We drove westwards to El Arish. A light breeze blew in from the Mediterranean. On either side of the road stretched the sand dunes, and from time to time we would pass a cluster of mud-huts, flocks of sheep and Bedouin women leading donkeys laden with water-skins. A more pastoral scene for a journey into battle it would be difficult to imagine.

We did not even have to miss breakfast, for before reaching the cross-roads, one of the Egyptian anti-tank gun crews who had not fled – there are exceptions in every group – opened fire on us and we had to spend a little time in a ditch on the side of the road.

The first Egyptian post where we expected to encounter opposition was Sheikh Zuweid, about six miles west of the cross-roads. The name was familiar to me from the episode of the 'Nili spies' (the Jewish group in Palestine who carried out missions for the Allies during the First World War). It was here, according to the story of Lishinsky, that Avshalom Feinberg was killed by Bedouin.

When we got there we found it empty. The fact is that we were not the first Israeli unit to reach it. Our Air Force had been here before us, and the signs of their visit were evident on the roadside – smoking vehicles and abandoned field and anti-tank guns whose crews had run off in panic.

We met enemy fire for the first time after we had travelled some twelve miles, just beyond the half-way mark from Rafah to El Arish. It came from the enemy look-out posts at El Burj. We were fired on again two miles farther on, from El Jeradi. El Jeradi was the salient guarding the approaches to El Arish, and it was selected for this task because it completely dominates

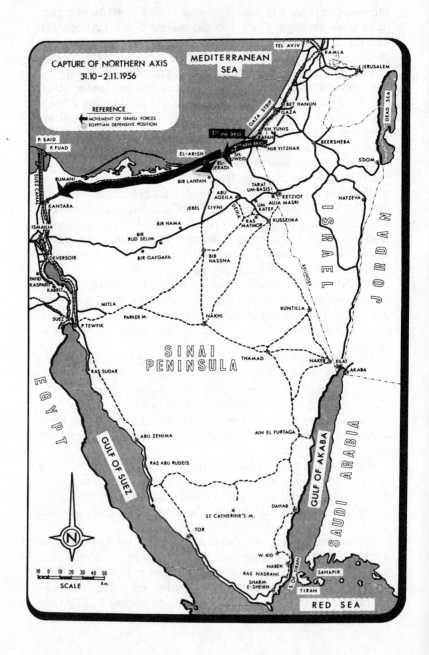

CAPTURE OF NORTHERN AXIS
31.10 - 2.11.1956

REFERENCE
MOVEMENT OF ISRAELI FORCES
EGYPTIAN DEFENSIVE POSITION

MEDITERRANEAN
SEA

TEL AVIV
RAMLA
JERUSALEM
DEAD SEA
GAZA STRIP
BET HANUN
GAZA
KH.YUNIS
1st INF BRIG
RAFAH
7th ARM BRIG
NIR YITZHAK
BEERSHEBA
EL-ARISH
SH. UWEID
EL-JERADI
P. SAID
P. FUAD
RUMANI
BIR LAHFAN
S'DOM
TARAT UM-BASIS
ABU AGEILA
KETZIOT
JEBEL LIVNI
UM AUJA MASRI
KANTARA
BIR HAMA
RAS MATMOR
KUSSEIMA
HATZEVA
ISMAILIA
BIR RUD SELIM
BIR HASSNA
DEVERSOIR
BIR GAFGAFA
FAYID
KASPARIT
KABRIT
MITLA
KUNTILLA
SUEZ
PARKER M.
P. TEWFIK
NAKHL

SUEZ CANAL
EGYPT

SINAI
PENINSULA

THAMAD
NAKEB
EILAT
AKABA

RAS SUDAR

ISRAEL
JORDAN
FRONTIER

GULF OF SUEZ

ABU ZENIMA
AIN EL FURTAGA

RAS ABU RUDEIS

DAHAB

ST. CATHERINE'S M.

TOR

W. KID
NABEK
RAS NASRANI
SHARM E-SHEIKH
STR.OF TIRAN
TIRAN
SANAPIR

SAUDI ARABIA
GULF OF AKABA

N

10 0 10 20 30 40 50
SCALE   Km.

RED SEA

this axis-route. On both sides of the highway here, and stretching far into the distance, are hills of soft sand which are extremely difficult to negotiate, so it was not possible to by-pass the Egyptian defences. The salient was held by an infantry company, a detachment of three 'Archer' anti-tank guns, and a troop of six 120-mm. mortars.

Our armoured attack on this strongpoint started at 14.30 and lasted more than an hour, largely because of the difficulty of movement through the dunes. (These are the very sand hills which so delighted Lawrence, who saw them as the last clean spot still left in the world.) Here, too, as at Rafah, as our tanks began to approach their emplacements, the Egyptian soldiers abandoned their weapons and ran. We suffered ten casualties.

We were now only nine miles from El Arish. As we moved towards the city, we came across more and more signs of the Egyptian units who had fled westwards from Rafah and been strafed by our aircraft. Ammunition cases, guns and vehicles of all types had been left at the side – and even in the centre – of the road.

We encountered the last Egyptian post about four miles from El Arish. This, too, like El Jeradi, was under the command of 11th Battalion of the Egyptian 4th Infantry Brigade. It comprised two infantry companies, anti-tank guns sited on both sides of the highway, and an artillery troop of eight 25-pounders.

The hour was now late, and our brigade convoy was too scattered to organize and deploy for attack in the last moments before nightfall. Energies had also slackened.

There was nothing for it but to postpone the attack, and the entry into El Arish, until morning, and during the night to let our crews refuel and do maintenance on their tanks, and get a little rest.

The night was cool and refreshing after the heat of the day and the dust of travel. We found a fold in the ground which sprouted a few low tamarisk bushes and got ourselves ready for the night. I looked through and replied to the last signals which had come in. I repeated my orders for the commencement at dawn next morning (2 November) of 9th Brigade's march on Sharm e-Sheikh and 11th Brigade's operation to secure control of the Gaza Strip. We are about to open the final phase of the campaign.

Supper was the traditional menu – rations of meat of doubtful

145

taste and tins of orange juice which is more heart-burn mixture than orange. The situation, as usual, was saved by the coffee – coffee hot and black, after which the world seems more rosy. Just as we had wrapped ourselves and started to doze off, the Egyptians started up their artillery again. The noise would not have disturbed our slumber, but the spurting into our faces of sand thrown up by the exploding shells prompted us to move to the protected reverse slope of the mound.

The next day at 06.00 we entered El Arish without opposition. We found it empty of troops. The last Egyptian units had withdrawn during the night.

At the thought that they had managed to evacuate it only a few hours before our arrival, we were naturally nagged by the idea that perhaps we should have made a special effort to press on and effect our entry at night. Had we done this, and then quickly advanced to the western exit of El Arish and sealed the road to Suez, we might have seized the bulk of the vehicles and weapons of 3rd Division and taken prisoner the Egyptian units who had in the meantime been moved to the Canal Zone.

None of us, of course, knew when the withdrawal had been carried out. From what we were told by prisoners, the Egyptian General Staff had issued the order to their forces in Sinai at noon on 1 November to withdraw immediately to the western bank of the Suez Canal. There is little doubt that the Egyptian units wasted not even a moment in executing the order – or rather in exercising the permission they had been given to retreat. As a matter of fact, both 3rd Division at El Arish and 1st Armoured Brigade team started retreating before the General Staff order was issued. Divisional HQ at El Arish sent a withdrawal order as early as the night of 31 October/1 November to its 5th Brigade at Rafah, but the brigade was in no position to carry it out, for, at the time, our attack on the Rafah defence area was at its height and the Egyptian troops could not break off to withdraw without turning retreat into panic flight.

1st Armoured Brigade team went even further. On the morning of 31 October, they received orders from Egyptian GHQ to advance with the utmost speed to the Jebel Livni cross-roads, engage the Israel armoured units (7th Brigade) and thereby help in the defence of Um Katef. According to an Egyptian tank officer whom we captured, the Egyptian armoured commander requested air cover, and when this was not forthcoming, not only did he fail to advance as he had been ordered but he instructed his unit to organize itself for a withdrawal from Sinai.

In the light of these facts, it is therefore possible that even if we had captured El Arish during the night, our arrival would still not have preceded the departure of most of the Egyptian armed forces from the city.

The El Arish evacuation was effected partly in organized manner but in the main it was a disordered flight. At dusk, two trains arrived from Egypt, but these could take only an insignificant part of the retreating force. Nor could the narrow road from El Arish to Kantara handle all the vehicles crowding to use it. The railway line and the road were accordingly reserved exclusively for the officers; other ranks were ordered to retreat on foot. In the event, the men on foot were more fortunate, for the vehicles on the highway received the attention of our Air Force, whereas our planes did not bother to attack the troops moving across the dunes.

These troops, abandoned by their officers, immediately shed all they wore and carried which hampered movement – weapons, military pack, uniform, and even their heavy army boots. They gathered in groups and made their way slowly westwards, in the direction of Egypt. Drinking-water was drawn from wells they came across, and hunger was satisfied by dates. The date plantations, stretching for miles along the coast, were now at the height of the season, and it was enough to cast a stone at a ripe cluster high on the palm to gather handfuls of fruit. From the air these troops looked like an endless procession of pilgrims, their white underwear conspicuous against the background of golden sand.

El Arish was evacuated without being destroyed or sabotaged. A few military stores had been set on fire, but these formed only a trifling part of the huge quantity of military equipment which was left. It was apparent that when the withdrawal order was given, everyone had simply left his post and rushed to join the convoys leaving the city. The hospital offered a gruesome sight. On the operating-table lay the body of a dead Egyptian soldier with a leg just amputated. He had been abandoned in the middle of the operation without doctor or nurse stopping to bandage him, and he died from loss of blood. The hospital wounded, some of them in the wards but most of them trying to hide in the courtyard and garden, told us that when the medical

147

personnel were informed that ambulances awaited them, they ran from whatever they were doing, pushed their way into the vehicles and vanished. Not even a single male nurse remained behind to treat the wounded, and casualties who were in need of immediate attention – eighteen men – expired during the night. They lay in the same position in which they had been left when the flight started.

The road out of El Arish towards Kantara was crammed with vehicles, some in going condition, most of them twisted or over-turned. This was not an intentional road-block; it was just that the flight had produced a bottleneck, and the heavy transport, half-tracks, Bren-carriers, tow-trucks and so on, had tried to smash out a path for themselves by pushing aside any light vehicle that stood in their way.

The southern road leading to the airfield and to Abu Ageila was also strewn with immobilized military vehicles; but these had been knocked out by our Air Force who made repeated attacks with rockets and cannon on the retreating army convoys.

The 27th Armoured Brigade did not linger in the city. Combat teams went off to seize the airfield and secure control of the road to Abu Ageila, and others hurried westwards to pursue the fleeing enemy and to reach Suez. Handling of the civilians of El Arish was left to Southern Command, who will appoint a military governor and deal with arrangements for ordered civilian life. I do not expect any special problems on this. As soon as we entered the city, what struck us were the white flags fluttering from roof-top and fence; and outside the Town Hall, awaiting our forces, stood a delegation of notables, come to express their loyalty to us and their readiness to co-operate.

The city square had been empty and silent when we arrived; within an hour it was bubbling with clamorous life. The rear and support echelons of 27th Brigade and service units from Southern Command came in and started getting some order into the city and taking control of its many army camps. Some of our troops recognized me and asked for autographs, offering for my signature military maps, soldiers' service books, first-aid kits and cigarette boxes. One quartermaster sergeant with novel ideas noticed a picture of Abdul Nasser in stunning colours hanging on a barbershop wall. He brought it to me and asked me to sign it, explaining that not only was there something special about the 'document', the signatory and the place; the date, too, was special: 2 November – anniversary of the Balfour Declaration!

It soon became evident that not all the Egyptian soldiers had left El Arish, and when they heard that a prison compound had been set up, they started streaming towards it and presenting themselves on their own initiative. Not all, however, did this. Some, bearing arms, hid in the city. At one point, while standing near the open window of a building looking out on the street, we were shot at by a sniper crouching behind a fence. He fired a burst from his machine-gun and hit my signalman, who fell dead at my side.

At 11.00, I took off in a Piper from the El Arish airfield to return to GHQ. I asked my pilot to circle the city flying low, but we quickly had to climb to get beyond the range of rifle and machine-gun fire being directed at us; the sand dunes east, south and west of El Arish were studded with Egyptian soldiers, singly and in groups, taking cover among bushes and in folds in the ground. But even from a height I was able to spot what I was looking for: the armoured column of 27th Brigade. It was moving westward without trouble. Now, five hours after our entry into El Arish, the brigade had managed to brush aside the obstacles and clear a path for itself. Its leading vehicles were already tens of miles west of the city, and the convoy looked as if it was proceeding down a boulevard of steel and smoke. The battle for the northern axis, Rafah–El Arish–Kantara, is over.

Into my mind came the recollection of the Egyptian documents which the intelligence officer had shown me in the morning. One was 'Directives by the Commander, 3rd Division' to his forces in northern Sinai. It read, in literal translation:

DIRECTIVES BY THE COMMANDER, 3rd INFANTRY DIVISION

Date: 15 February 1956.

To: Commander, Egyptian District in Palestine.
    Commander, 5th Reinforced Infantry Brigade.

Herewith summary of directives by 3rd Division transmitted to commanders and officers on the dates detailed below:

| El Arish | 1 February 1956 | Rafah | 3 February 1956 |
| Khan Yunis | 4 February 1956 | Gaza | 4 February 1956 |

Please ensure execution of these directives by all officers and make certain that these directives are not published in writing to ranks below battalion commander or comparable rank in other units.

1 INTRODUCTION

Every commander must prepare himself and his command for the inevitable campaign against Israel, with the intention of fulfilling our exalted aim, namely, the destruction and annihilation of Israel in the shortest possible time and in the most brutal and cruel of battles.

2 FAITH

(a) Faith is the basic element in the fulfilment of our aim. Without it, victory cannot be achieved.

(b) Our faith in battle must, in all ranks, express itself in faith in aggressiveness and speed.

(c) Faith must contain the following factors:

 (i) Perseverance and the powerful will to fight in the most brutal manner.

 (ii) Self-confidence in leadership to secure the trust of the troops in their commanders. Within the realm of safeguarding discipline, any breach between officers and men must be avoided.

 (iii) Seriousness and realism in all our deeds . . .

We turned eastwards and flew back towards Israel. Beneath us wound Wadi El Arish. This low-lying strip alone was marked by the chequered pattern of cultivated fields, and the rest of the landscape was bare wilderness. Close to the Israeli border sprawled a Bedouin encampment. As we passed over it, we flew through a light cloud of smoke that rose from the cooking fires below. The pungent smell of burning juniper twigs filled the cockpit of our plane, and for a moment I was transported on a wave of memories to other bonfires and other experiences of another world.

*   *   *

Yesterday and the day before, simultaneously with 27th Armoured Brigade's actions securing the northern axis, 7th Armoured Brigade completed its capture of the central axis, Kussei ma-Jebel Livni–Ismailia. The conquest of this central axis has also brought to an end the vain attempts of the Egyptian General Staff to activate its main operational force, its 1st Armoured Brigade Group, against our army.

The brigade team was the most powerful mobile force the Egyptians had in Sinai. It was organized as an independent formation, and it had enough provisions, equipment and service units to enable it to operate without reliance on bases inside Egypt for current supplies. It carried sufficient fuel and ammunition for its first line, and at its base in Sinai, Bir Rud Selim, were stored large stocks of fuel, ammunition and spare parts.

A captured Egyptian tank officer told us that on 31 October, the brigade commander received orders from Egyptian GHQ to proceed immediately eastwards to give support to Um Katef, and also to send an armoured unit to attack our paratroopers at Mitla. Units of the brigade did in fact start moving in accordance with these orders, but owing to the repeated attacks by our Air Force, they had difficulty in reaching their objectives. The brigade commander signalled for air cover, but when it became apparent to him that this request would not be fulfilled, he decided to return to Egypt without even making an attempt to attack a single one of our units.

The only contact between our forces and this Egyptian brigade group occurred after it had started its retreat. It occurred two days ago, 1 November at 06.00, when one of our armoured battalion teams reached the vicinity of Bir Rud Selim – twenty-five miles west of Jebel Livni – it met with fire from the armoured unit serving as rearguard of the retreating Egyptian brigade. Our tanks replied, knocking out three of their T-34 tanks with direct hits. The motorized infantry with the Egyptian unit jumped from their vehicles and dispersed among the sand dunes, while the rest of the armoured force sped westwards in great haste. Half an hour later, at 06.30, our men entered the Egyptian tank base, Bir Rud Selim, and found there a number of wounded as well as several able-bodied officers and men who for some reason had not escaped with their unit.

Our battalion team went chasing the Egyptians. After driving a few miles westward, it encountered heavy fire from artillery and tanks. The exchange lasted about an hour, and our unit then found itself unable to continue the pursuit. Its armour had almost run out of fuel, and two of its nine tanks had been hit and rendered unserviceable. There was nothing for it to do but return to Bir Rud Selim, tend its wounded and refuel. (In the fuel-storage chambers of this Egyptian camp were found large quantities of fuel for tanks.) By now day had ended and there was no point in trying to pursue the Egyptian armour in the dark.

This was resumed at dawn next day, 2 November. Apart from a single Egyptian tank which was seen moving near the road and was shot-up immediately, there was no sign of any Egyptian armour throughout the day. The Bir Gafgafa camp was empty, and so was the area to its immediate west. Scattered along the route lay trucks, anti-tank guns, and abandoned personal equipment. Our unit also passed several groups of Egyptian soldiers in flight, but of the enemy's 1st Armoured Brigade, there was no trace. Only at 16.00, when our men reached Katib el-Sabha (about thirty miles east of the Suez Canal), did they catch up with the tail of the Egyptian column. This turned out to be a troop of T-34 tanks, dug in at the side of the road in hull-down position to hold up our forces. Sited as they were in a dip in the ground, their field of vision was limited, and our reconnaissance jeeps managed to get within 300 yards of them without being spotted. One of the jeep scouts off-loaded a bazooka and had just started to take aim at the nearest enemy tank when he was noticed by another Egyptian tank which immediately swivelled its gun turret in his direction. It looked as if our scout was as good as dead; but, in standard fairy-tale fashion, help came literally at the last moment, in the form of one of our Shermans, whose crew saw what was happening and managed to get off a shell at the Egyptian tank in time. The scout whose life had been saved had got his bazooka ready by now, and he fired at – and hit – the first enemy tank. The surviving crewmen of the two damaged tanks jumped out and fled. So did the men of a third tank, which had not been hit at all, leaving it to fall into our hands.

This in fact was our last encounter with the Egyptian armoured formation, for with dusk the pace of the pursuit slackened, and when our reconnaissance unit reached the end of its journey – ten miles from Suez – the Egyptian 1st Armoured Brigade team was already on the other side of the Canal. Casualties to our armoured battalion were one killed and ten wounded. They also lost one tank and one half-track. But most of these casualties were suffered in their attack on Um Shihan and not in their pursuit of the Egyptian armour. Losses to the enemy brigade were thirty T-34 tanks (eight of them knocked out by the armoured battalion and the rest by our Air Force); five SU-100 self-propelled guns; and about forty armoured troop-carriers – most of them hit in air attacks.

When the official figures came in of losses inflicted on the enemy's armour, I could feel the disappointment of our men. Between the youthful enthusiasm of the battle reports and the grey statistical facts, the gap is often wide. A characteristic illustration is the account of an air attack on the Egyptian 1st Brigade near Bir Gafgafa on 31 October. After the action, Lieutenant Z.K. reported:

Suddenly we spotted an armoured column on the central axis. Things became lively. Truck after truck and tank after tank went up in flames. It seemed at first like a practice range in peace-time; but after bullets began exploding all round us, it got more serious. Captain G. and Lieutenant P., their windshields covered with oil, swooped blindly on where they expected the targets to be, and the rest of us tried to fill in the gaps . . .

G. and I went in to attack a concentration of tanks. I suddenly saw puffs of exploding 40-mm. shells flicking into the air near us. In a second I located the firing gun and began diving on it. The gun crew tried to keep their barrel trained on me, but when they found they were too late, they jumped and started crawling on the ground. A short burst from the 0.5 Browning took care of them. A similar incident almost led to a crash, when I fired on an ammunition truck and it exploded. The blast lifted me into the line of flight of another plane, and we nearly collided. All but one of us ran out of ammunition, and Lieutenant S. stayed behind to finish his rounds after our five other planes turned for home.

To this report was added a prosaic hand-written postscript by the squadron commander: 'I must point out that despite the exciting description, the enemy losses, as recorded in the opening paragraph, were two tanks and two trucks.'

*   *   *

This morning we completed the capture of the Gaza Strip. The Egyptian units did not show stiff opposition. Their morale was not up to it, after the defeat of Rafah and El Arish; nor were they capable militarily of organizing themselves for consolidated and concerted defence. The force in the Strip was split into small units dispersed in scores of separate outposts, none able to rush to the help of another and none capable singly of withstanding an attack by tanks or half-tracks. Even from the overall point of view of the campaign, this was not a decisive battle. This narrow coastal strip, twenty-five miles in length and averaging six miles in width, could not hold out independently after the fall of Rafah and El Arish; and the 8th Palestinian Division garrisoned there was not built as an operational force able to act beyond the bounds of the Strip. True, it numbered more than 10,000 troops (including the 87th Palestinian Brigade at Rafah), but it was possible to employ them only when each was in his accustomed post, doing the job with which he was familiar. The 'brigades', 'battalions' and 'companies' were simply organizational frameworks and not operational formations, and they could not be used as military units.

The basic value of our control of Gaza is that it has rid the area of Egyptians. At the end of our war of independence in 1948, the Gaza Strip was handed over to Egypt, and she saw it as a bridge-head on the other side of the Sinai desert for a military attack on Israel, and, in time of 'peace', as a base for terrorist and sabotage operations. Unlike the Government of Jordan, which joined the west bank of the river Jordan to her territory and gave its Palestinian inhabitants Jordanian nationality, the Egyptian Government was most careful to consider the Gaza Strip as separate from Egypt. This was prompted no doubt partly by her political approach, which viewed 'conquered Palestine' as a national and political entity whose independence should be restored, but, perhaps more particularly, by the presence in the Strip of close to 200,000 Arab refugees, people whom Egypt does not wish to and cannot absorb or even support economically. (Ben Gurion, too, feels that Israel should not agree – if she is ever offered the proposal – to attach the Gaza Strip to her territory because of its numerous refugees whom Israel cannot accept.) No one can forecast today what will be the future of the Strip, but Israel seeks to ensure that it will cease to serve the aggressive designs of Egypt.

The Egyptian defence of the Strip was divided into two sectors, north and south. The northern sector included the town of

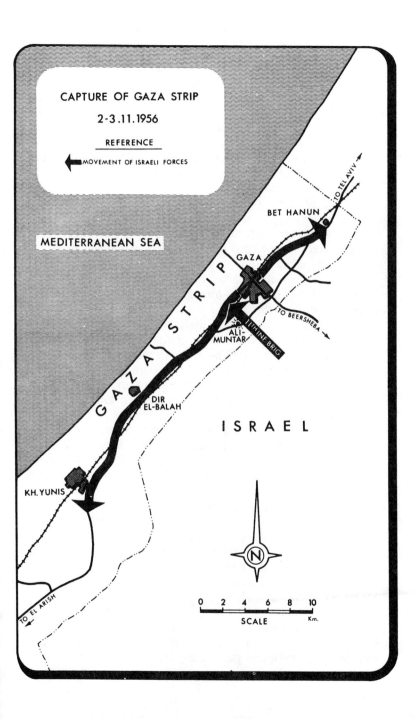

CAPTURE OF GAZA STRIP

2-3.11.1956

REFERENCE

MOVEMENT OF ISRAELI FORCES

MEDITERRANEAN SEA

GAZA STRIP

BET HANUN

TO TEL AVIV

GAZA

TO BEERSHEBA

ALI-MUNTAR

11TH INF BRIG

DIR EL-BALAH

ISRAEL

KH. YUNIS

TO EL ARISH

N

0 2 4 6 8 10
SCALE   Km.

Gaza, and its protection was entrusted to the Egyptian National Guard Brigade. This brigade, consisting of fourteen 'battalions" numbered some 3,500 troops who manned numerous defence posts of company strength, crowded together, all along the Israel border. In addition to these infantry 'battalions', the brigade was given command of a troop (eight) of 120-mm. heavy mortars and two platoons of the Motorized Border unit. The mortar detachment was broken up and distributed in pairs among the outposts, and the Motorized Border platoons were held as a mobile reserve.

The centre of the southern sector was the townlet of Khan Yunis. Defence of this area was in the hands of 86th Palestinian Brigade (whose other ranks were Palestinians but whose commanders were professional Egyptian officers) and was based on three strongpoints of battalion strength plus artillery support. These positions were held by 11th, 34th and 44th Battalions, and the artillery unit, 120-mm. mortars, was located in the middle to serve all three.

Capture of the Strip was assigned to our 11th Infantry Brigade. It comprised two infantry battalions together with an armoured combat team from 37th Armoured Brigade which was put under its command for this operation. This ACT had one squadron of medium tanks (Sherman) and one company of infantry on half-tracks, but of its thirteen tanks, only six were serviceable.

The attack was launched at 06.00 on 2 November. It was decided to breach the enemy defence line where it was held by the cluster of outposts Nos. 122, 123 and 125, situated some two miles to the south of Tell Ali Muntar, the salient dominating the approaches to the city. This was the route followed throughout the centuries by the armies who sought to capture Gaza. Tradition has it that Tell Ali Muntar was the hill to which Samson carried the 'doors of the gate of the city' of Gaza; and it was at the foot of this hill that the British Army in the First World War lost about ten thousand men in the two unsuccessful attacks against the Turkish forces in Gaza by Sir Archibald Murray. (Murray himself sat sixty miles away from the front, in a railway coach at El Arish.)

The tank squadron and the half-track company broke into Post 122; and although they encountered heavy fire from the neighbouring posts, and particularly from the positions on the ridge of Ali Muntar, they pressed on and advanced into the city of Gaza, right up to the main square. After a brief exchange of fire, this armoured combat team pushed north, captured all the enemy positions along the highway and reached the village of Bet Hanun, on the northern border of the Strip. At the same time, the infantry battalion which had followed on the heels of the ACT into Gaza, dealt with those enemy positions which continued to show resistance in various parts of the city. By about noontime the fire died down and responsibility for Gaza was passed to our military governor and to the police force which took over from the fighting units.

The advance of the ACT southwards to the sector of Khan Yunis was held up by the need to do maintenance on the tanks and above all to replenish the ammunition belts – more than 80,000 rounds had been fired during the morning. Clearing the Egyptian posts in the southern part of the Gaza (northern) sector had occasioned no difficulty. An Egyptian Lieut.-Colonel travelled with the Operations Officer of our 11th Brigade in an UNWRA jeep – UNWRA was the UN agency dealing with the Arab refugees – and ordered the soldiers in Egyptian emplacements who still kept up sporadic fire to lay down their arms.

The southern sector, however, (held by the 86th Palestinian Brigade) refused to surrender. When the ACT reached the approaches to Khan Yunis at dawn on 3 November, they were met with machine-gun and anti-tank fire. One half-track was hit by an anti-tank shell and one tank struck a mine. The heavy exchange of fire was kept up, and only after our tanks had scored several hits on the enemy positions and our infantry went into the assault was a breach made in the Egyptian defences. The ACT went through, and in their wake the second infantry battalion, penetrating to the heart of the defended locality. After this, resistance petered out.

The mopping up of the enemy posts in the rest of this sector – and the continued exchange of fire – lasted all morning. Only at 13.30 was the last of the Egyptian positions in the Strip taken, and the men of 11th Brigade linked up with the infantry units of our 1st Brigade at Rafah.

Casualties to 11th Brigade were eleven killed and sixty-five wounded. Two of their tanks and one half-track had been hit, but these were soon repaired and restored to service.

The two surrender requests we received from the Egyptian

civilian and military chiefs in the Gaza Strip were accepted.
They read as follows:

SURRENDER REQUEST BY THE
ADMINISTRATIVE GOVERNOR-GENERAL
OF THE GAZA STRIP

I, Brigadier-General Mahmed Fuad e-Dagawi, Administrative Governor-General of the Gaza Strip on behalf of the
Minister of War, hereby request from the front commander
of the Israel Army forces, Colonel Asaf Simhoni, that he
accept my *unconditional* surrender together with the entire
administration in Gaza and the whole of the Strip.

The Hebrew copy is binding.

14.20 hours, 2 November 1956
Accepted, signed
GOC Southern Command

Signed   Colonel Asaf Simhoni

Brigadier-General Mahmed Fuad e-Dagawi
Administrative Governor of the Gaza Strip
on behalf of the Egyptian Ministry of War.

SURRENDER REQUEST BY THE
COMMANDER OF THE EGYPTIAN ARMED
FORCES IN THE GAZA SECTOR

I, Gamal Adin Ali, 855, Colonel (Bigbashi), Commander
of the Egyptian armed forces in the sector of the city of Gaza,
hereby request from the senior commander of the Israel
armed forces, Colonel Asaf Simhoni, his acceptance of my
unconditional surrender and that of all the forces under my
command in the sector of the city of Gaza and its surroundings, regular forces, volunteers and irregulars.

(Signature)
2 November 1956

We have received the surrender on behalf of the GOC
Southern Command.

Mishael Shaham, Colonel
Aharon Doron, Colonel

The capture of the northern part of Sinai has been completed.
Our units have reached Suez: our paratroopers by the southern
axis through Mitla; 7th Armoured Brigade by the central axis
through Jebel Livni; and 27th Armoured Brigade by the

northern axis through El Arish. It is now possible to drive from Tel Aviv to Suez along three routes: the Gaza–Kantara highway; the Beersheba–Ismailia road; and the less comfortable dirt track from Kuntilla to Port Tewfik.

* * *

The British and French today transmitted to Hammarskjöld their reply to his demand following the UN Assembly resolution of 1 November (immediate cease-fire). Like us, they, too, say 'Yes, but':

1 Israel and Egypt must agree to the entry into the region of United Nations Emergency Forces in order to safeguard peace.
2 The UN must agree that its forces shall remain in the region until final peace arrangements are concluded between Israel and Egypt and until reasonable arrangements are effected over the status of the Suez Canal.
3 Egypt must agree to the immediate entry of French and British forces into the Canal Zone. These forces shall remain there until the UNEF is organized and is capable of replacing them.

The significance of the third clause is that Britain and France stand by their plan to land forces in the Canal Zone. The weakness of their position is that their landing forces are still aboard ship somewhere between Malta and Cyprus and cannot be landed on the Egyptian coast before the 6th. Until then, Britain and France will have to counter the pressure on them not with a *fait accompli* but with empty words.

Ben Gurion has grave doubts that Britain and France can withstand the constraining influence of the United States. He would very much like them to carry out their plan and he would like Israel not to be the sole target of the political pressure (particularly from the United States and the Soviet Union) demanding withdrawal. On the other hand, he does not agree that Israel should be involved in any way with the Suez problem. At our meeting today, he repeated his order scrupulously to ensure that our units do not move any nearer to the Canal. 'We have enough problems without Suez,' he said, 'and I see no point in joining a coalition on an issue which is opposed by the entire world. We should concern ourselves with Sinai, and not interfere in the Suez question, not become hitched to that wagon.'

* * *

Last night at 21.00 hours a representative of the French Military Attaché's office came to see me urgently. He said that the French command in the Anglo–French operation feel frustrated by the obstinacy of the British in refusing to advance the date of their landings in the Canal Zone. The date fixed is 6 November, but the day before, on the 5th, the UN Assembly is to reconvene to consider Suez, and the French would like at that time to be already in the Canal Zone, and then they can comply with the decision of the Assembly who will certainly repeat their demand for an immediate cease-fire. They would therefore like to advance the landings by two days, and they are now investigating the possibilities of doing this with their own forces alone, without the British.

Their plan for independent action was to land south of Port Said early in the morning of 4 November, and then to capture the port. To do this, they would wish us, at about noon on the same day, to capture eastern Kantara, which lies on the east bank of the Canal, east of the designated area for their paratroop landing. Our entry into Kantara would cover their paratroop drop, protect their flanks, and exert pressure on the Egyptian forces in the zone. The French representative added that he knew our commanders prefer to operate at night, and, having no alternative, the French would fight alone during the daylight hours knowing that at night we would join them.

I replied that I would naturally have to refer this proposal to the Minister of Defence, but from the military point of view I could give him my agreement immediately. We would be prepared to capture eastern Kantara at noon, night or in the morning, whichever they thought most helpful. Moreover, I could suggest to the French – and the British, too, if they wished to join in – that they use the El Arish–Kantara highway, which was now in our hands, or any other axis of movement in Sinai, in order to move their forces to the Canal.

It was evident that this possibility had not occurred to him, and he could not decide whether he was being offered an absurdity or the egg of Columbus. From the military aspect, if the French wished to use the routes we now control, they could seize key positions in the Canal Zone without any special difficulty. They could get to the regions of Port Said, Kantara, Ismailia and Suez in armoured vehicles and secure mastery over all or part of them before the UN Assembly meets.

We reviewed several items connected with my suggestion, and the French representative then hurried off to report what I had told him to his command. He promised to let me know their final decision during the night.

I went over to Ben Gurion and found him relaxed and in good spirits. Although several times during our conversation he stressed the need to speed up the capture of Sharm e-Sheikh, he showed no sign of tenseness. To the French request he gave his immediate and wholehearted agreement. Mention of Kantara released a flood of memories from the days of the First World War when he had attended a conference there of representatives of the Jewish battalions. He remembers exactly what was said by each speaker from the 'Young Worker's' movement and the 'Workers of Zion' party forty years ago!

I returned to GHQ and notified the French that I could now confirm my earlier reply agreeing to their proposal. My private belief, however, was that their plan would not be put into effect. The situation is too complicated. The Anglo–French Suez Operation, 'Musketeer', is dependent more on political than on military factors. From the military point of view they have no difficulty in overwhelming the Egyptian Army and capturing the Canal Zone; but from the political point of view, they must stand up to the United States and the Soviet Union and – more serious still – hostile public opinion in Britain itself. I do not think that the British will agree to co-operate with us as suggested by the French Army representative. After all, they went into this operation ostensibly on the basis of their ultimatum to Egypt and to us, and, seemingly, to establish order in the Canal Zone and prevent fighting there between us and the Egyptians. They demanded of us (and of Egypt) that we do not move any closer to the Canal, so how can they suddenly agree to our capture of eastern Kantara which is right on the banks of Suez? How can they conceivably co-operate with us on a military operation when they are explaining to the world that their own armed action is designed to arrest our advance to the Suez Canal?

I was not surprised, therefore, when a few hours later I

received the French reply stating that their request was cancelled, since it appeared that they could not act without the British, and the British were not prepared under any circumstances to give up their 'hundred-ship plan' – the French officer's derisory term for the British military plan based on the employment of a complete armada – and certainly not to maintain any military contact or co-operation whatsoever with Israel. Israel, according to the British commander, is a state whose soldiers are illegally approaching Suez, and it is the task of the British forces to open fire on them should they cross the ten-mile line from the Canal!

Incidentally, this is not only the political concept of the British but also their behaviour in practice. This morning a British plane was shot down over Kantara and the pilot managed to bale out, landing only a few miles from detachments of our armoured unit controlling this axis. Our men, who saw the flier coming down, naturally rushed to his assistance, but British fighters swooped low and raked the road in front of our vehicles with machine-gun fire. The hint was clear, and the men of our ACT turned round and went back. A little while later a British helicopter arrived and took off the downed pilot.

I am very sorry that the Anglo–French forces are not advancing the date of their entry into the Canal Zone. According to the cables we are getting from our representatives at the UN, the storm and pressure against the use of military force in the Suez crisis are not only not abating but are becoming increasingly vigorous. I only hope that by 6 November, when the British and French finally begin their landings, we shall already have completed our campaign.

*　　　*　　　*

As soon as I had returned from El Arish, I had gone to see Ben Gurion and found him fully recovered from his 'flu and in high spirits. He questioned me about the battles of Rafah and El Arish and also on what was happening on the other fronts. He asked to see separately the commanders of the Air Force, Southern Command, the Armoured formation and the Paratroop Brigade so that he could hear directly from them about the fighting in which their units had been involved.

I sought Ben Gurion's instructions on several matters. General Burns, head of the UN Truce Supervision Organization, demands that his UN observers be allowed to return to the Gaza Strip. Ben Gurion instructed me to refuse permission. We shall let the UN teams dealing with the Arab refugee camps remain, but not the observers supervising the truce. 'Between Israel and Egypt there is now no truce,' said Ben Gurion, 'and we do not recognize the armistice lines. Our forces are in Sinai, so what will the observers supervise?' I kept asking him what were the chances that our forces would remain in Sinai, and Ben Gurion answered that he hoped they would but he was not certain. 'We shall not hold out for this with the same obduracy with which we held out for Jerusalem,' he said. As to the suggestion – not mine; it never seemed feasible to me – that we evacuate the Arab refugees from Gaza and transfer them to the neighbouring Arab States, Ben Gurion rejected it completely. It is true that there are no settlement possibilities for the refugees in Gaza and it would be better to take them out and settle them in Lebanon, Syria and Jordan; but only with the approval of these countries.

I told Ben Gurion that British naval vessels were patrolling the waters near Sharm e-Sheikh and I asked whether he thought the British were likely to shell our forces. 'About the British,' he replied, 'I do not know, but about the British Foreign Office I am prepared to believe anything.'

Before leaving his room, I heard Ben Gurion amiably chiding officials who had come to him with Job-like tales of what was happening at the UN Assembly. 'Why are you so worried?' he asked. 'So long as they are sitting in New York, and we in Sinai, the situation is not bad!'

The task remaining to be accomplished is the capture of Sharm e-Sheikh. The 9th Brigade, which has been given this mission, set out from Ras en-Nakeb at 05.00 hours yesterday morning, 2 November, and moved south along the western shore of the Gulf of Akaba. The distance from its assembly area to Sharm e-Sheikh is more than 250 miles (sixty inside Israel territory). On its first day, yesterday, the brigade covered ninety miles. This was a very rough section of the route, deep sand for the most part, difficult to negotiate, and uphill all the way.

In addition to these stubborn problems of movement and the slow pace of the advance, we are also worried by the question of what support will be available to the brigade when it goes into combat. So far, with all due respect to the 'king of combat' –

the infantry – most of our conquests have been accomplished by our armoured units and Air Force, whereas 9th Brigade possesses no armoured detachment. The light tanks the Navy was to have brought them have not yet reached them. And the activity of our Air Force in this region is very restricted – five to seven minutes – because of the great distance from their bases.

We do not know of course how strong an opposition the Egyptian forces at Sharm e-Sheikh will put up, but the fact that their escape and retreat route is blocked may stiffen them to dogged and bitter fighting. I was sorry that our Air Force had been given orders to sink Egyptian vessels which may have come to evacuate their troops to Saudi Arabia. What good will it do us to take another thousand Egyptians prisoner? I would rather that 9th Brigade arrived at Sharm e-Sheikh to find it empty. Our purpose is to secure control of the Straits of Tiran and not to seek a military contest with the Egyptian Army.

We decided that we had better strengthen the forces designated to take Sharm e-Sheikh, and that units of the paratroop brigade will attack it from the south while 9th Brigade comes in from the north. Orders (Kadesh 6) were therefore issued to the paratroopers to hand over responsibility for the Mitla–Nakhl axis to 4th Infantry Brigade, who were at Kusseima, and to start advancing southwards. The plan was for a paratroop battalion to leave the Parker Memorial last night, 2 November, and move southwards in vehicles along the Ras Sudar–Abu Zenima road which runs along the eastern shore of the Gulf of Suez. At the same time, a detachment from another battalion was to be parachuted on the airfield of Tor, and with this in our hands, an infantry battalion was to be flown in. We hoped we would surprise the Egyptian unit at Tor and capture the place before it could receive reinforcements.

The thirty miles from the Parker Memorial to Ras Sudar is difficult terrain; but from Ras Sudar to Tor, about 105 miles, there is a tarred road. It is thus not improbable that the paratroop units may reach Sharm e-Sheikh at the same time as 9th Brigade, or even before. I decided yesterday that as soon as possible I would fly over to 9th Brigade and talk directly to the brigade commander. Then, if everything worked out according to plan and Tor was captured at night, I would fly on to meet the paratroopers there. The pressure on us to cease fire gets stronger all the time and each additional day of fighting involves us in heavy political difficulties. Everything must therefore be done to hasten the completion of the campaign, and it is as well that in addition to orders in this vein sent to the commanders, I should also meet and talk to them.

At midnight I held a meeting of the General Staff. Even though less than a week has passed since our previous session, when we were concerned with the opening of the campaign, this session was already devoted to activities associated with its end.

In two or three days we shall begin releasing our reservists. Control of conquered territory in Sinai will be maintained largely with armour, Air Force and patrol units on light vehicles.

Another problem which requires speedy action is the collection of enemy equipment. The retreating Egyptian units left behind considerable quantities of weapons in their defence posts, their camps and along their escape routes. The Sinai Peninsula is full of Bedouin and fleeing Egyptian soldiers. Our men have already on two occasions caught Bedouin with camel caravans heavily laden with arms and ammunition. We must make a serious effort to gather up and store the enemy weapons in guarded compounds.

Our overall casualties so far are a little more than 100 killed and almost 700 wounded – including the sick and those injured in traffic accidents. As to Egyptian casualties, we have no idea. Our units do not count the enemy fallen nor send reports on them. Prisoners we have, despite all our efforts not to accept them. They apparently number several thousand. It is not yet clear what we shall do with them or where we shall house them. It is just as well that at this time of the year (the dry season) they can be kept in the open. The Adjutant General assures me that the behaviour of our troops towards them is good, and that possible revenge takes only one form – the prisoners are being fed Israel Army rations!

*   *   *

This morning I took off in a Dakota for 9th Brigade and the paratroopers. We flew low both to avoid the 'evil eye' of enemy fighters and also to enable me to get a close-up view of the terrain. Near Dahab, ninety miles south of Eilat and about forty-five north of Sharm e-Sheikh, we spotted the 9th Brigade convoy.

I contacted the brigade commander by radio. Dahab was captured this morning by the brigade reconnaissance company in a short engagement with the Bedouin unit of the Egyptian Motorized Border Battalion. We lost three killed and three wounded. The column was now waiting for fuel which is due to arrive from Eilat in the Navy's landing craft. The advance detachments have in the meantime pressed on southwards. I again urged upon the brigade commander the necessity to capture Sharm e-Sheikh quickly. I have no doubt that he will do everything possible, but my visit and the talk have not resolved my anxiety. The route has proved much tougher than we expected, and who knows what hold-ups lie ahead. Moreover, now that the brigade has already encountered Egyptian troops, the commander of Sharm e-Sheikh must be aware of its approach and he may try to block its path. As far as I could judge from the air, nothing would be easier. There is no possibility for the convoy to get off the narrow track through the wadi, or, farther south, between the mountains and the sea. The Egyptian forces have enough appropriate weapons for such blocking action – mines, artillery, anti-tank guns and Bren-carriers which can move in sand.

We cannot change the situation of 9th Brigade. We shall therefore have to give them as much air support as we can, and also ensure a simultaneous attack on Sharm e-Sheikh by the paratroopers from the south.

From Dahab we flew westwards, rising above the high mountains of central Sinai and landing at Tor on the Gulf of Suez. Southern Sinai is totally different from the north. The mountains in the centre rise to a height of more than 6,500 feet and from the air they seem to form one powerful complex of pyramidal rocks crowding against each other. Only along the seashore which frames the southern rugged triangle of the Peninsula is the bleakness broken by strips of sand and narrow stretches of level ground.

Tor was seized during the night by two paratroop companies. They were dropped at last light in a strong wind, and in landing several were injured, among them the battalion commander who suffered a badly fractured ankle and had to be evacuated for treatment. After the paratroopers had secured control of the airfield, it was repaired and rendered serviceable by men of the Air Force – who had jumped with the unit – and the 'air-railway' of transport planes from Israel was soon in operation. In the course of the night our Dakotas and Nords made twenty-three flights, and even an El Al Constellation was pressed into service and made two flights. These planes brought in a complete infantry battalion with all its equipment, and they also delivered the remaining weapons and ammunition for the paratroopers.

I outlined the situation to the paratroop company commanders and I ordered them to start moving before nightfall and advance to the outposts of Sharm e-Sheikh. They cannot in fact capture it on their own, but their move will be helpful to the paratroop battalion that is due in from Mitla; and it is also good that the Egyptian troops in Sharm e-Sheikh should know that our forces are coming at them from two directions. This will ease the fighting for 9th Brigade.

Because of the strong wind, the jeeps that were parachuted were damaged on landing. The paratroopers managed to repair several of them, and they can also get a few more vehicles from the infantry battalion commander, who was appointed 'governor' of Tor and who, on a foraging expedition in the townlet and its surroundings, collected a number of light trucks and civilian jeeps.

I did not get the feeling that the paratroop officers were 'biting at the bit' and eager to rush into battle. On other occasions it would be they who were pressing me to let them advance and attack, and now, even after my orders, they did not seem enthusiastic. This may be due to the absence of their battalion commander; and it may be that they are not as self-confident as usual because of the paucity of appropriate vehicles and the hasty planning of their action at Tor. I must confess that this time we really overreached ourselves. Not only was the order to capture Tor given on the very day of the action, so that the paratroopers went into the operation without any preparation and without any knowledge of the terrain, but under the first order, only one company was designated to be dropped at Tor and the second in the vicinity of Sharm e-Sheikh. The reports we received on the situation in Sharm e-Sheikh were contradictory, and they kept changing. We were first told that the place had been evacuated and its defence posts were empty; then our pilots returned from a sortie and reported that they had met there with strong anti-aircraft fire and noticed large Egyptian forces. It was in the light of this last piece of information that we changed our paratroop plan. Indeed, the second paratroop company was already on its way to be dropped at Sharm e-Sheikh, and was almost there, when its planes were overtaken by a Meteor jet which had been specially sent after them and which managed, literally at the last moment, to signal them to parachute the company at Tor instead.

In the event, it is good that the two companies are concentrated in the same spot, and together with the paratroop battalion, which reached Tor in the late-afternoon (after I had already left), they will be a formidable force.

After my talk with the paratroopers, I discussed with the commander of the infantry battalion a number of civilian problems which have cropped up. Tor is a central station on the pilgrimage route to Mecca. It has a port with a small jetty, quarantine quarters, a leper hospital and a tumbledown hotel. The inhabitants are employed in fishing and in tending the date plantations in the area. As usual a small army detachment was stationed there, but the men apparently fled when they saw our planes approaching. I ordered the battalion commander to cancel the curfew that was imposed by the paratroopers last night, and to help the villagers return to normal life as far as possible – to allow them to go to their work in the groves and to fish near the coast. I then met with a delegation of Greek-Orthodox monks. They have a community of seventy Christian families in Tor, and they also deal with the food supplies from Egypt to the Monastery of St Catherine. At the moment they need nothing, but in time we shall ourselves have to see that they get supplies.

I wanted to go out and inspect the cultivated fields at the foot of the mountains, but there was no time. I shall do so on my next visit.

At noon we took off on our return journey, making several stops on the way. We landed first at Mitla, where I met the commander of the paratroop brigade, explained to him the situation at Sharm e-Sheikh, and told him of my meeting with his company commanders at Tor. He promised to deal with the matter and expressed his confidence that when his battalion – which left Mitla last night – reached Tor, the paratroop forces would be consolidated and readied to mount the attack. I asked him to ensure that his men do not tamper with the property of foreign companies, Italian, British and others, who have oil installations and manganese quarries in the region of Ras

Sudar. We have enough troubles and there is no need to add to them by complications over petty matters.

From Mitla we flew east. Here in central Sinai we were back in our familiar landscape – flat expanses of sand dunes, and stretches of loess ringed by white limestone hills. At the air strip of Bir Hama I met with the command of 7th Armoured Brigade. This brigade fought and captured more in this campaign than any other unit. They now hold the central axis and await the arrival of the infantry battalions who will take over from them. Their tanks and half-tracks need basic maintenance, and the men themselves also need some real rest.

The next and last stop was El Arish. I had a short session with the formation commander who reported on the position and state of his units, the steps he has taken to restore normal civilian life to the city, the setting up of prisoner-of-war camps, and, above all, the handling of the military equipment left here, at Abu Ageila and at Rafah, by the Egyptians. It is good that this sector with its tough problems should be in such competent hands. Our ability to meet the problems of the refugees in the Gaza Strip, to prevent pillage and hooliganism, and to safeguard the valuable Egyptian equipment, represented a challenge no less serious than the test of battle.

Though the hour was late, I went to inspect the date plantations. These veritable forests of El Arish date palms stretch for several miles to the west, covering narrow strips along the seashore. The Arab peasants dig deep ditches – up to ten to fifteen feet – to plant the palm-cuttings, so that their roots reach the subterranean water. During the years, as the palms grow, the ditches get filled in and covered by sand, but the roots continue to suck up and supply the trees with plenty of water. Neither in the Araba Plain near the Dead Sea nor in the Beth She'an Valley, nor yet on the shores of the Sea of Galilee, have I seen date plantations of such freshness and vitality.

At 19.00 that evening I arrived back at GHQ command post. On the main subject – the capture of Sharm e-Sheikh – my inspection visit has not allayed my anxieties.

4 November 1956

A meeting of the General Staff at 08.00 hours. After Eden's speech last night, we can expect that the Anglo–French forces will after all carry out their landings at Port Said the day after tomorrow. Our men should capture Sharm e-Sheikh today or, at the latest, tomorrow, and this will end the combat part of the Sinai Campaign. In the neighbouring Arab States (apart from Egypt) there is no recognizable sign of impending military activity. In Jordan, domestic trouble is on the increase and the King has dismissed his Chief of Staff, Ali Abu Nawar, and appointed Al Hiari in his place.

In this situation there is no reason not to hasten the release of our reservists. The civilian economy needs them. We therefore decided to release three infantry brigades by the end of the week, one from each Command (Southern, Central and Northern), as well as many other units of support (artillery, engineers) and service troops. The State of Israel will again have need to mobilize its reservists from time to time, and it is right that the nation should be assured that this is done only in emergency and only for the period it is essential, and that the moment it becomes possible, they are released and returned to their homes and their work.

In the afternoon I drove to the Gaza Strip. At the border between Israel and the Strip, over Wadi Hasi, a Bailey-bridge had been erected, and after crossing it we found ourselves on the old Gaza–Tel Aviv highway. Workers are busy tarring the road, which has not received any maintenance for eight years, and also laying sleepers along the railway track which runs parallel to the highway. The Egyptian authorities – or the local peasants – dismantled the rails and sleepers along a four-and-a-half-mile stretch; but the repairs will not take long. In another week it will be possible to travel by train from El Arish through Rafah and Gaza to Tel Aviv, Jerusalem and Haifa. This is particularly important in view of the approaching citrus season. There are numerous orange-groves in the Strip and it will be necessary to ship something like 300,000 cases of citrus fruit from Gaza to Europe through the port of Haifa.

The land on both sides of the road is scrupulously and intensively cultivated. It is divided into small plots planted with vegetables, fruit trees and citrus; not an inch of soil is left bare. Small wonder. I doubt whether there is another piece of territory in the world where the density of the population is so high. In an area of 330,000 dunams (four dunams equal one acre), of which more than half are sand dunes, dwell more than 100,000 permanent settlers and 180,000 refugees – nearly two persons per agricultural dunam.

In the city of Gaza the curfew for civilians, imposed two days ago after the capture, continues. The tank that was hit by a bazooka during the assault still stands in the central square, like a monument. Endless streams of soldiers mill through the foul-smelling streets – it is already a week that the garbage has not been cleared. It is a sorry sight. And unnecessary. The battle is over and the inhabitants of Gaza should be allowed to get back to work and to their normal lives. There is not the slightest fear that they will revolt. If their army did not wish to fight, the civilians certainly will not.

We spent an hour roaming the city. Apart from a small number of beautiful villas, with flower gardens in their open courts, most of the buildings are dilapidated. On the seashore were several fishing boats and a troop of guns which the Egyptians managed to spike before they withdrew. The streets offer glaring evidence of the prolonged (eight years) absence of city government interested in municipal development. This is not the Gaza which drew Samson from the hills of Jerusalem with the promise of an agreeable stay.

Headquarters of the military governor were set up in the police building. That too has not yet been cleaned and made orderly. The rooms are a mess of overturned cupboards, drawers flung helter skelter, and mounds of paper. I do not know whether these are the signs of Egyptian flight or the work of the conquering soldiers.

We dragged some old Arab armchairs, upholstered in tradi-tional, but now faded, velvet, into one of the rooms and sat down to review the main problems. The most urgent and import-ant concerns the 180,000 Arab refugees. About half – 95,000 – are housed in eight camps scattered along the length of the Strip. The remainder live among the local population. Up to now, it has not been Egypt but the United Nations Relief and Works Agency (UNRWA) which has assumed responsibility for the refugees – for their food, health and education. We must try and arrange for UNRWA to continue caring and being responsible for them. It has the necessary staff – a personnel of some 3,000, foreigners and local employees – and large ware-houses with supplies which will last until the arrival of the next food shipments. Of course this raises many questions: the status of the UNRWA staff (who include local Arabs, Lebanese and others); the route by which they are to receive their future supplies (up to now they have come through Egypt); what currency will be used; and a host of other problems for which we shall have to find answers. In the meantime, however, the important thing is for the daily care of the refugees to continue as usual. This is a humane problem – 180,000 persons on relief; an economic problem – Israel cannot assume the burden of maintaining them; and a front rank political problem. So far, UNRWA has not notified us that it intends to abandon its mission, and its work proceeds in orderly fashion. Only on the first day of the capture were there disturbances when the refugees tried to break open and raid the food and clothing stores of UNRWA, but the damage was not too heavy.

The local population of the Strip are largely urban, and their centre, the city of Gaza, has about 60,000 permanent inhabitants and two refugee camps numbering some 50,000.

Egypt looked upon the Gaza Strip as an Egyptian colony. Under Egyptian law it came within the authority of the Minister of War and Minister of the Navy, and their powers were similar to those of Britain's Colonial Minister in her overseas colonies. In practice, too, the Egyptians behaved as the British. In the administration, the senior officials were Egyptian and serving under them were local Palestinians. (Though the Egyptians had a personnel of 3,000 as against 1,000 who administered the Strip during the British Mandate.) In their policy towards the local population, too, the Egyptians followed the British pattern. They handed economic control – not without benefit to themselves – to a thin stratum of city notables, and these grew rich, largely through the appallingly low wage of seven to ten Egyptian piastres a day paid to their workers. This intensified the social extremes between the downtrodden and poverty-stricken refugees and the group of wealthy landowners, merchants and government officials (who would make frequent pleasure trips to Egypt – during which they would also renew their contacts). The centre of those close to governmental authority was the suburb of handsome villas built amid the sand dunes, separated from the other quarters of the city. The most magnificent villa of all was of course the residence of the Egyptian Governor, though when I saw it, it was not at its best; for the refugees had seized the opportunity during the interregnum of breaking into it, stealing all there was to steal, and shattering its windows and doors.

The mayor appointed by the Egyptians was also, of course, someone close to them: Munir el-Ra'is, formerly a senior official of the Municipality. Our military governor now wants to replace him by another Gaza notable, Rushdi el-Shawa, who is considered a straightforward man and acceptable to the populace. In general these local notables show no reservations whatsoever about co-operating with us. On the contrary, the moment after our capture, most of them came knocking at the doors of our representatives begging to be given some communal job or be taken on as officials on the staff of the new governor. Some of the more subtle among them went further, hinting that it would be useful if we could arrest and imprison them for a short while first so as to give them a nationalist halo (provided of course that we did not carry it too far; five or six days in prison would be quite sufficient).

The readiness of the locals to co-operate with us eases the situation considerably. So far there has been only one case where our troops were fired on from an Arab house (they were fedayun in hiding). The local Municipality was told to continue operating from the first day of the capture, and it is supposed to concern itself with the water and electricity supply and with public health. It has also been entrusted with the burial of Egyptian and Palestinian soldiers who were killed in combat in the city and in the border posts.

The most complicated problem at the moment is rounding up the Egyptian soldiers who are hiding in the city, and collecting the enemy arms. There is no difficulty about the heavy weapons left by the Egyptians in their defence posts; but most of their small-arms have disappeared. In addition, a few days before the battle, the Egyptian authorities distributed large quantities of rifles and sub-machine-guns to the local inhabitants in the hope that they would join in the fighting against us. Immediately after the capture, our governor ordered all civilians to hand in their weapons. So far about one thousand pieces have been given up – machine-guns, rifles and revolvers; but there is no doubt that a great number are still being withheld. We have been told that in Jordan the price of rifles and ammunition is very high, and Bedouin as well as just plain smugglers undertake gun-running trips night after night to Mount Hebron. (The distance between the Gaza Strip and the Jordan border is twenty to thirty miles.)

The interesting part of this business is that our men, who have had so much experience over so many years of fruitless arms searches conducted against them by the British during the Mandatory Administration, now find themselves in Gaza repeating the same methods – and, of course, getting the same results!

As to the Egyptian troops, some of them, mostly the officers, moved off along the seashore towards Egypt; but the rest mingled with the population of Gaza, Khan Yunis, Rafah and the rural villages. Those who did not manage to acquire civilian clothing threw away their uniforms and are wandering about in their vests and underpants, and some even in striped pyjamas. In addition to them there are the fedayun (in hiding), who were attached to the Egyptian Intelligence staff, and several hundred criminals, for whom the prison gates were opened by the Egyptian authorities in honour of our arrival.

The last problem we dealt with was that of looting by our own men (both uniformed and civilian). At first they broke open shops to see if there were any armed enemy troops in hiding; but afterwards groups of our soldiers and also civilians from the settlements in the region began laying their hands on property which, because of the curfew, remained unguarded. Our military police finally got the stiuation in hand and stopped it, but not before much damage was done to Arab belongings and much shame to ourselves.

Later in the afternoon, as I was about to leave for GHQ the curfew was lifted and the people streamed out of their homes to visit relatives, make purchases, but mostly just to be out in the open and meander through the streets. At first they walked like thieves in the night, eyes furtive, heads bent, voices low. But after a few minutes, subdued murmur burst into tumultuous noise, the sound of shouting, laughing, clamorous crowds, and the dead city sprang suddenly to life. All that was missing were the mounds of giant juicy water-melons that are the pride of Gaza. (Apart from local guzzling, the Gaza Strip annually exports some 5,000 tons of these melons to the Arab States!)

On leaving the city I climbed Tell Ali Muntar. Quite rightly has this long ridge been regarded in every war in this region as the key to the capture of Gaza. From the top you can see how

174

completely it dominates the whole of the plain to the east. (Gaza is protected on the west by the sea. North and south stretch sand dunes.) The Egyptians fortified this ridge and established artillery and machine-gun posts, linking them by communications trenches. I was careful not to go too near the fence in case there were mines which had not yet been defused, but I examined the earth in the trenches dug by the Egyptians – and I was not disappointed. In one of them, on the north side of Ali Muntar, I spotted what looked like human bones. Digging down a little deeper, I uncovered a Canaanite grave – about 1300 B.C. In it I found a jug and a plate that had held a meal-offering to the deceased. The vessels are characteristic of the period. The edge of the plate curls inwards; the jug is cone-shaped, with a round base, and has shoulder-handles. I have not yet cleared the dirt off the jug. This must be done very carefully. One often finds at the bottom of such jugs a small flask or vial with which they would draw oil or wine from the larger container.

During the six days of fighting I have managed to see and speak with all our brigade commanders, except the commander of 1st Brigade. It is precisely to him that I should like to say a good word. He certainly deserves it after the battle of Rafah, which was the key action in the fighting for the northern axis and in which his brigade played the principal part. I would have preferred to congratulate him orally, and I shall; but in the meantime I have sent him this note:

Dear B.,

In the chance developments of 'fire and movement', I have not managed to see you during the last four days of fighting, and this I regret. Even in El Arish, where I have just been, I missed you. I think you were with H.B.L. I just wanted two things: first, to see you and hear how you are faring 'in these days'; second, to shake your hand as a comrade and as one who is delighted with the actions of your brigade.

When you get to Tel Aviv, come in and see me. If not, I will try and catch you in El Arish.

In the meantime, Shalom.

*　　*　　*

Information reaching us from various sources – British, Egyptian and reports from our own pilots – tells of battles and incidents in the last few days involving British warships, our own fighter planes, and Egyptian naval vessels.

The whole affair started with the Egyptian frigate *Domiat*, which was to have transported an Egyptian military unit from Suez to Sharm e-Sheikh as reinforcements to the garrison there. Our Air Force got ready to deal with it, but a British naval squadron patrolling the southern approaches to the Gulf of Suez got there first and sank the *Domiat* in the hours of darkness of 1 November.

The British squadron picked up survivors from the Egyptian frigate and continued patrolling the area. In the afternoon of 3 November, its vessels were in the Straits of Tiran, near Sharm e-Sheikh. At just about this time, two flights of four Mystères from our Air Force took off to attack an Egyptian vessel that was spotted near Ras Natsrani, nine miles north of Sharm e-Sheikh. The first four Mystères attacked their target, and the ship, which must have been made of poor wood, split in two and sank. When our planes were turning to get back to base after finishing their job, the pilots sighted a large warship near the coast. They could not get close to it as their fuel was running low, but they passed on the information to their sister flight that followed them. When these four planes reached the spot, they saw a white foamy wake being churned up in the sea, indicating that the warship had just changed course and was now racing away from Sharm e-Sheikh. The flight commander had no doubt what was the good deed it was his duty to perform that day, and despite the heavy fire directed at him from the ship, he nose-dived and, with a single pressure on the button, released all thirty-eight of his rockets. The other three Mystères did the same. The vessel under attack turned out to be the British frigate HMS *Crane*. She was hit but not badly, for the rockets were not armour-piercing. The attack planes also emerged without damage, in spite of the heavy fire from the guns of the *Crane*.

The report of another mishap, which occurred in the same region the previous day when one of our Mystères was brought down, has apparently crept into the report of the *Crane* incident. Somewhere in the Intelligence room the two incidents have become one, and the downing of the Mystère has been chalked up to the *Crane*. The fact is that there is no connection between the two actions. The shooting down of the Mystère is a story on its own. The day before yesterday, 2 November, at 12 noon, a flight of four Mystères took off to attack ground targets at Ras Natsrani and Sharm e-Sheikh. They flew low, and two of them were hit by Egyptian anti-aircraft fire. One of the damaged planes managed to return to base, but fire broke out in the second, and the pilot, Major Benny Peled, was forced to bale out. The plane flew on for a few seconds and then crashed and exploded. Benny was blown by a strong wind towards the Egyptian camp and he landed about a mile and a half from its defence posts. He hit the ground hard and damaged his knee. He was in acute pain, but slight reflection on what he could expect if he were caught prodded him to scramble some two miles through the chain of mountains that rose in the west. The Egyptian unit that went searching for the pilot they had seen jumping from the burning Mystère chased after his abandoned parachute, which the wind had lifted and was blowing in the opposite direction. Benny therefore succeeded in reaching a small hill at the foot of the mountains. When he got to the top, he saw to his astonishment, only 200 yards away, a guard hut; sitting beside it were two Egyptian soldiers. But by then he was utterly exhausted and he decided to stay where he was. After a short time a Piper plane arrived and circled above the burnt-out Mystère. Benny made signals with the parachute sleeve which he had taken with him, but the pilot of the Piper did not spot him and flew away. Two hours later, at 17.00, the Piper returned and this time made a wider sweep, coming closer to the mountains. The pilot now noticed Peled's waving. Just to make sure, though, he shut off his motor, flew low and shouted 'Are you Benny?' When he saw the nodding head, he proceeded to land on the seashore, coming to rest less than 550 yards from the Egyptian camp. He then taxied towards Benny while Benny crawled towards him. The pilot and a scout who was with him pulled Benny aboard and made a hurried getaway with their 'booty'.

Worthy of special mention are the two Egyptian soldiers who sat near the hut on the hill. Throughout the entire protracted operation – signalling, waving, identification, landing, crawling, loading and take-off – these two men sat, leaning on their rifles, in stoic silence, following with keen interest, and with intense passivity, all that was happening.

Major Peled's Mystère is the only one of our jet planes which has been shot down so far. We have lost another nine planes, all piston-engined: seven Mustangs and two Harvards. Of particular interest are the facts that all our downed planes were hit by the anti-aircraft fire of enemy ground units and not in aerial battle; and that most of them – seven out of the ten – were shot down on 30 and 31 October, namely before the Anglo French forces went into action. The commander of the Egyptian ground forces has every right to complain that the Egyptian Air Force does not trouble to protect his infantry units and that they have to fight off Israeli planes themselves, alone.

Our piston-engined aircraft were hit because they made so many sorties against ground targets from a low altitude. The fact is, also, that they were flown by young pilots who lack combat experience, and they start flying low even before they reach their target, which makes it easier for the Egyptian anti-aircraft gunners to get them accurately within their sights.

Among our pilots – apart from those in the Piper squadron – six have been wounded and two killed. One of the wounded fell prisoner to the Egyptians, but the other five all returned to base, three on their own, and two who were evacuated from enemy territory by rescue planes.

The 'long-distance record' for an escape from enemy territory and a safe return to base is held by Captain Paz. He walked; and it took him almost thirty hours to get back to our lines. His plane was hit by enemy anti-aircraft fire on 31 October when he and two other Mustang pilots were attacking an armoured Egyptian column in the area of Bir Gafgafa. When he noticed his oil pressure approaching zero and black smoke coming from his engine, he climbed to 1,300 feet, picked out a more or less level stretch of ground, cut his engine and did a belly-landing. Under other circumstances he would have chosen to bale out, but here he thought that his parachute would attract the attention of the near-by Egyptian soldiers and he would probably be shot before he reached the ground.

As soon as his plane came to a stop, Paz jumped out and hid among the bushes in the adjoining wadi. When he found that he was not being pursued, he considered his situation and decided to start walking in the direction of Bir Hassna in the hope of finding there an Israeli unit. He walked the whole of the night, arriving close to Bir Hassna shortly before dawn. Just to be on the safe side, he hid behind a near-by hill and decided to wait until it got light. He was not sorry he had done so, for with the first glimmerings of day, he crept towards the camp and to his astonishment found it teeming with Egyptian troops. There was nothing for it but to continue walking towards Israel. On the second night, he changed direction and instead of moving south-east, he walked north-east to try and reach Jebel Livni. And, indeed, after this additional night of tough marching he reached his goal and was welcomed by Israeli troops.

The main problem of such journeys in the desert is, of course, water. As with all pilots, Paz carried on his person a small box containing two hundred grams of water – about two cupfuls – and a packet of boiled sweets. He finished the water within two hours of his crash-landing, for at the very beginning of his march he had to climb a steep 1,000-foot hill in order to avoid Jebel Yalek, and when he got to the top he was so dry inside that he thought it better to enjoy a hearty thirst-quencher and remain without water than to stretch it out and take an occasional sip without satisfaction.

To avoid both the heat and the danger of encountering Bedouin or Egyptian soldiers, Paz decided not to move during the day. He therefore hid among the boulders, made himself a hollow in the sand and lay there until sundown.

He overcame thirst by sucking the sweets. Indeed, when he returned, he could not stop singing their praises – even though they do not, he said, necessarily have to be of the cheapest kind that stick to the wrapping paper! He divided these sweets into rations of two and supplemented them with the small leaves of a fleshy desert plant that grows in the wadis. The leaves were bitter as gall, but they were juicy, and taken together with the sweets they were just about bearable.

Paz also noticed that during the night, on bushes which had been covered with dust, there was particularly heavy dew. It was apparently formed round the dust particles, and although one could not drink or suck it, the moist muddy solution could be smeared over the exposed parts of the body, hands, neck, fore-head. When Captain Paz reached his journey's end, he still had four sweets left. He had planned, if there were no Israeli soldiers even at Jebel Livni, to walk on to Kusseima. With his four remaining sweets, divided into even smaller rations, the bitter juice of the leaves and the 'lotion' of muddy dew, he believed he would be able to walk another night, and even two.

179

6 November 1956

In the last forty-eight hours, the three campaigns have reached their peak – the military ('Kadesh'), the international and the Anglo–French.

The session of the UN Assembly in New York was resumed on 3 November, and the Secretary-General, Dag Hammarskjöld, opened by announcing that Britain, France and Israel had given negative replies to the Assembly demand of the previous day for a cease-fire and the withdrawal of their forces. On the other hand, he reported, the Government of Egypt had announced her acceptance, and was prepared to order her Army to cease fire.

The Soviet Union, her satellites and the Afro-Asian bloc demanded full compliance with the Assembly resolution on the part of the three aggressors (Britain, France and Israel). The United States representative, Henry Cabot Lodge, suggested the establishment of two international committees, one to find a solution to the Arab–Israel conflict and the other to deal with the Suez problem. What was accepted was the third suggestion, presented by the Canadian Foreign Minister, Lester Pearson, and supported by Hammarskjöld. Under this proposal, an international military force would be set up to secure the fulfilment of the resolution of the Assembly. The text of the Pearson resolution reads:

> Bearing in mind the urgent necessity of facilitating compliance with the resolution adopted by the Assembly on 2 November 1956 (A/3256), the Assembly requests, as a matter of priority, the Secretary-General to submit to it within forty-eight hours a plan for the setting up, with the consent of the nations concerned, of an emergency international United Nations force to secure and supervise the cessation of hostilities in accordance with the terms of the aforementioned resolution.

Britain and France, who had demanded international supervision of Suez, could not very well oppose the Canadian suggestion, and so they, together with Israel, abstained in the voting. Even for Egypt this was, in the present circumstances, the lesser of two evils, and so she too abstained. The Soviet bloc, New Zealand and South Africa also abstained, so the resolution was carried with no opposition votes and with sixteen abstentions.

Adoption of this resolution did not of course prevent India from proposing and the Assembly from accepting a further resolution repeating the call to the parties engaged in the fighting to comply immediately with the UN resolution of 2 November on cease-fire and military withdrawal.

Towards the end of the Assembly session, which was adjourned in the early hours of 4 November, there was renewed pressure on Britain, France and Israel to declare their acceptance of the UN resolutions. The Israel representative asked for the floor and he announced that 'Israel agrees to an immediate cease-fire provided that a similar answer is forthcoming from Egypt'. I imagine that our representative assumed that by the time the Egyptian reply came in, we would have succeeded in capturing Sharm e-Sheikh. And even if the cease-fire went into effect with a delay of a few hours, it would not be so bad. The main point was that in principle we had announced our readiness to carry out UN resolutions.

The Governments of Britain and France, however, almost jumped out of their skins when they learned of the statement by the Israel representative. After all, they have repeatedly announced that the whole purpose of the entry of their forces into the Canal Zone is to separate the belligerent Israel and Egyptian Armies; now, if the two combatants cease fire, what justification is there for Anglo–French intervention? In this circumstance, the situation of the British Prime Minister is particularly difficult. Public opinion in his country is against the war in Egypt, and this opposition is mounting daily, erupting in demonstrations demanding that 'Eden must go!'. Britain therefore asked France to use the full weight of her influence to persuade us to retract our announcement agreeing to a cease-fire. France has done this, begging us to do nothing which may shake the tottering foundations underlying Eden's position on Suez. As our friends, the French, explained it, if we did not accede to Britain's request, Eden would be compelled to abandon completely his military plan on Suez.

After reviewing and weighing up all the factors, Ben Gurion decided to respond to the French entreaties, and at noon on 4 November, our UN representative notified Hammarskjöld that his announcement at the Assembly had not been properly understood. What he had meant was that at the moment there was a *de facto* cease-fire on the fighting fronts. As to Israel's compliance with the Assembly resolution, this was conditional on the acceptance of satisfactory positive replies to the following five questions:

1 Is there clear and unequivocal agreement on the part of the Government of Egypt to a cease-fire?
2 Does Egypt still adhere to the position declared and maintained by her over the years that she is in a state of war with Israel?
3 Is Egypt prepared to enter into immediate negotiations with Israel with a view to the establishment of peace between the two countries as indicated in the aide-mémoire of the Government of Israel of 4 November to the Secretary-General of the UN?
4 Does Egypt agree to cease the economic boycott against Israel and lift the blockade of Israel shipping in the Suez Canal?
5 Does Egypt undertake to recall the fedayun gangs under her control in other Arab countries?

Although Ben Gurion met the request of the French Government, he was most angry. If Britain and France had wished to exploit the fact that hostilities had broken out between Israel and Egypt, they had had six days at their disposal, from 29 October to 4 November, during which there was fighting between Israeli and Egyptian forces near the east bank of the Suez Canal. But throughout that period the British Army occupied themselves with their meticulous preparations for Operation 'Musketeer' as if they had all the time in the world. Now, when the UN Assembly called for a cease-fire, Britain was asking Israel to reject it for the sake of her (Britain's) political convenience. Israel had done her utmost, made a supreme effort, to end the campaign before finding herself in grave conflict with resolutions of the UN – and she had in fact succeeded. Of course she had no alternative but to refuse the demand to pull her forces back to the armistice lines; but she could at least have accepted the second demand of the resolution, the cease-fire. Now she had to add to her burdens by rejecting even that, which she would not, for herself, have needed to do.

What prompted Ben Gurion to agree was, of course, not only the desire to respond to the request of France, who in the last few years has shown such sincere friendship for us. He was also actuated by the cold calculation that it is better for Israel not to appear alone as an aggressor who disturbs the peace and ignores UN resolutions. It is better that Britain and France should be with her on this front.

The matter, however, did not end there. The French sensed that the final moments of their political time were upon them and that if they wished to land their forces on Egyptian soil, they had to do so immediately. France's Defence Minister, Bourges-Maunoury, and Foreign Minister, Christian Pineau, therefore flew to London to spur the British for the n'th time to advance the date of their landing. This time, apparently, the British realized that the twelfth hour had indeed arrived, but they searched for a formula which would justify their action in the eyes of the world. The formula agreed on by the British and the French was, inevitably, at the expense of Israel. The reply handed by Britain and France to the UN Secretary-General, following the Assembly resolution of 4 November, included the following sentence: 'The two Governments continue to believe that it is necessary to interpose an international force to prevent the continuance of hostilities between Egypt and Israel, *to secure the speedy withdrawal of Israel forces*, to take the necessary measures to remove obstructions to traffic through the Suez Canal, and to promote a settlement of the problems in the area.'

The phrase about the withdrawal of Israel forces (my italics) was inserted at the urgent behest of the British, and the French acquiesced because they were ready to endorse any formula in the world if only it would get the British moving and prod them to carry out the landings.

Ben Gurion, who cannot be surprised by any new expression of British hypocrisy, was most sorry that the French had agreed to this text, which presents Israel before the world as an aggressor against whom they, the French and British, must take military action to ensure her withdrawal to her own border. And this is done when only a few hours earlier Israel had agreed, at their urgent entreaty and to ease their problems, to retract her acceptance of a cease-fire. Not without bitterness did Ben Gurion send the following cable to our representative in Paris to be brought to the attention of the French Government:

Have read with astonishment your cable on text of Anglo–French reply to Hammarskjöld. They have no authority to make such announcement and am amazed that our friends in France are party to such a proposal. It will be act of unfriendliness against us if they base their entry into Suez as protection from Israel and no declaration on their part will be binding on us. We urge them in all friendship not to do this thing.

The only course seen by the French Prime Minister as possible in the circumstances was to instruct his representative at the United Nations that the official interpretation of the Anglo–French announcement on the withdrawal of Israeli forces was withdrawal from the Suez Canal Zone. This interpretation did not satisfy Israel and has not dispersed the atmosphere of bitterness. As for Britain and France, it is doubtful whether clutching at this straw will help them out of the morass.

At all events, yesterday, 5 November, at dawn, came the signal, and after the lengthy incubation, two chicks finally burst through. A French paratroop battalion landed and captured the bridges linking Port Said to the mainland, and a British paratroop battalion seized the Gamil airfield at Port Said.

But in the meantime something else happened. The Soviet Union, which at first acted with restraint – perhaps on account of the Hungarian uprising which broke out at the same time – decided that the moment had come to react forcefully, and her President, Marshal Bulganin, sent sharp and threatening notes to Britain, France and Israel. The letters were delivered last night, 5 November. The one to Israel reads:

Mr Prime Minister,
    The Soviet Government has already expressed its unqualified condemnation of the armed aggression of Israel, as well as of Britain and France, against Egypt, which constitutes a direct and open violation of the Charter and the principles of the United Nations. At the special emergency session of the Assembly, the great majority of the countries of the world have also condemned the act of aggression that was perpetrated on the Egyptian Republic and called on the Governments of Israel, Britain and France to put an end to the military operations without delay, and to withdraw the invading armies from Egyptian territory. The whole of peace-loving humanity indignantly condemns the criminal acts of the aggressors who have violated the territorial integrity, the sovereignty and the independence of the Egyptian Republic.
    Without taking this into account, the Government of

General Dayan on a flight between battle areas during the campaign

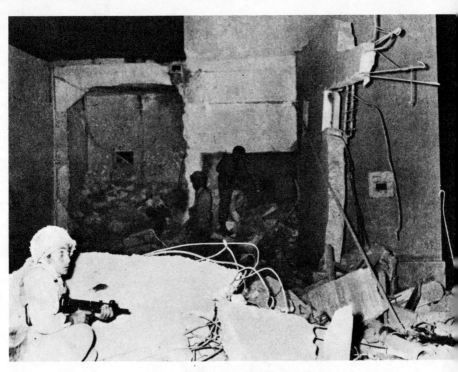

The raid on the Kalkiliah police fort

An Israeli column moves through Sinai

General Dayan (centre) with some of the men who broke through the
Egyptian lines

General Mahmed Fuad e-Dagawi, the captured Egyptian Governor of the Gaza Strip

Egyptian prisoners of war

The Egyptian destroyer *Ibrahim el-Awal* being towed to Haifa after its capture

Sherman tanks captured by the Israelis

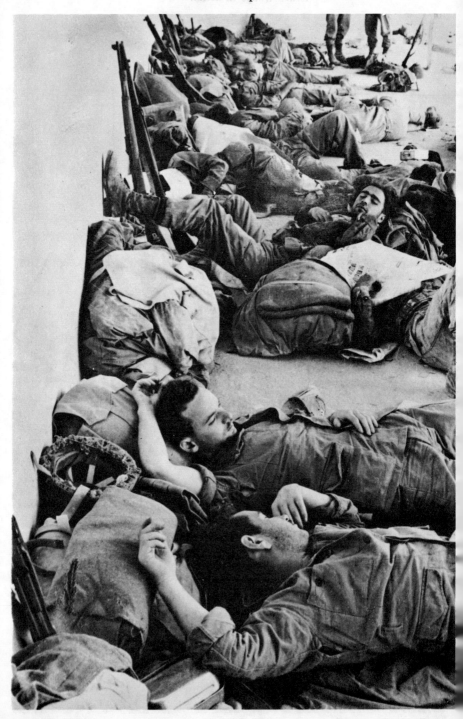

General Dayan, with the late General Asaf Simhoni, GOC Southern
Command (on his right) and General Avraham Yoffe, addressing the
victory parade at Sharm e-Sheikh

Prime Minister David Ben Gurion flies south to visit the troops

The Israeli flag being raised at Sharm e-Sheikh, marking the end of the campaign

The aftermath: a desert casualty

Israel, acting as an instrument of external imperialistic forces, perseveres in the senseless adventure, thus defying all the peoples of the East who are conducting a struggle against colonialism and for freedom and independence for all peace-loving peoples in the world.

These acts of the Government of Israel clearly demonstrate the value to be attached to all its false declarations about Israel's love of peace and her aspirations to peaceful co-existence with the neighbouring Arab countries. In these declarations the Government of Israel in effect aimed only at dulling the vigilance of the other peoples, while she prepared a treacherous attack on her neighbours in obedience to a foreign will and acting in accordance with outside orders.

The Government of Israel is criminally and irresponsibly playing with the fate of peace and with the fate of its own people. It is sowing hatred of the State of Israel among the Eastern peoples, which cannot but leave its impression on the future of Israel and which puts a question mark against the very existence of Israel as a State. Vitally interested in the maintenance of peace and the preservation of tranquillity in the Middle East, the Soviet Government is at this moment taking steps to put an end to the war and to restrain the aggressors.

We suggest that the Government of Israel should consider, before it is too late, and put an end to her military measures against Egypt. We appeal to you, to Parliament, to the workers of the Israel State, to all the people of Israel: stop the aggression, stop the bloodshed, withdraw your armies from Egyptian territory.

In view of the situation which has been created, the Soviet Government has decided to ask its Ambassador in Tel Aviv to leave Israel and set out for Moscow without delay. We hope that the Government of Israel will properly understand and appreciate this notification of ours.

N. Bulganin.

Ben Gurion did not hide his deep concern over the Soviet stand, nor did he seek to ignore the full gravity of its significance; but his reaction was not a trembling at the knees. He was not seized with panic. On the contrary, the emotional effect of the Soviet ultimatum was to spur him to struggle. What particularly infuriated him was the difference between the letters sent to

Britain and France and that sent to Israel. The one to us is couched in terms of contempt and scorn, and it threatens the very existence of Israel as a State. The messages to France and Britain also contain the clear and explicit threat to use military force and to bombard them with ballistic missiles, but there is calumny, no threat to their political independence, and there is none of the coarse mockery that marks the text of the ultimatum to Israel.

I was very happy at the cool composure with which Ben Gurion analysed this new development. I can think of several people who might have filled the position of Premier if Ben Gurion were not exercising this function, and whose reactions in such a situation would have reflected more than a slight dash of panic.

It is perhaps just as well that owing to the situation in Hungary, Russia's threatening messages were delayed until this date, the night of 5 November, twelve hours after the last shot was fired in Operation 'Kadesh'. Who knows whether this Sinai Campaign would have been launched if the Russian messages had been sent to Britain, France and Israel before the 29th of October.

*

SHARM E-SHEIKH

6 November 1956

During the day of 4 November and the night that followed, we received conflicting reports of 9th Brigade's progress in capturing Sharm e-Sheikh. Twice we were informed that it had been taken and found empty, and later it transpired that only Ras Natsrani had been evacuated and that the Egyptian force had been concentrated at Sharm e-Sheikh. Even an army commander more long-suffering than I would have lost his patience. I resolved to take off on the morrow – yesterday – in a Dakota for Tor, and from there fly by Piper to 9th Brigade in order to ensure that the attack on Sharm e-Sheikh would be mounted the same day. It was pretty certain that this would be done even without me, but I wanted to leave no doubts on this score. Now that the paratroop battalion was at Tor, less than sixty-five miles west of Sharm e-Sheikh, and 9th Brigade, with all its units, had already passed Ras Natsrani and had had its first engagements with the northern outposts of Sharm e-Sheikh, we should – and we should be able to – attack and capture this southernmost defended locality immediately.

I left early in the morning, and after a two-hour flight, landed at Tor. According to the arrangements, there should have been a Piper Cub waiting to fly me to 9th Brigade, but it had not yet arrived. Under other circumstances I should have been delighted to have a free hour and been happy at the slip-up in army procedures, but this time I was preoccupied with one thought alone – the capture of Sharm e-Sheikh.

The paratroop battalion was no longer there. It had already set off from Tor (before dawn, at 03.30) with the object of seizing the southern opening to Sharm e-Sheikh, which is bounded on the west and south by mountains.

After an hour of vain expectation, I decided to wait no longer

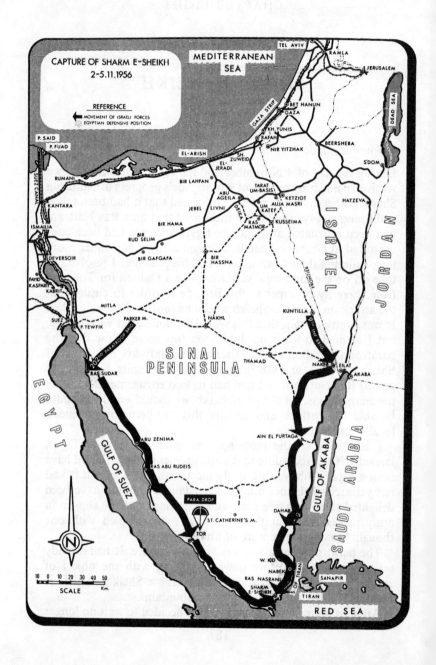

CAPTURE OF SHARM E-SHEIKH
2-5.11.1956

REFERENCE

← MOVEMENT OF ISRAELI FORCES
EGYPTIAN DEFENSIVE POSITION

MEDITERRANEAN
SEA

TEL AVIV
RAMLA
JERUSALEM
DEAD SEA

GAZA STRIP
BET HANUN
GAZA
KH. YUNIS
RAFAH
BEERSHEBA
NIR YITZHAK
S'DOM

EL-ARISH
SH. ZUWEID
EL-JERADI
BIR LAHFAN
TARAT
UM-BASIS
KETZIOT
ABU
AGEILA
UM AUJA MASRI
HATZEVA
JEBEL
LIVNI
RAS
MATMOR
KUSSEIMA
BIR HAMA
BIR
RUD SELIM
BIR
HASSNA
BIR GAFGAFA

P. SAID
P. FUAD

RUMANI

KANTARA

ISMAILIA

BIR
RUD SELIM

DEVERSOIR

FAYID
KASPARIT
KABRIT

MITLA

SUEZ
P. TEWFIK

PARKER M.

NAKHL

KUNTILLA

202ND PARATROOP BRIG.

RAS SUDAR

PARKER M.

SINAI
PENINSULA

THAMAD

NAKEB
AKABA
EILAT

ISRAEL

JORDAN

SAUDI ARABIA

EGYPT

GULF OF SUEZ

ABU ZENIMA

RAS ABU RUDEIS

AIN EL FURTAGA

GULF OF AKABA

PARA. DROP

ST. CATHERINE'S M.

TOR

DAHAB

W. KID

NABEK

RAS NASRANI

SHARM
E-SHEIKH

STR. OF TIRAN

SANAPIR

TIRAN

RED SEA

N

10 0 10 20 30 40 50

SCALE   Km.

for the Piper, to abandon my plan of reaching 9th Brigade, and to leave instead by vehicle and try to overtake the paratroopers. Their battalion was at full strength, comprising four companies, one on half-tracks and three on trucks. These were our finest troops and they were fighting fit. I therefore resolved that if Sharm e-Sheikh had not yet been taken by 9th Brigade, I would order these paratroopers to attack it and try and capture it alone.

The Aide to my Chief of Operations, who had come with me, went off to organize transport and an escort while I waited on the airfield. After an hour he returned with three vehicles and several soldiers from the reserve battalion holding Tor. We climbed aboard – there was one command car and two rather doubtful civilian vans – and off we drove.

The road was good, but the vehicles were dreadful, and we were afraid to overtax them with fast driving; they just would not have stood up to it. At the beginning of the journey we did not meet a living soul. The black strip of road unwound before us, on our right the waters of the Gulf of Suez and on our left, beyond the sand, the rising mountain range. But after covering some thirty miles, about half-way, we began to pass Egyptian soldiers coming singly and in groups from the direction of Sharm e-Sheikh. These soldiers (from the National Guard Battalion) had started escaping from the defended locality the night before. Here and there we also came across killed and wounded lying near the road, casualties from clashes with the paratroop battalion which had passed by a few hours earlier. The closer we got to Sharm e-Sheikh, the more Egyptian troops we encountered. I ordered our escort not to reply if we should be fired on with isolated shots. The last thing I wanted was to get stuck that day between Tor and Sharm e-Sheikh, and become involved in skirmishes with fleeing Egyptian soldiers.

I got out of the driver's cab – from inside I could not tell what was happening on the sides of the road – and mounted the open rear of the vehicle where I could stand and get an all-round view. There was, of course, nothing to stop any of the groups of Egyptian soldiers from taking cover behind the bushes or a fold in the ground and riddling us with machine-gun fire. But none did.

The whole picture – though it was the middle of the day – had a nightmarish quality. The scorching desert sun blazed without pity. One could see the heat haze rising from the melting surface of the tarred road. The Egyptian troops in khaki fatigues merged with the sandy landscape and only at the last moment did they spring into sight amidst the dunes. There is no doubt that they knew we were Israeli soldiers, but they neither fired at us nor did they seek to hide from us. They simply let us pass by, their faces a study in feebleness and exhaustion. The wounded among them dragged one foot after the other with difficulty, and some who were on the road did not even bother to move aside to let our vehicles pass. We had to move round them.

Nevertheless, the thought never left me that if anything happened to make us stop, it would be the end. We were so few, exposed and vulnerable, that even if all they had were their bare hands they would tear us apart. I knew that our chances of reaching Sharm e-Sheikh depended on not a shot being fired and on our not pausing for a moment; each meeting with an escaping enemy group should pass in a flash so that by the time they digested what they had seen, we would be out of range of their fire.

At last the road curved and turned towards the hills, and we could breathe again. In the distance we saw the trucks and half-tracks of the paratroop battalion.

The commander of the company assigned to protect the newly seized road told us that the battalion had captured this southern defile leading up to Sharm e-Sheikh at about 05.00 hours. At 06.30 a Piper had flown in from 9th Brigade requesting the battalion to advance up to a point about 2,000 yards from the defended locality of Sharm e-Sheikh. The commander decided to break through into the locality. The battalion advanced, the half-tracks leading and after them the motorized companies. Resistance was not stiff – the Air Force had given close, powerful and effective support – and by 09.30, the battalion commander with the first half-tracks reached the entrance to the locality, while the dominant defence positions opposite him were already in the hands of units of 9th Brigade.

After hearing this roadside report, we pushed on to the Egyptian base. The sight that greeted us was a combination of battle-ground and enchanting scenery. The Sharm e-Sheikh harbour, at the southern tip of the Sinai Peninsula where the Gulf of Suez and the Gulf of Akaba meet and join the Red Sea, offers one of the most spectacular views I have ever seen. Its waters are deep blue (Egyptian prisoners warned us against swimming there for they are teeming with sharks) and they are framed by hills of crimson rock. Even the building on the shore, the white mosque with its tall minaret, matches the picture of a wonderland hidden among lofty mountains.

On the ground, however, there were still fresh signs of battle. Smoke was rising from the defence posts and stores which had been bombed a few hours before by the Air Force. Numerous Egyptian Bren-carriers, some damaged, others serviceable, lay scattered in confusion in the port area. And troops of 9th Brigade could be seen moving over the surrounding ridges, their weapons at the ready, combing the region and assembling the prisoners.

*　　*　　*

The most ambitious mission in Operation 'Kadesh' was undoubtedly the one entrusted to 9th Brigade. Both in the first phase – the 185 miles march over trackless ground through enemy territory – and in the second – the assault on a defended locality of two-battalion strength, fortified and organized for lengthy siege – the brigade could have met with serious misadventure, and even failure.

Its convoy consisted of some 200 vehicles and almost 1,800 men – two infantry battalions, one artillery battery, one heavy-mortar battalion, a reconnaissance unit, an anti-aircraft troop, and engineer, workshop and service detachments. It was self-sufficient, carrying its own supplies. It had food for five days, fuel for 375 miles, and enough water – carried in eighteen tankers – to provide five litres a day per man and four per vehicle for five days. Neither in the course of its march nor in battle would it be possible to send it reinforcements. The 9th Brigade was thus an expeditionary force which had to rely on itself alone, and which had to succeed in its mission. If it captured its objective, Sharm e-Sheikh, it would have at its disposal a port, an airfield and a landward route to Israel. If it was blocked on its way south, or defeated in combat, it could expect to be cut off, for it would be unable to return to Israel by retracing its steps. Not only would it lack the necessary water, fuel and spare parts, but there were lengthy stretches along the route which could be negotiated only from north to south but not from the reverse direction. (These were sandy inclines which could be traversed only downhill.)

From the political point of view, securing control of the Straits of Tiran was of supreme importance. This was, in fact, the primary aim of the campaign. If the fighting had stopped when we had in our possession the whole of the Sinai Peninsula but not Sharm e-Sheikh, the Egyptian blockade of Israeli shipping through the Gulf of Akaba would continue, and this would have meant that we had lost the campaign.

The time element was crucial. It is doubtful whether Israel could have continued fighting, in violation of UN Assembly resolutions, when even powers like Britain and France eventually found themselves compelled to accept the verdict and halt their military operations. It is not inconceivable, therefore, that if Egyptian forces at the Straits of Tiran could have held up 9th Brigade while it was on the march, or could have staved off its attack on their defence positions for a few days, a political situation would have been created in which Israel would have been forced to stop fighting before gaining possession of Sharm e-Sheikh.

The special importance of the Straits of Tiran, the military difficulties involved in their capture and the likely political complications, were not absent from the minds of the General Staff, and it was for this reason that we planned the advance of the paratroop units from Mitla to Sharm e-Sheikh through Tor. But if pressing an additional formation into service for this engagement acting independently of 9th Brigade was a correct step from the point of view of GHQ, this arrangement did not meet the brigade's problems, and, in the event, it was helped by the paratroopers only on the last day, when the battle for Sharm e-Sheikh was already at its height.

The brigade attacked this defended locality on 5 November instead of on 3 November as called for in the first plan. The reason for the delay was two-fold. First, as a result of the postponement of the Anglo–French bombardment of the Egyption airfields, the start of 9th Brigade's march was also put off for one day. Second, part of the route the brigade had to take was very much worse than we had thought, and the rate of movement was slower than had been estimated.

The going was easiest along the first section, from Ras en-Nakeb to the oasis of Ain Furtaga. Here the convoy proceeded at an average speed of seven and a half miles an hour and had covered sixty-two miles by 13.00 hours on 2 November. During this part of the journey, too, nothing untoward occurred, and apart from the vehicle which an Egyptian patrol had abandoned the day before when it encountered our reconnaissance unit, there was no sign of the Egyptian Army.

But immediately after Ain Furtaga came the toughest part of the journey. The next nine miles were uphill (one of the few N–S uphill sections), and the route lay through deep sand which, apart from half-tracks, no vehicle could traverse under its own power. The most difficult items to move were the field guns (25-pounders) which sank up to their axles. But even with the other vehicles the tyres had to be deflated so that the wheels could get a better grip. The average speed of the convoy along this stretch from Ain Furtaga to the next stop, the 'watershed', was two and a half miles an hour, and even this was attained only by supreme efforts of pushing and towing both by hand and with the aid of half-tracks. The brigade reached the 'watershed' – the peak of the ascent, after which it was almost all downhill – two hours after midnight. Eight vehicles which had got stuck in the sand and could not be pulled out quickly were left behind, after whatever could be dismantled was removed. The men were utterly exhausted.

Even the next section had a five-mile stretch which was sandy, but now, with the 'watershed' behind them, they were on a slight descent and their vehicles could move with less difficulty. They covered the next thirty miles in five hours, and shortly before noon (3 November) reached Dahab, the largest oasis on the Gulf of Akaba.

The Egyptian guard unit at Dahab was the first enemy detachment encountered by the brigade. It consisted of ten camel-mounted soldiers and a radio transmitter. They occupied a tented camp on the seashore, and their task was to carry out patrols in the area and report their findings to headquarters at Sharm e-Sheikh. (Similar units were stationed on the islands of Tiran and Sanapir – twelve soldiers on each – and at Teba and Boasit, on the Gulf between Eilat and Dahab.) When the brigade reconnaissance unit arrived (earlier than the main body), the Egyptian detachment split up. A group of three took cover among the bushes near the road and when the reconnaissance scouts started combing the area, one of them, a Sudanese sergeant, opened fire, killing one of our men and wounding another. He did not manage to get off a third shot. Another scout, spotting his rifle-barrel peeping out of the bushes, silenced him with a burst from his Uzi sub-machine-gun.

The remaining seven men of the enemy section hid in a tent. Here, too, our men made the same mistake, entering the tents to search before first opening fire. When they reached the one with the enemy, they were met by a hand-grenade. Two of our troops were killed and one was wounded. The Egyptians fled but were soon overtaken by machine-gun fire.

At Dahab the brigade enjoyed its first long rest. The men were able to wash in the waters of the abundant springs and to relax in the shade of date palm and tamarisk. The vehicles, too, were in need of maintenance and refuelling. During the evening, two naval landing craft arrived, according to plan, laden with fuel. This was most timely, for owing to the unexpectedly stubborn track, far more fuel had been expended than the prescribed allowance.

The brigade set out on the third stage of its journey at 18.00 hours (3 November), reaching its next stop, Wadi Kid, at 02.00. The grimmest problem here was getting through the rocky section. The route is a 'goats'-pass' on the mountain slope, less than two yards wide and in some parts even narrower, and strewn with boulders. There was nothing to do but widen the narrow sections and blast the obstructing rock. The dynamiting was done by the engineers, and then the rest of the men were mobilized; not this time, however, to push and pull immobilized vehicles out of sand but to remove the blasted rocks and level the track.

Apparently the Egyptians also knew that this narrow defile in the Wadi Kid was a most difficult stretch to cross, and when the reconnaissance unit – which was again several hours ahead of the convoy – got to a point about one and a quarter miles from the exit, they ran into an ambush. Their first jeep went up on a mine, and this was immediately followed by a hail of fire from enemy machine-guns and bazookas and the tossing of hand-grenades. Our unit returned the fire, left the damaged jeep behind, and retired. It was now 20.00 hours, and in the thick darkness of the wadi, they could see nothing. They could certainly not spot mines or locate the Egyptian positions.

At first light (4 November) the reconnaissance scouts returned to the road-block, while ahead of them flew a Piper examining the ground. The pilot reported that he could not see a soul and the enemy must have left. He was right. Apart from a large bloodstain – doubtless one of the Egyptians had been wounded during the night-engagement – there was no sign of enemy troops. The abandoned jeep lay where it had been hit, and just opposite, on the mountain slope, could be seen the empty positions of the Egyptian unit (a platoon). Farther along the wadi a large number of vehicle-mines were detected, hidden just beneath the surface of the ground; also found was a pile of mines which the Egyptians had apparently not had time to lay. The mines were located, a path marked through them, and at 09.00 on 4 November, the brigade went forth on the final stage of its advance, with only twenty-five miles more to go. At 11.45, it reached the end of its journey, coming within sight of the Egyptian defence positions of Ras Natsrani and Sharm e-Sheikh. The men had been *en route* to their objective three days and two nights. They now faced the decisive phase of the expedition – the battle for the Straits of Tiran.

The arrival of the brigade from the direction of Eilat was a complete surprise to the Egyptian command. In planning the defences of the Straits, the Egyptian General Staff had proceeded on the assumption that no sizeable Israeli force could possibly reach them by this route. When the Egyptian guard unit at Boasit, about forty miles south of Eilat, reported to Sharm e-Sheikh that an Israeli brigade was advancing southwards along the shore of the Gulf, the commander there assumed that the information was exaggerated, since he was convinced that only a very small force would be capable of crossing this trail. Later, when he received similar reports from his unit at Dahab, he began to suspect that he had perhaps been mistaken. The full measure of his mistake, however, became apparent to him only at noon on 4 November, when his eyes took in the sight of some 200 Israeli vehicles approaching Ras Natsrani.

Nevertheless, this surprise brought almost no tactical advantage to 9th Brigade. While the Egyptian command did not expect an attack on such a scale by an overland force, they did take into account the possibility of an Israeli attempt by air and by sea to capture the Straits of Tiran. The defended localities of Sharm e-Sheikh and Ras Natsrani were accordingly organized for all-round defence, to meet attack from all directions, and particularly from the north, where there is a flat expanse suitable for paratroop landings.

9th Brigade did not therefore find the northern flank of Sharm e-Sheikh exposed and unprepared. It was organized for defence, and, objectively, it made no difference whether attack came from paratroopers dropping from the skies – as their commander expected – or from an infantry brigade which had made a 185-mile (inside enemy territory) trek across what they, the Egyptians, had believed was an impassable route.

The sole advantage enjoyed by 9th Brigade over a parachuted force was their possession of armoured vehicles. A paratroop force, with the flight means available to the Israelis, could not have included armour, whereas a land force could, and the brigade's light-armoured half-tracks played a decisive part in storming the Egyptian defences. (The four tanks which naval landing craft were to have brought to 9th Brigade arrived only after Sharm e-Sheikh had fallen.)

In terms both of its topographical features and its length, the route of the brigade trek was an ideal target for enemy road-block, ambush and harassment. I have little doubt that the brigade would eventually have overcome such hostile activities, had they been encountered; but I have equally little doubt that on so lengthy a march over so vulnerable a route, it would have been possible to sabotage and weaken and hold up the brigade, and thereby postpone the attack on Sharm e-Sheikh.

The most appropriate weapon for harassing a long and complex convoy like that of 9th Brigade was of course aircraft, and this, after the opening of the Anglo–French attack, was no longer at the disposal of the Egyptians. But there were other ways in which the brigade could have been struck while it was on the march. These need not have duplicated exactly the methods of Lawrence on the Hejaz railway, but they could have followed the same principle – hit and run. The enemy could have organized ambushes along the route and fired on the slow-moving vehicles; they could have thoroughly mined the sandy stretches, blocked the narrow defiles by blasting the rocky hillsides, and sealed the track in other ways.

But the capacity to carry out such actions depended on advance intelligence that the brigade would use this route and on the availability of a force trained in guerrilla tactics. The Egyptian commander at Sharm e-Sheikh possessed neither the advance information nor the appropriate units, so that even when he did send a platoon to block Wadi Kid, its action was pretty worthless.

The decision of the Egyptian commander to evacuate Ras Natsrani and concentrate his forces within Sharm e-Sheikh may be justified. With the units at his command, he could not think it possible to hold both defended localities, and he had to decide which one to give up. The advantages of the Ras Natsrani position lay in its fortifications and its anti-aircraft defences which were more powerful than those at Sharm e-Sheikh; but Sharm e-Sheikh had the port and the airfield. These were important not only for their military value. The Egyptian commander certainly realized that we would use them if they were in our hands; but what he also took into account – and this may well have been his determining consideration – was the hope of using them himself to evacuate his forces to Egypt or Saudi Arabia.

The withdrawal order reached Sharm e-Sheikh on 1 November, when the Egyptian General Staff ordered all its forces in Sinai to retire to Egypt. But at the time the local commander did not have the means of getting his men away. At his suggestion, therefore, GHQ in Cairo endorsed his plan to defend himself until a transport unit could reach him to evacuate his troops. But nothing came of this because of the speedy advance of our forces. Tor was taken on 2 November, thereby sealing the overland route from the Straits of Tiran to Egypt. And by the sea route, only two small sailing boats managed to reach Sharm e-Sheikh and return to Egypt with some of the civilians and the wounded. (Among them was the wounded Israeli pilot, Captain Atkes, who had been brought down and captured at Ras Natsrani on 2 November.)

As to the defence plan of Sharm e-Sheikh, the main emphasis was on fitting it to hold out under prolonged siege and not on fortifying it and organizing its fighting capacity to throw back an assault. Underground store-chambers were dug, and stocked with enough water, food, fuel and ammunition to last several months. A deep harbour was constructed, an air strip laid, an electric power station built, and the site was equipped with all the other installations and amenities which an isolated fortress would require. But only comparatively scant attention was given to the combat part of its defence. Trenches, minefields, fences, and the outposts dominating the approaches to the area were not sufficiently powerful to withstand a determined attack. Neither in its southern sector, to meet assault from the direction of Tor, nor in its northern sector, to meet it from the direction of Eilat, was this Egyptian defence base fortified and secured as it should have been. It was clear that those responsible for preparing Sharm e-Sheikh for war were more concerned with the day-to-day business of living than they were with the urgencies of decisive combat. They thought in terms of meat rations and allocations of flour and not of quantities of mines and tonnage of barbed wire.

The 9th Brigade passed through empty Ras Natsrani without stopping and pressed on without opposition to the chain of hills, Tzafrat el-At, about three miles north of Sharm e-Sheikh. The Egyptians had evacuated Ras Natsrani the night before, upon learning that in addition to the brigade which had passed Dahab and was approaching them from the north, they could also expect attack from the south by the paratroop unit which had landed at Tor. It was following this information that the Egyptian commander decided to concentrate all his forces at Sharm e-Sheikh, judging that he could not defend that as well as Natsrani against a simultaneous onslaught from north and south.

Before moving out of Ras Natsrani, the Egyptians spiked their coastal guns – two 6-inch and four 3-inch guns – which controlled the straits between the coast and the Isle of Tiran and which had barred the passage of Israeli shipping to Eilat.

The first Egyptian emplacement on Tzafrat el-At was captured without difficulty. Aircraft (Mustangs) directed from the ground attacked it with rockets and machine-gun fire, and when the leading detachment of the reconnaissance company rushed in to storm it, they found it empty. The Egyptians had left behind their weapons – several medium machine-guns and anti-tank guns.

But the attempts of the unit to follow through and get into 'the city' failed. (Sharm e-Sheikh was referred to as 'the city' by the men of the brigade, and many of them really thought that beyond the barren cliffs there would be something to see other than barbed wire and machine-gun posts.) The fire directed at them from the posts on the neighbouring ridge was heavy and accurate, and without air support – with dusk approaching the aircraft had to return to base – advance would have been too costly. The reconnaissance company therefore decided to break off the action, and retire for the moment. On their way back they rounded up and brought in the Egyptian soldiers who had fled from their emplacement. These were the first prisoners from this locality, and the brigade intelligence officer welcomed them with open arms.

The brigade command now had to choose between alternative possibilities: to launch the attack on Sharm e-Sheikh proper that night, or to do so in the morning at dawn. The arguments in support of the night action was avoidance of delay. Those favouring this course pointed out that each hour that went by would be exploited by the Egyptians to improve the organization of their defences. The unit evacuated from Ras Natsrani had reached Sharm e-Sheikh only the previous night and had probably not yet been properly deployed. It could also be expected that the arrival of the brigade, the capture of the Tzafrat el-At outpost, and the air attacks had shaken the morale of the Egyptian troops and this should be exploited before they could recover.

The principal drawback to this proposal was the absence of air support. The night operation would have to proceed without the participation of the Air Force, whereas a dawn attack on the morrow could be aided by aircraft.

It was finally resolved not to delay the attack but to launch it immediately, at night. What probably tipped the scales was the fact that many of the brigade's senior officers were reservists who had acquired their combat experience during the 1948 war of independence, when the Army operated without air support and attacked mostly at night.

The assault was mounted just after midnight in battalion strength. The objective was a defensive position held by two companies on the western flank of Sharm e-Sheikh. Our D Company made two charges, reaching the fence round the Egyptian emplacements, but they were unable to develop a passage through the minefields. The terrain was not in their favour, and they were exposed to heavy machine-gun fire from the post under attack and from neighbouring positions. In a short time the company suffered fourteen casualties, who included six section commanders. 'A' Company, which moved parallel to D Company, also had casualties – one killed and five wounded, among them the battalion commander.

At 04.20 the order was given to withdraw. It was impossible to dig in, because of the rocky ground, and advantage was taken of the remaining hour of darkness to remove themselves from enemy range. The half-tracks collected the casualties and the battalion retired to its base, two miles north of Sharm e-Sheikh.

At first light, 05.30, the attack was renewed, this time with the accurate support of the heavy mortars (120 mm.) and with the participation of the Air Force. Leading the attack were the half-track company and the reconnaissance unit, with the infantry units right behind. The fighting was stiff and lasted about fifty minutes, after which the jeep detachment of the reconnaissance unit, with covering fire from the half-tracks, stormed and broke right into the Egyptian emplacements, and the enemy troops started to run. In large measure, the morning assault reaped the fruits of the earlier action, for the collapse of the enemy defences had begun during the night attack, and only when the Egyptian troops had then seen the battalion withdrawing did they recover and remain at their emplacements which they had been on the point of abandoning. Now, with the attack renewed, and this time with greater power, they were no longer capable of maintaining their resistance.

This 'steamroller' operation of diving attack planes followed by assaulting half-tracks and jeeps rolled forward along the entire stretch of road that runs through the defended locality of Sharm e-Sheikh, and one after another, the emplacements in the western flank, which dominate the whole locality, were captured. At the same time, a second battalion, moving parallel to the half-track and jeep units, advanced along the eastern flank and cleaned up the enemy posts there. One emplacement near the harbour showed particularly sharp opposition and let fly with bazookas and machine-guns at anyone trying to approach it. But this position, too, was eventually silenced by a direct hit from a bazooka through its embrasure. By 09.30, surrender came from the last Egyptian outpost in Sinai – Sharm e-Sheikh.

Casualties to the brigade were ten killed (including the three at Dahab) and thirty-two wounded (five at Dahab). The Egyptians suffered about one hundred killed and thirty-one wounded. 864 were taken prisoner. These included forty-two officers of various ranks, among them the Egyptian force commander and his second-in-command, both Lieut.-Colonels.

Although the main assaults and breakthroughs in the mid-night to 09.30 battle for Sharm e-Sheikh were effected by the reconnaissance unit and the half-track company, the decisive element which brought about the speedy collapse of the enemy was the Air Force. The Egyptians had neither effective weapons nor the spirit to withstand the air attacks.

I do not know how the Egyptian officers behaved, whether or not they fought side by side with their men in the emplacements and set an example. As to the commander himself, the moment the battle was over, he appeared all ready for captivity – together with half a dozen suitcases, well and properly packed.

*　　*　　*

Yesterday, 5 November, after meeting with the men of 9th Brigade and hearing from them a hasty account of their trek and their battles, I rushed back to Tel Aviv. This new 'empire' of ours – Gaza, El Arish, the POW camps (we have some 4,000 Egyptian prisoners as against fewer than twenty Israelis in their hands) – raises problems that need urgent attention. The political campaign, too, is becoming more serious than ever. The British and French have promised the UN Secretary-General that they are complying with the cease-fire order with effect from midnight tonight, without the apparent likelihood of their managing to put a foot down in the Canal Zone proper (i.e. the mainland). I share their disappointment. I am glad, however, that although we ourselves ceased fire yesterday, we did so after we had carried out our aim in its entirety.

This morning I returned to Sharm e-Sheikh. At 13.00 there was a ceremonial parade by 9th Brigade to mark the end of their operation, which also marked the end of the Sinai Campaign. Ben Gurion was unable to come, and he gave me a moving and congratulatory letter for the men and officers of the brigade. Attending the parade were all the senior commanders of the Israel Defence Forces. The place was also thick with photographers and correspondents. The ceremony was short and informal. Serving as the dais were two command-cars parked back to back. In front, formed up as three sides of a square, stood the troops, their faces bearded, still wearing their battle garb. The brigade commander spoke briefly. I read out Ben Gurion's message and also the Order of the Day on the conquest of Sinai.

Then came the review of the troops, the raising of the flag, and . . . the Sinai Campaign was over.

At 16.00 we took off in a Dakota for Tel Aviv. All the way up the Gulf to Eilat I could not tear my eyes from the window. We flew low, and the reefs of coral skirting the coast below the limpid surface of the shallow water were clearly visible. Near Dahab I could even pick out the wreck of a sunken fishing vessel, nestling against the coral.

It was getting dark when we reached Eilat, so I moved into the pilot's cabin and by the light of the lamp on the radio operator's table went over the latest cables to brief myself for this evening at Ben Gurion's.

In New York, at the UN, heavy pressure is being exerted against us. They are demanding our withdrawal without guaranteeing freedom of navigation for our ships in the Red Sea, and without ensuring that Sinai will not again become a base for Egyptian aggression.

I recalled that last night, when I reported to Ben Gurion that Sharm e-Sheikh had been captured and the campaign was now over, he said, half-joking, half-serious: 'And I suppose you can't bear that, can you?'

I said nothing. He knows well that what disturbs me is not the end of the fighting but my apprehension about our capacity to hold our own in the political campaign which now begins.

CHAPTER NINE

*

EPILOGUE

1

THIS 'Diary' is presented for publication nine-and-a-half years after the campaign. It is therefore now possible to make an appreciation of the results, significance and influence of that campaign.

It may be said right away that its three major purposes were achieved: freedom of shipping for Israeli vessels in the Gulf of Aqaba; an end to the fedayun terrorism; and a neutralization of the threat of attack on Israel by the joint Egypt–Syria–Jordan military command.

Israel, however, did not gain its 'war aims' by direct negotiation with Egypt. The Sinai Campaign did not end with victor and vanquished seated together at the negotiating table, signing a mutual agreement. The arrangement was tripartite, with the Secretary-General of the United Nations serving as intermediary separating the two sides.

His liaison (or insulation?) mission was not that of a neutral mediator. By virtue of the authority vested in him by the United Nations, and with the force of the Powers who backed him – the United States and the Soviet Union – the Secretary-General became a third party (and, as far as Israel was concerned, the only other party) in negotiating the conditions for ending the war.

Moreover, the intense activity of the UN over the Israel–Egyptian dispute and its intervention in the Anglo–French Suez operation finally turned it from a body which simply 'called upon' the parties to act in a certain way into an institution bearing direct responsibility for a settlement of the conflict. It will be recalled that the UN General Assembly resolved on

4 November 1956, to request the Secretary-General to present a plan to establish an international emergency force which would guarantee a cessation of hostilities and supervise it. This force was indeed brought into being. General E. L. M. Burns was appointed its Commander and at the beginning of 1957 seven infantry units were placed at his disposal – one battalion each from India, Sweden, Denmark–Norway, Colombia, Finland, Indonesia and Brazil.

Through this international force – the United Nations Emergency Force (UNEF) – the differences were formally resolved between the UN Secretary-General and the Israel Government. The Secretary-General had demanded the unconditional withdrawal of the Israel Army from Sinai; the Israel Government had insisted, as a condition of evacuation, on guarantees for the freedom of her shipping through the Gulf and a cessation of Egyptian acts of hostility.

Thus, on 16 March 1957, four-and-a-half months after it had begun, the Sinai conflict was brought to an end. The Israeli units returned to their borders, but their positions in the Sharm e-Sheikh area and the Gaza Strip were not re-taken by the Egyptian Army; UNEF took control of the evacuated sectors. It is doubtful whether Egypt regards the transference of these regions to the control of the UNEF as a surrender of her sovereignty (to this day, more than nine years later, units of the UNEF are still stationed there); but Egyptian consent to this arrangement at all events signifies acceptance of the decision giving freedom of shipping to Israel and ending the terrorism against Israel.

2

The decision to order the Israel Army into action without adequate preparation – primarily in order not to lose the element of surprise – and the concomitant need to conduct the campaign at a fast pace, had their repercussions in battle. 'Adequate preparation' is not just a phrase; its absence produced very tangible effects – some reservists failing to present themselves because the mobilization procedures needed more time; vehicles not quite ready; equipment failing to reach units from the stores; failure to carry out air reconnaissance and ground patrols; hasty posting of unit commanders who thus had no time properly to study their new assignments. Doing without 'adequate preparation' cost us dearly; but it made victory possible.

Hanging over the military operations was a political sword of Damocles. Advance revelation of the Israeli plan, or an extension of the campaign by a few days, was liable to bring pressures from the United States and the Soviet Union upon Israel and put her in the position of violating a resolution of the UN Assembly. Waiting until all the required preparations for battle were properly completed, or conducting the campaign in a more orthodox manner, would have brought to the Israel Army the same fate as that suffered by the Anglo–French forces. By the time the opening phases of their campaign were over, their political time had run out, and before they had even begun the actual conquest of Suez, their Governments were compelled to order them to halt.

There may be Powers to-day who can undertake warfare on the assumption that they can go on fighting until victory is theirs, that they alone can decide when to stop, knowing that no one can force them to do so against their will. The State of Israel in 1956 was far indeed from being in such a position. The real military problem which faced her army in Sinai was not how to overcome the Egyptian forces, but how to do so within the restrictive political framework by which she was circumscribed.

In a basic sense one could say, therefore, that the Israel Army achieved its aims in Sinai not in spite of the misadventures but because of them. Such misadventures and obstacles were inevitable once everything centred on speed – and speed was integral to the solution adopted by the Israel Army to meet its military and political problems. There is no doubt that there were great risks attendant on this solution; but given the political circumstances in which Israel found herself at the time, failure to take the risk would have been still more risky.

Opening the campaign with the drop of a paratroop battalion near the Mitla Pass and refraining from bombing the Egyptian airfields meant endangering the isolated paratroopers and losing the only opportunity of destroying the Egyptian aircraft while still on the ground. But to avoid this danger and to adopt a 'classic' opening with an attack on the Egyptian air force would have made the failure of our campaign aims almost certain. For Egypt, without doubt, would have summoned the international organizations the same night, and Israel would have been branded an aggressor and compelled to evacuate her army immediately.

The Order of Battle of the Sinai Campaign assigned to each force its own axis, so that the advance of one was not dependent on the advance of another. The purpose of this plan was to secure the speediest possible progress of each force, even if by so advancing its flanks were exposed and it became isolated.

This plan, however, could never have been carried out if it were not for the courageous spirit and character of the fighting units. Privates and generals alike were imbued with this spirit, the spirit that could prompt wounded soldiers to escape from hospital in order to rejoin their fighting comrades, and move commanders of armoured battalions to storm heavily fortified enemy positions at the head of their men.

It was these soldiers and officers who moulded the character of the Israel Army in the Sinai Campaign; and it would not be proper to isolate from the total campaign picture such incidents as a commanding general's launching of an attack before the prescribed time, or the refusal of a brigade commander to delay an assault (in which he was killed) until the arrival of reinforcements. The backbone of the army's strength was the urge and readiness of all participants to push ahead despite all obstacles, recognizing that thereon hung the fate of the campaign.

If no such spirit had permeated the ranks of the Israel Army, it is likely that fewer mistakes would have been made; but Sinai would not have been won.

3

The military victory in Sinai brought Israel not only direct gains – freedom of navigation, cessation of terrorism – but, more important, a heightened prestige among friends and enemies alike. Israel emerged as a state that would be welcomed as a valued friend and ally, and her army was regarded as the strongest in the Middle East. Friendly Powers no longer looked upon her as an infant incapable of assuming responsibility for her own fate. And the sale of arms for her forces ceased to be conditional upon prior agreement among the 'Big Powers' – the United States, Britain and France.

The main change in the situation achieved by Israel, however, was manifested among her Arab neighbours. Israel's readiness to take to the sword to secure her rights at sea and her safety on land, and the capacity of her army to defeat the Egyptian forces, deterred the Arab rulers in the years that followed from renewing their acts of hostility. The Sinai Campaign was not intended as a preventive war. It was not meant to forestall a sickness but to cure a situation already sick – to breach an existing blockade of Israel's southern waters, and to put an end to rampant terrorism and sabotage. But in fact it did have the effect of checking Arab ambitions to do harm to Israel. It is not by chance that the President of Egypt, Gamal Abdul Nasser, bids the Arab States to refrain from attacking Israel as long as they have not strengthened their forces. He makes this plea not because he has stopped seeking Israel's destruction but because he has learned to respect the power of her army.

APPENDIX 1

MOST SECRET
Operations Branch/GHQ
5 October 1956

'*Kadesh*'
Planning Order No. 1

INFORMATION:

1. See intelligence summary.

INTENTION

2. Forces of the IDF (Israel Defence Forces) will capture Northern Sinai, establish a defence line on the east bank of the Suez Canal, and give protection to the State on its other sectors.

METHOD

3. GENERAL:

a. The conquest of Northern Sinai will be carried out by Southern Command with a force of 6 infantry brigades and 3 armoured brigades.

b. Northern and Central Commands will defend their regions with the following forces:

  i. Northern Command: 2 infantry brigades plus 1 battalion.
  2 additional battalions (elderly reservists);
  1 battalion Border Guards.
  Command armoured battalion.

  ii. Central Command: 2 infantry brigades plus 1 battalion.
  4 additional battalions (elderly reservists);
  2 battalions Border Guards.
  Command armoured battalion.

c. 202nd Paratroop Infantry Brigade will capture El Arish in a parachute landing.

d. 2 infantry brigades will serve as GHQ reserves.

e. Phases:

  i. Capture of Northern Sinai up to El Arish–Jebel Livni–Bir Hassna–Nakhl line, and continuance of advance. (D-day to D plus 1.)

  ii. Advance towards the Suez Canal and completion of clearance of Gaza Strip. (D plus 1 to D plus 3.)

  iii. Capture of Straits of Tiran.

209

APPENDIX 2

To: Chief of Operations Branch
25th October 1956

Subject: *Directives for Operational Order*

INTENTION

1. To create a military threat to the Suez Canal by seizing objectives in its proximity.
2. To capture the Straits of Tiran.
3. To confound the organization of the Egyptian forces in Sinai and bring about their collapse.

METHOD

General: D-day: Monday, 29.10.1956
H-hour: 17.00 hours

PHASES:

Phase 1. Night of D-day (29/30.10):

  a. Seizure by parachuted force of crossroads at Suder el-Heitan [Mitla] on the Nakhl–Suez axis.
  b. Capture of Nakhl.
  c. Capture of Kuntilla and Ras en-Nakeb.
  d. Opening of Kusseima–Nakhl axis.
  e. Opening of Kuntilla–Nakhl axis.
  f. Opening of Ras en-Nakeb–Nakhl axis.
  g. Defence readiness in other Regional Commands as from dawn on 30.10.
  h. Readiness of Air Force and Navy for full action as from H-hour to carry out the following tasks: Defence of Israel skies; support for ground forces; attack on Egyptian airfields.

Phase 2. Night of D plus 1 (30/31.10):

  a. Advance along Ras en-Nakeb–Sharm e-Sheikh axis with the intention of capturing Sharm e-Sheikh.
  b. Readiness for counter-attack on Jordanian sector.
  c. Capture of Kusseima.
  d. Defence readiness on the Syrian and Lebanese borders.

Phase 3. Night of D plus 2 (31.10/1.11) and following:

  a. Capture of Straits of Tiran.
  b. Capture of Rafah, Abu Ageila and El Arish.
  c. Establishment of line parallel to, and at distance of not less than 15 kilometers east of, the Suez Canal.
  d. Opening of axis from Suder el-Heitan through Bir Mor and Tor to Sharm e-Sheikh, and axis from Abu Zenima to Dahab.

Moshe Dayan, Major-General
Chief of the General Staff.

210

APPENDIX 3

Egyptian Order of Battle in Sinai (on eve of the Sinai Campaign)

GENERAL:

   a. Commander: General Ali Ali Amer

   b. Functions:

      1. Defence of Sinai and the Gaza Strip against possible Israeli attack;

      2. Defence of the Canal Zone against aggressive action on the part of Britain and France.

   c. Forces and tasks:

      1. 2nd Infantry Division – defence of Canal Zone;

      2. 3rd Infantry Division – defence of northern and central Sinai;

      3. 8th Palestinian Division – defence of Gaza Strip;

      4. 2nd Motorized Border Battalion – defence of Southern Sinai sector;

      5. 1st Armoured Brigade Team – Command reserves.

3rd INFANTRY DIVISION

General:

   a. Commander: Brigadier-General Abd el Wahab Alkadi

   b. Functions: Defence of northern and central Sinai

   c. Sectors of responsibility: the length of the international boundary from, and including, Rafah, up to, and including, Kusseima and the defended locality of Um Katef–Abu Ageila

   d. Method: Stubborn defence based on positions of battalion-strength in the sectors of Rafah–El Arish and Um Katef–Abu Ageila, with divisional reserves, and plan for counter-attacks in the event of attack

FORCES AND TASKS

A. *General:*

      1. 5th Brigade (reinforced) plus tank squadron [Shermans] – defence of Rafah region.

      2. 6th Brigade (reinforced) – defence of Um Katef–Abu Ageila defended locality.

      3. Reinforced infantry battalion – defence of El Arish.

      4. Reservist brigade – general defence duties at Abu Ageila and El Arish.

      5. Divisional reserves – 2 tank squadrons [Shermans] plus one infantry battalion.

B. *Rafah Sector:*

      1. Commander: Colonel Jafr el Majid, Commander 5th Infantry Brigade.

2. Forces: 5th Infantry Brigade plus attached units.
3. Tasks: a. Manning of Rafah's defence posts and defence of Rafah camps;
      b. Action against enemy forces parachuted or landed by sea in the brigade sector.
4. Boundaries:
East: From point where Danegor track cuts Armistice Line 2356/2396 up to point on Mediterranean coast 2278/2492 – inclusive.
West: Coordinate line 216.
North:Mediterranean coast.
South:Wadi el Haridin.

C. *Abu Ageila–Kusseima Sector:*
1. Commander: Brigadier-General Sami Yam Boletz, Commander 6th Infantry Brigade.
2. Forces: 6th Infantry Brigade plus attached units.
3. Tasks:
a. Be on alert for Israel army coming from direction of Kusseima, and hold up advance by:
(i) Stationing National Guards units at Kusseima and surroundings;
(ii) sending elements from reconnaissance company to support the National Guards at Kusseima, carrying out delaying actions at Ras Matmor and Deika and undertaking dynamiting operations.
b. Manning of Um Katef defence position.
c. Destruction of enemy force which may advance through Wadi Jemal.
d. Destruction of enemy force which may be parachuted in the brigade sector.
4. Boundaries:
North: Wadi el Haridin and the whole length of the wadi to the west.
South: Jebel Haruf (25741550) – Jebel al-Marafek (243153) – Jebel al-Sharif (219146) – Jebel Katima (173146 – Point 916 (162146) – Point 409 (135146) – Point 430 (803856) – up to co-ordinate line 770.
East: The political boundary.
West: Co-ordinate line 770.

D. *El Arish Sector:*
1. Commander: Lieut. Colonel Selim Makor Bashchara, Commander 11th Infantry Battalion.
2. Forces: 11th Infantry Battalion plus attached units.
3. Tasks:
a. Defence of El Arish.

b. Protection of Sheikh Zuweid by reinforced infantry company.

c. Destruction of enemy ground forces and forces parachuted or landed by sea.

4. Boundaries:

North: Mediterranean coast.

South: Wadi el Haridin.

East: Co-ordinate line 216.

West: Co-ordinate line 178.

E. *Divisional Reserves:*

1. Commander: Colonel Saad el-Din Metuli, Commander 4th Infantry Brigade.

2. Forces: 12th Battalion of 4th Brigade plus attached units.

3. Location: El Arish defence position or any other location in accordance with developments.

4. Tasks: a. Recovery of Rafah and any other defence post which may be captured in this sector.

b. Engagement of enemy which may attack Rafah with the intention of lightening the pressure on Rafah.

c. Prevention of enemy advance westward towards El Arish.

d. Defence of El Arish in the event of attack (to aid the garrison within).

e. Recovery of Um Katef defence position.

f. Prevention of enemy advance northward towards El Arish.

g. Action to cut off any force which may advance westward in the direction of Ismailia.

F. *Forces under Divisional Command:*

1. 1st Motorized Border Battalion (less one company).

2. Jeep company.

3. 43rd Battalion from 86th Palestinian Brigade.

4. 247th Guard Battalion.

5. 289th Infantry Battalion (Reservists).

6. National Guards Brigade plus one battalion.

7. 295th and 297th Battalions (Reservists) of 9th Brigade.

8th PALESTINIAN DIVISION

General:

a. Commander: Major-General Yussef Abdullah Agrudi.

b. Functions: Defence of Gaza Strip against Israeli attack.

c. Method:

(i) Line of defence posts along the whole of border between Israel and the Strip;

(ii) Allocation of reserve force within the framework of the brigades for small-scale counter-attacks.

d. Forces and Tasks:

26th Egyptian National Guards Brigade – defence of northern sector of Strip (including the city of Gaza);

86th Palestinian Brigade – defence of Khan Yunis region and surroundings.

87th Palestinian Brigade – organisation and training in Rafah camps. In event of war, to come under command of 5th Infantry Brigade.

Disposition of Forces

a. HQ of 8th Palestinian Division – Khan Yunis.

b. 86th Palestinian Brigade – Khan Yunis region; comprises 11th Battalion, 32nd Battalion; 44th Battalion (from 87th Brigade).

c. 26th Egyptian National Guards Brigade – northern sector of Strip; comprises battalion group in northern section of this sector and similar formation in southern section, with a reserve unit located near the coast. [There is no specific establishment for the National Guards Brigade. It is determined in accordance with local needs.] 20th Mortar Battery (120 mm.) – dispersed in northern sector. 2 platoons of Border Guards – dispersed in northern sector.

d. 87th Palestinian Brigade – organization and training in Rafah camps.

Forces and Tasks

a. 86th Palestinian Brigade:

1. Commander of Sector: Lieut. Colonel Lutfi el-Burini.

2. Task: Defence of Khan Yunis region to the very end.

3. Boundaries:

South: contiguous to 3rd Division's eastern boundary of Rafah Sector. (23562396 to 22782492)

West: Coast

East: Armistice Line.

North: North of Khan Yunis to level-crossing on the main road. (From 090868 to 050912)

4. Dispositions:

i. HQ of 86th Palestinian Brigade – Khan Yunis.

ii. 32nd Battalion in defended locality north and northeast of Khan Yunis. 3 companies to man company-strength defence positions: one company to man three platoon-strength posts in the north, at level-crossing on the main road; a second company to man three posts in the north-east. [in the hilly area]; the third to hold three posts in the east. A fourth company to be held in reserve under battalion command, ready to man second-line defence posts.

iii. 11th Battalion to be located south and southeast of Khan Yunis, also manning platoon-strength posts. One company to man defence posts on the highway to Rafah.

iv. 44th Battalion – 3 companies to be held in reserve; the fourth to man the post on the sea-shore at 08100855.

v. Heavy mortar battery at 08600840.

b. 26th National Guards Brigade – northern sector of Strip:

1. Commander of Sector: Lieut. Colonel Gamal e-Din Ali.
2. Task: Defence of Strip against Israeli raids and incursions.
3. Boundaries:
   South: Contiguous to northern boundary of 86th Palestinian Brigade from 090868 to 050912.
   East: Armistice Line.
   North: Boundary of the Gaza Strip.
   West: Coast.
4. Dispositions:
   [The area between Dir el Balah and Bet Hanun is divided by Wadi Gaza into a northern and southern section. The Egyptian document called for two 'battalions' to man the northern section, but these were small units; one 'battalion' was located in the southern section as a reserve unit, and 250 men in a camp on the sea-shore were held as brigade reserves. Another group of 'battalions' garrisoned the sector south of Dir el Balah. One 'battalion' was responsible for defence of the coast.] 20th Heavy Mortar Battery to be distributed among defence posts: 1st Troop – north of Gaza; 2nd – south of Gaza; 3rd – north of Khan Yunis. [Each troop was stationed in a separate defence position along the Strip border, serving as artillery support for the National Guards forces manning the border posts.] One troop of coastal artillery from 4th Battalion. [2 three-inch guns, 2 searchlights, sited on sea-shore.]
   4 six-pounder anti-tank guns.
   One detachment of Border Guards to patrol the dunes in the northern part of the Strip.

2nd MOTORIZED BORDER BATTALION – (southern Sinai sector)

a. Forces: Directly responsible to Eastern Command.
   3 motorized companies.
   1 battalion [about 250 men] of Egyptian National Guard.

b. Sector of responsibility: The Kuntilla–Nakhl-Mitla axis and the Ras en-Nakeb–Thamad–Nakhl axis, and the area as far north as Bir Hassna. Also responsible for protection of installations on the Jebel Livni–Bir Gafgafa axis.

c. Tasks: i. Protection of the area from incursions by Israeli forces and guarding of Egyptian southern flank [on the supposition that the operational intention of the Israeli army may be to outflank 3rd Division from the south].

ii. Warning to forces in northern Sinai in event of an Israeli invasion [so that they can engage the enemy in time].

iii. Delaying actions on southern axis, in event of emergency, to enable organization of defence in depth.

iv. Protection of installations in vicinity of Bir Gafgafa; and patrols.

d. Dispositions: i. Battalion HQ at Nakhl [Nakhl was the meeting-point of several tracks in the southern Sinai sector] plus one motorized company and two companies of National Guard battalion. Nakhl also battalion supply base.

ii. Thamad entrenched defence position, manned by two companies, one motorized, one National Guards. The motorized company responsible for Thamad–Ras en-Nakeb–Kuntilla sector, sending out small forces to warn against impending approach of enemy troops. A third company to patrol the Nakhl–Bir Hassna–Bir Gafgafa axis.

e. Neighbouring forces: i. Shlufa–Suez sector (Canal Zone): 2nd Infantry Brigade: 5 battalions, 2 batteries of heavy mortars, units of Border Guards and Egyptian National Guards, 1 light anti-aircraft regiment (54 pieces), 1 heavy anti-aircraft battery, 2 troops of coastal guns.

ii. 3rd Division in northern Sinai.

f. Tasks of Nakhl sub-sector (Commander: Lieut. Colonel Fuad Hakla Jerajes): Regional defence, with special reference to defence of Nakhl air-strip against enemy parachute action.

g. Tasks of Thamad sub-sector (Commander: Major Mahmad Abd el-Mejid Mari):

i. Detachment to man following 'early warning' positions: Um Makrut, Jebel Um Haluf, entrance to Wadi Jerafi, Kuntilla, Jebel el Risha, Ras en-Nakeb.

ii. To give early warning of major enemy attack.

iii. Delaying enemy advance within sector.

iv. Defence of approaches to Thamad and protection of Thamad village.

    v. Daily patrols from Thamad to maintain contact with forward 'early warning' positions. Unit at Um Makrut to maintain daily patrols along Wadi el-Bida up to Bir Ma'ain or along Wadi Lusan up to the international frontier.

GULF OF AKABA

    a. Forces (Sharm e-Sheikh–Ras Natsrani region):

       21st Infantry Battalion

       National Guards Battalion

       Two 6-inch coastal guns

       Four 3-inch H.A.A. guns

       Six 30 mm. L.A.A. guns

       1 troop of 57 mm. anti-tank guns

       Look-out posts along the western shore of Gulf.

       2 platoons Border Guards

       The frigate *Rashid*

    b. Command: Commander: Colonel Raif Mahfouz Zaki. Directly under GHQ command. HQ – Sharm e-Sheikh.

    c. Area of responsibility: From Sharm e-Sheikh in the south to the northern section of the Gulf.

    d. Dispositions. Ras Natsrani: [Ras Natsrani was the key site to blockade the Straits of Tiran, its guns completely dominating the entrance to the Gulf of Akaba.]

    HQ of 21st Infantry Battalion plus 2 companies; 2 sections of 81 mm. mortars; 1 platoon medium machine-guns; the 6-inch and 3-inch guns and 3 of the 30 mm guns; and 2 searchlights.

    One company responsible for defence of route to Sharm e-Sheikh and protection of coastal and anti-aircraft guns.

    Second company responsible for remaining sector, with special reference to coast and prevention of sea-borne landings.

    Sharm e-Sheikh:

    Area Command plus 1 company from 21st Battalion; 1 platoon of medium machine-guns; three 30-mm. and two 57-mm. guns; 10 Bren-carriers.

    Responsible for defence of airfield (with special reference to prevention of seizure by parachute forces); protection of route to Ras Natsrani and on alert for possible airborne landings to the immediate north.

    [A fourth company of Bren-carriers plus light and heavy mortar detachments were based at Kaida and in radio touch with special look-out posts located in sites to the north of Sharm e-Sheikh which could serve as possible landing grounds for enemy paratroopers.]

The Coasts [Defence of the coasts of the Sinai Peninsula was the responsibility of the Egyptian Border Guards, comprising camel-mounted troops (Jana) and motorized infantry. (A camel-mounted platoon consisted of 30 troops and 45 camels.) The Border Guards maintained look-out posts along the east coast of the Gulf of Suez and the west coast of the Gulf of Akaba. They came under Suez Regional Command.]

Gulf of Suez: Border Guards positions at El Shatt, Abu Zenima, Tor, Sharm e-Sheikh.

Gulf of Akaba: Positions at Teba, Boasit, Dahab and on the islands of Tiran and Sanapir [all maintaining radio contact with Sharm e-Sheikh].

1st ARMOURED BRIGADE TEAM

Forces: 4th Armoured Battalion [Soviet T-34 tanks]
6th Armoured Battalion [motorized infantry on Soviet armoured troop-carriers]
53rd Artillery Battery [Soviet SU-100 self-propelled guns]
1 battery of light anti-aircraft guns

Tasks: Command reserve. To check advance of Israeli armour, to engage enemy, stabilize line in first phase and then go over to counter-attack.

THE AIR FORCE [Egyptian dispositions on eve of Campaign]

Abu Suweir air base	30th Squadron	Mig-15s	15 aircraft
Fayid	40th ,,	Vampires	10 ,,
		Meteors	20 ,,
,,	5th ,,	Meteors	12 ,,
,,	2nd ,,	Vampires	15 ,,
Kasparit	31st ,,	Vampires	15 ,,
Kabrit	20th ,,	Mig-15s	15 ,,
,,	1st ,,	Mig-15s	15 ,,
Cairo West	8th ,,	Ilyushin-28s	12 (in organizational phase)
,,	9th ,,	Ilyushin-28s	12 (plus 5 in reserve)
Almaza	3rd ,,	Ilyushin-14s	20 aircraft
,,	7th ,,	Commandos	20 ,,
,,	11th ,,	Dakotas	20 ,,

[Almaza also had 6 Meteor NP-13 night-fighters and 8 Furies]

Luxor		Ilyushin-28s	20 aircraft

[Not all these squadrons were operational. The operational force consisted of: 2 Mig squadrons (30 aircraft); 1 Vampire squadron (15 aircraft); 1 Meteor squadron (12 aircraft); 1 Ilyushin-28 squadron (12 aircraft); and 3 transport squadrons (about 60 aircraft).

Almaza, Cairo West and Luxor were the bases used for jet bombers and transport planes.

Almaza and Cairo West also served together with Inchas as fighter bases for the air defence of Cairo and the nearby populated region. These airfields were improved and made operational for Soviet-type planes.

The air bases of the Canal Zone were Kabrit, Abu Suweir and Fayid. Most of the fighter planes took off from there. Their mission was to maintain control of the Zone and give support and cover for the ground forces stationed there.

Emergency airfields in Sinai were at El Arish, Bir Hama and Bir Gafgafa. These were made ready for fighters to afford close support and air defence in Sinai. At the Bir Hama field, work was started to make it operational for MIGs.

There were additional airfields for dispersal of planes.]

APPENDIX 4

ISRAEL ARMY FORMATIONS TAKING PART IN OPERATION 'KADESH'

FORMATION	BATTLE
202nd Paratroop Brigade (3 battalions 2 companies 'Nahal' 1 tank squadron (AMXs) 1 battery field artillery 1 battery heavy mortars)	Capture of Kuntilla, Thamad, Nakhl, Mitla, Ras Sudar, Tor, participated in capture of Sharm e-Sheikh.
4th Infantry Brigade (reinforced) (3 battalions 1 battery field artillery 1 battery medium artillery 1 battery heavy mortars)	Capture of Kusseima defence positions; held Jebel Livni, Nakhl and Mitla.
10th Infantry Brigade (reinforced) (3 battalions 1 battery field artillery 1 battery heavy mortars) (The artillery batteries serving with 4th Brigade also served with 10th Brigade.)	Capture of Auja Masri and Tarat Um Basis, and attempt to capture Um Katef.
1st Infantry Brigade (reinforced) (4 battalions 1 battery field artillery 1 battery heavy mortars 1 battalion engineers)	Capture of some of positions at Rafah; held El Arish.
11th Infantry Brigade (reinforced) (2 infantry battalions 1 armoured battalion combat team 1 battery heavy mortars 1 anti-tank battery)	Capture of the Gaza Strip
9th Infantry Brigade (reinforced) (3 battalions 1 battery field artillery 1 battalion engineers	Capture of Ras en-Nakeb, Ras Natsrani and Sharm e-Sheikh
12th Infantry Brigade 1 battalion	Landing at Tor (following its capture by the paratroopers); mopping-up operations in Gaza Strip.

7th Armoured Brigade (1 armoured battalion [Shermans] 1 armoured battalion [AMXs] 1 battalion half-tracks 1 battalion motorized infantry 1 battery field artillery)	Capture of defence posts at Abu Ageila crossroads; capture of defence posts at Ruafa dam; battles with enemy armour in areas of Bir Rud Selim, Gafgafa and Jebel Livni.

27th Armoured Brigade
(1 armoured battalion
  combat team:
  1 squadron light tanks
  1 half-track company
  1 troop self-propelled guns (105 mm)
  1 reconnaissance unit
  1 section engineers.
1 armoured battalion
  combat team:
  1 squadron heavy tanks
  1 half-track company
  1 troop self-propelled guns (105 mm)
  1 reconnaissance unit
  1 tank-recovery detachment
  1 section engineers.
1 battalion motorized infantry)
	Capture of some of positions at Rafah; capture of El Jeradi and El Arish; advance up to Suez.

37th Armoured Brigade (1 armoured battalion (Shermans and Super- Shermans) 1 squadron light tanks (AMXs) 1 battalion half-tracks 1 battalion motorized infantry 1 company engineers)	Battle for defence posts of Um Katef; participated in capture of the Gaza Strip under command of 11th Brigade.

Israel Air Force	Operational aircraft on D-day:
Mystères	16
Ouragans	22
Meteors	15
Mustangs	29
Harvards	17
Mosquitos	16
Dakotas	16
Nords	3
B-17s	2
	136

APPENDIX 5

Dates of major actions by Israel formations (ground forces)

No.	Formation	Monday 29 Oct 56	Tuesday 30 Oct	Wednesday 31 Oct	Thursday 1 Nov	Friday 2 Nov	Saturday 3 Nov	Sunday 4 Nov	Monday 5 Nov	Casualties Killed	Casualties Wounded	Casualties Total
1	202nd Paratroop Brigade	Evening: 1 Capture of Kuntilla. 2 Battalion parachute drop at Mitla	Before dawn: Capture of Thamad. Afternoon: Capture of Nakhl. 18.00 hours: Link-up with parachuted battalion	Attempt to advance through Mitla Pass while under air attack. Trapped and em-battled in Pass	Battle of Mitla Pass	1 Reconnaissance to find route to Ras Sudar. 2 Two companies parachuted at Tor, followed by airborne landing of infantry battalion	1 Seizure of oil-fields in Western Sinai. 2 Reconnaissance from Tor towards Sharm e-Sheikh	Battalion reaches Tor from Ras Sudar and advances towards Sharm e-Sheikh	Break-through from South into Sharm e-Sheikh	42	120	162
2	9th Infantry Brigade	Evening: Capture of Ras en-Nakeb by two companies			1 Brigade moves to area of Ras en-Nakeb. 2 Reconnaissance up to 25 miles south	1 Advance up to 22 miles north of Dahab. 2 Capture of Teba by unit from Eilat	1 Capture of Dahab and advance southwards. 2 Reconnaissance unit reaches point 12½ miles north of Ras Natsrani	1 Capture of Ras Natsrani, 2 Advance to Sharm e-Sheikh	Morning: Capture of Sharm e-Sheikh	10	32	42

No.	Formation	Monday 29 Oct 56	Tuesday 30 Oct	Wednesday 31 Oct	Thursday 1 Nov	Friday 2 Nov	Saturday 3 Nov	Sunday 4 Nov	Monday 5 Nov	Casualties		
3	4th Infantry Brigade		Before dawn: 1 Seizure of Sabha. 2 Capture of Kusseima 3 Reconnaissance unit moves towards Nakhl		One Battalion transferred to hold Nakhl, replacing paratroop unit					3	23	26
4	7th Armoured Brigade		Advance through Kusseima towards Abu Ageila along two axes (towards Um Shihan and through Deika defile)	1 Capture of Abu Ageila cross-roads 2 Capture of Ruafa dam 3 Capture of Jebel Livni	Before dawn: Battle with enemy armoured brigade combat team at Bir Rud Selim	Tank battle west of Gafgafa. Advance to Suez Canal on central axis				15	88	103

APPENDIX 5 – continued

No.	Formation	Monday 29 Oct 56	Tuesday 30 Oct	Wednesday 31 Oct	Thursday 1 Nov	Friday 2 Nov	Saturday 3 Nov	Sunday 4 Nov	Monday 5 Nov	Casualties		
4 (cont.)	7th Armoured Brigade (cont.)			cross-roads; holds off armoured counter-attacks. 4 Capture of Bir Hassna. 5 Reconnaissance up to Mitla								
5	10th Infantry Brigade		Evening: Capture of Auja Masri and Tarat Um Basis	Attempt to capture Um Katef		Seizure of Um Shihan				4	47 (1 missing)	52
6	37th Armoured Brigade (less one armoured battalion)				Night and early morning: Attempt to capture Um Katef by half-track battalion		(Participated in capture of Gaza Strip under Command of 11th Infantry Brigade)			28	94	122

No.	Formation	Monday 29 Oct 56	Tuesday 30 Oct	Wednesday 31 Oct	Thursday 1 Nov	Friday 2 Nov	Saturday 3 Nov	Sunday 4 Nov	Monday 5 Nov	Casualties		
7	1st Infantry Brigade				Before dawn: Captured some of defence posts of Rafah					15	79	94
8	27th Armoured Brigade				Early morning till nightfall: 1 Breakthrough defence positions of Rafah 2 Battle of El Jeradi 3 Advance to approaches to El Arish	Morning: Capture of El Arish. Advance up to 9½ miles from Suez Canal				16	82	98

225

APPENDIX 5 – *continued*

No.	Formation	Monday 29 Oct 56	Tuesday 30 Oct	Wednesday 31 Oct	Thursday 1 Nov	Friday 2 Nov	Saturday 3 Nov	Sunday 4 Nov	Monday 5 Nov	Casualties		
9	11th Infantry Brigade (plus one armoured battalion team from 37th Brigade)					Morning: Capture of Gaza and northern part of Strip: and advance towards Khan Yunis	Capture of Khan Yunis			10	63	73
10	12th Infantry Brigade					Evening: Airborne landing of one battalion at Tor in wake of two parachuted companies of 202 Brigade	Entry into Gaza Strip for mopping-up operations			7	22	29

NOTE:: The casualty figures in the above table are not complete. Total casualties suffered by the Israel Defence Forces, including the Air Force, were: 172 killed; 817 wounded (29% medium and severe wounds); 3 missing; 1 captured.

APPENDIX 6

CAPTURED EGYPTIAN WEAPONS AND EQUIPMENT IN SINAI CAMPAIGN

NAVAL VESSELS:	1 destroyer (*Ibrahim el-Awal*)
RADAR:	1 mobile radar station

LIGHT WEAPONS:

Revolvers	300
Sub-machine-guns	1170
Rifles	4300
Light machine-guns	550
Medium machine-guns	290
Mortars (from 2-inch to 81 mm.)	220
Bazookas	260
Anti-tank rifles	320
Recoilless guns (Czech, 82 mm.)	200

ARTILLERY:

25-pounders (British)	55
Coastal guns	6
Anti-tank guns (6-pounders and Soviet 57 mm.)	110
Anti-aircraft guns (various)	100
Mortars (120 mm.)	18

ARMOUR:

T-34 tanks	26
Self-propelled SU-100	6
Sherman tanks	40
Shermans with special turret	12
Valentine tanks (without guns)	15
'Archer' anti-tank guns (17-pounder)	40
Armoured troop-carriers (full track, fully covered, Soviet)	60
Bren-carriers	260
T-34 (Soviet) command tank	1
Tank-recovery tank (Sherman)	3
Tank-dozer (recovery)	3
Dummy Shermans	16
Dummy guns	16

227

VEHICLES:	Motor-cycles	155
	Passenger vehicles	50
	Jeeps (Willys)	470
	Landrovers	34
	Light trucks (various)	700
	Heavy trucks	820
	Gun-trucks	60
	Vehicles of various types . . .	200
	Tank-transporters	3
	Trailers (various)	480
	Tank-trailers	12
AMMUNITION:	Hand-grenades (Mills)	25,000
	9 mm.	8,000,000
	.303-inch	5,000,000
	7.62 mm.(short and long) . .	6,000,000
	7.92 mm.	21,000,000
	20 mm.	20,000
	30 mm.	70,000
	40 mm.	22,000
	37 mm. (Soviet)	13,500
	23 mm. ,, ...	14,000
	6-pounder	22,000
	57 mm. (Soviet)	13,500
	75 mm.	15,000
	85 mm. (Soviet)	30,000
	100 mm. ,, ...	6,500
	102 mm.(coastal)	390
	100 mm.(naval)	940
	25-pounder (British)	75,000
	17-pounder ,, ...	35,000
	122 mm. (Soviet)	3,000
	20-pounder	15,000
	3-inch (anti-aircraft)	3,000
	3.7-inch ,, ...	400
	12.7 mm.	15,000
	Bazooka 85 mm.	8,000
	Rifle-grenades and mortars (up to 81 mm.)	100,000
	120 mm mortar	15,000
	80 mm. aircraft rockets	850
	82 mm. recoilless shells (Czech)	1,700
	Depth charges	20

228

APPENDIX 6

ENGINEERS EQUIPMENT :   Plastic anti-vehicle mines...   35,000
Other mines..............   20,000
Blocks of explosives.......   25,000

SIGNALS EQUIPMENT :   Radio sets   300

OTHER EQUIPMENT :   Binoculars   100
Telescopes and compasses..   200
Searchlights   2

(The Egyptians also lost the following aircraft: 4 MIG-15s
3 Vampires
1 Meteor)

INDEX

231